THE DRIVE-IN, THE SUPERMARKET, AND THE
TRANSFORMATION OF COMMERCIAL SPACE IN
LOS ANGELES, 1914–1941

THE DRIVE-IN, THE SUPERMARKET, AND THE TRANSFORMATION OF COMMERCIAL SPACE IN LOS ANGELES, 1914–1941

RICHARD LONGSTRETH

THE MIT PRESS
CAMBRIDGE, MASSACHUSETTS
LONDON, ENGLAND

This book was set in Bembo by Graphic Composition, Inc., and was printed and bound in the United States of America.

Library of Congress Cataloging-in-Publication Data

Longstreth, Richard W.
    The drive-in, the supermarket, and the transformation of commercial space in Los Angeles, 1914–1941 / Richard Longstreth.
      p. cm.
    Includes bibliographical references and index.
    ISBN 0-262-12214-6 (hc : alk. paper)
    1. Retail trade—California—Los Angeles Metropolitan Area—History.   2. Drive-in facilities—California—Los Angeles Metropolitan Area—History.   3. Supermarkets—California—Los Angeles Metropolitan Area—History.   4. Commercial buildings—California—Los Angeles Metropolitan Area—History.   I. Title.
HF5429.5.L7L663   1999
381'.1—dc21   98-39140
                                                              CIP

for Cinda

Contents

ACKNOWLEDGMENTS

I began this study over a decade ago, with the modest intention of examining the long-forgotten phenomenon of the drive-in market. The parameters soon expanded, for initial probing made clear that analysis of the drive-in necessitated close investigation of the service station, which provided an essential precedent, of the supermarket, which quickly rendered the drive-in obsolete, and also of a series of broader business, cultural, and urban issues. After a few years, material gathered to provide a framework for this sequence of developments led to a much more encompassing study of retail decentralization in southern California, which was published as City Center to Regional Mall *by the MIT Press in 1997. The time and research on that project, in turn, enabled clarification of some key points related to the subject of this book. Many of those who assisted me in preparing* City Center to Regional Mall *deserve thanks here as well.*

I am especially indebted to the late David Gebhard, not only for advice and encouragement but also for supporting the publication of this study in its early stages. Robert Winter was equally enthusiastic from the outset. Besides his encouragement, J. B. Jackson offered an intellectual perspective that was essential for embarking on a project of this kind. Others have assisted in important ways. Robert Bruegmann, Howard Gillette, Thomas Hines, Chester Liebs, and Dell Upton read an early draft of the manuscript, when the two studies were still one, and gave invaluable suggestions for taming what seemed an overwhelming array of information. Without Ed Whittington there would be no book, for his vast collection of negatives and prints, then housed at the library at California State University, Long Beach, afforded an essential basis for the project in its current form. He also kindly introduced me to others who helped immeasurably with information and insights. Dace Taube at the University of Southern California's special collections has likewise gone out of her way to assist me with the Whittington material, which now resides there, as well as with many additional photographs.

The architects, real estate brokers, retailers, and others who agreed to be interviewed offered insights that would have been impossible to glean otherwise. I am thus indebted to Albert Frey, the late Regula Fybel, the late Frederick Gutheim, the late S. Charles Lee, Walter Leimert, Jr., Milton and Burke McGinty, Edward Schmidt, and Ben Schwartz. Many others have helped in ways too numerous to mention: Carson Anderson, Scott Bottles, Barbara Boyd, Kenneth Breisch, Lauren Weiss Bricker, the late David Cameron, Margaret Crawford, David De Long, George Ehrlich, Stephen Fox, Marilyn Harper, Maurice Hattem, Greg Hise, Preston Kaufmann, Antoinette Lee, Steven Levin, Brita Mack, Megs Merriwether, Frank Mittlebach, the late Dione Neutra, Tom Owen, Beth Savage, Richard and Sarah Striner, Michael Tomlan, Richard Wagner, Mary Jo Winder, Mrs. Oliver Winston, Kathy Wood, and David Zeidberg. The staff of Ralphs Grocery Company supplied me with photographs and additional material on their stores. Equally important is the photo archive of Progressive Grocer in Stamford, Connecticut, overseen by Shirley Palmer, who allowed me access. Lee Fowler and Barbara Barrickman of the J. C. Nichols Company in Kansas City, Missouri, have given me material for many projects, of which this is only the latest. Don M. Casto III and Carla Chuirazzi of the Don M. Casto Organization in Columbus, Ohio, were generous with material in their files. Thanks also go to Margo Stipe of the Frank Lloyd Wright Archives and to James V. Miller of the University of Akron Archives.

I am grateful to the staffs of the many institutions in which my research was conducted. Without the vast collections of the Library of Congress—including those in the Geography and Maps, Newspapers and Current Periodicals, and Prints and Photographs divisions—the task would have been far more difficult, time-consuming, and expensive. In southern California, the Los Angeles Public Library, the Los Angeles Municipal Library, the Sever Center at the Los Angeles County Museum of Natural History, the Huntington Library, and several libraries each at the University of Southern California and the University of California, Los Angeles, were major sources. Others in the region included the public libraries of Alhambra, Anaheim, Beverly Hills, Glendale, Huntington Park, Inglewood, Long Beach, Montebello, Norwalk, Pasadena, Santa Ana, Santa Monica, and South Gate, as well as the Architectural Drawing Collection at the University of California, Santa Barbara. Elsewhere, the public libraries of Houston, Texas; New York, New York; Philadelphia, Pennsylvania; Shreveport, Louisiana; and Washington, D.C., as well as the library of the University of Akron, all contained important information.

The initial trip to Los Angeles for this study was underwritten by the National Main Street Center of the National Trust for Historic Preservation. Lectures at the Foundation for San Francisco's Architectural Heritage, California State University at San Luis Obispo, the Southern California Institute of Architecture, and UCLA facilitated additional trips. Generous funding for the illustrations and other facets of my research was provided by several grants from George Washington University.

Time spent in southern California was greatly enhanced by the hospitality of friends, including Kenneth Breisch and Judy Keller, the late David Cameron, John and Nadine Dillon, the late Hans and Regula Fybel, the late David and Patricia Gebhard, Thomas and Carol Hanchett, Thomas Hines, Tom Owen, Gene Waddell, and Robert Winter. Randell Makinson and Edward Bosley greatly facilitated the project by allowing me to reside at the Gamble House on several occasions.

I am grateful to Roger Conover and others at the MIT Press, most especially Julie Grimaldi, Matthew Abbate, Paula Woolley, and Jim McWethy, for the care they have lavished on the manuscript and for making the whole production process a pleasure.

My father, the late Thaddeus Longstreth, was tireless in his interest, and it is my great regret that he did not live to see this work completed. My daughter, Elizabeth, introduced me to a world of contemporary shopping I otherwise would have known little about. My wife, Cinda, has been generous with her love and understanding. Nothing pleases me more than to dedicate this book to her.

INTRODUCTION

The experience is so commonplace and seems so mundane as to be taken
for granted. For most Americans, shopping entails movement through two
kinds of space, exterior and interior, in sequence. The exterior space, the
parking lot, appears amorphous, but is in fact carefully calculated to accommodate the motor vehicles of customers, staff, and delivery personnel
alike—while moving and while stationary—with efficiency and convenience. The requirements of this space weigh heavily in the selection of the
site and in the configuration of the building, which in many cases occupies
but a small portion of the acreage. While not accorded any stature by the
public, even if it is adorned with landscaping and other embellishments,
the large open space is considered absolutely essential by consumers. Without it, they would not come. There would be no store.

   The inside space, the selling area, is neutral. It is generally limited to a single floor. It lacks a hierarchy—all parts are more or less equally
important. It is also nondirectional in that there is no single route of preference, but rather a series of similar aisles, most, if not all, running parallel
to one another. Movement within this space is unencumbered; patrons may
go anywhere in any sequence as often as they choose. Contact with store personnel is minimal, often nonexistent, and almost always at the customer's
initiative, until one finishes selecting merchandise and approaches the
checkout stands.

   This couplet of today's retail spaces is significant in several ways.
First, it is entirely different from that generally experienced by consumers

of all kinds only two generations ago. As late as 1950, most shopping precincts remained pedestrian-oriented. Even when driving was involved, as it was with increasing frequency, space to park the car tended to remain separate from the store. In the majority of cases, selling space was also more confined. Space divided among several floors was a sign of stature. The taller the emporium, the more important it must be, according to the then conventional wisdom of urban retail development. Space was more hierarchically divided and also more directional. Customer movement was directed toward sales personnel, who usually occupied designated stations. Contact with the sales force was necessary if one wanted to inspect many of the goods. If the store was departmentalized, payment took place at multiple points instead of one.

A second matter of significance is that this transformation has occurred in a sweeping array of retail spheres. Hardware stores, furniture stores, drug stores, convenience stores, appliance stores, auto accessory stores, computer stores, toy stores, food stores, discount variety stores, record stores, bookstores, video stores, office supply stores, home furnishing stores, and even many clothing stores are among those where this pattern is now commonplace. The process of shopping, and the physical environment in which it occurs, have tended toward homogeneity irrespective of the type of product. Furthermore, this leveling has become relatively classless. New retail development, from low-income, inner-city districts to posh outlying ones, may differ in its trappings, but the basic nature of space, movement, and transactions are much the same. Although retail precincts orient themselves according to numerous and often-changing target consumer groups, in physical organization the variations are increasingly on a single theme.

Third, the shift in the configuration of retail spaces, which has occurred mostly during the second half of the twentieth century, represents basic changes in retailing practices that are aimed at efficiency and economy. In the simplest terms, the objective is to sell more goods more often at lower cost. But consumer preferences also enter the equation, for most Americans have favored maximum selection, minimum intervention by salesclerks, and shopping spaces that are unencumbered. The shopper is in effect free to make choices without feeling obliged to buy, without feeling pressure to select quickly, without feeling embarrassed about ignorance of details or about rummaging through an assortment of goods, and without having to wait for service. This move to self-service was perhaps an inevitable outcome, given a consumption-oriented, relatively well-informed populace with increasing amounts of disposable income.

Fourth, the shift also entails a profound change in the landscape, both in the location and the character of shopping districts. The demand for copious amounts of space—inside and out—has rendered many long-established retail districts obsolete, or at least has consigned them to second-class status. Whereas downtown once dominated retail functions for all save the lower tiers of the consumption chain, today many core precincts hold a marginal place. Only in the largest cities and in a few other places where attachment to the urban center remains unusually strong is down-town still a shopping destination of consequence, and even then its role has become more specialized. Many outlying retail districts created during the first six decades of the twentieth century are likewise in decline. New loci of commerce, in shopping centers and in less planned stretches along traffic arteries, are low-density, sprawling affairs whose buildings are visually dwarfed by the open spaces—the parking lots, circulation paths, and arte-rial routes—that serve them. Most of today's major retail concentrations exist on land that had little or no development on it four, perhaps even two, decades ago. People flock to such precincts, but have almost no attachment to them as permanent definers of place or community.[1]

This study focuses on a little-known series of developments that were key to laying the foundation for these dramatic changes in retail space. The important early innovations took place during a short period of time, most intensely during the 1920s and 1930s, and entailed buildings of rela-tively modest function—servicing automobiles and selling food.[2] Most of those innovations occurred in a single metropolitan area, Los Angeles. Yet what started as local anomalies soon had an impact on practices elsewhere, eventually becoming national phenomena.

Initially the transformation of exterior space and of interior space occurred independently, and their relationship was considered somewhat ad-versarial. Allocating prime space to cars limited the capacity to sell goods, critics charged. Greater emphasis on selling space, on the other hand, could reduce the convenience to motorists. Only with time were the attributes of each seen as contributing to the other. An approach to organizing space that today may seem straightforward and obvious had a difficult, circuitous evolution.

Each chapter in this book analyzes a major component of the se-quence, in more or less chronological order. The first chapter focuses on the earliest transformation of exterior space according to what I call the drive-in concept: the arrangement of functions on a site to accommodate the move-ment and parking of customers' automobiles. This idea began in an elemen-tary way during the 1910s with the filling station, and soon was applied in a more significant way to the development of what was known as the su-per service station. The latter facilities were arranged for motorists' conve-nience and included a wide range of auto-related goods and services, organized around a sizable forecourt.

Beginning in the mid-1920s, both the physical form and organi-zational structure of the super station were directly applied to the drive-in market. The second chapter examines these buildings, which constituted the first widespread application of the drive-in concept to a nonautomotive business. Like the super station, these markets combined related functions at a time when such practices were rare and made this amenity available citywide, not just in a few central locations. Here the forecourt played an even more important role from the customer's perspective, allowing what was then considered a very generous area for off-street parking. With the

*proliferation of these outlets at the decade's end, retail-related space cater-
ing to the automobile became a common feature of the landscape in that distinguished the Los Angeles metropolitan area from all others in the
country.*

   *The third chapter analyzes the rise of the supermarket, which
quickly eclipsed the drive-in locally as a standard outlet for food in the
early 1930s. Examples built in the Los Angeles area were arguably the
most important in defining what the type became nationally by the 1940s.
In certain respects, the supermarket was more traditional in form, its front
oriented to the sidewalk and street and set at the property line. Early buildings often excluded the car lot altogether; later, as consumer demand made
off-street parking standard for supermarkets, it generally was relegated to
a utilitarian side yard, not given prime space in front of the lot.*

   *The major spatial innovation of the supermarket occurred inside,
where a large selling area, uninterrupted by structural supports, was configured to foster self-service and a high-volume turnover of a large inventory
of goods. In developing this arrangement, ideas were drawn from that well-
established institution, the public market, among other sources. But the attributes found at the supermarket made it distinct, both in concept and use.*

   *The final chapter discusses key ways in which the drive-in and the
supermarket influenced other retail development patterns nationwide. The
drive-in itself had a very limited impact outside California, but its basic
form and concept were directly adapted for the neighborhood shopping center, a transfer that began on the east coast in 1930 and diffused to other
parts of the country by the eve of World War II. After the war, the drive-in
concept was applied to shopping centers of all sizes, which became a major
form of retail growth within a decade. Drawing in large part from precedents set in California, the supermarket also began to have an important
impact on other retail types as early as the 1930s. The drug store and the
variety store were the most prominent among these to adopt the supermarket's expansive, nondirectional space as well as its practice of self-service.*

   *The fact that one region was the primary spawning ground for the
super service station, the drive-in market, and the supermarket is far from
coincidental. A confluence of factors there provided ideal circumstances for
innovation. During the 1910s and especially during the 1920s, Los
Angeles experienced unprecedented development that rendered it a major
metropolis. At the same time, an abundance of land and water fostered
low-density growth that outdistanced transit lines beginning in the 1910s.
The swelling population mostly consisted of American-born men and
women who came with skills and often with reserve capital. This burgeoning middle class created one of the highest incidences of automobile
ownership in the nation, and both the diffuse nature of settlement and a
mild climate year-round yielded an equally high rate of automobile use.
Driving the car to purchase goods, even routine ones, was a favorite
pastime.*[3]

   *Equally important, oil and agriculture were two of southern Cali-
fornia's foremost industries, and the abundance of their products generated*

a highly competitive climate among retailers. Each of the three building types studied in this book was largely the product of one merchant group seeking to gain an edge over others. The super station was created by independent filling-station operators pursuing greater revenues than the sale of gas and motor oil alone allowed, and the type's ultimate demise was in part due to major oil companies searching for a more economical arrangement by which they could capture some of the independents' business. The drive-in market was developed by real estate entrepreneurs as a profitable way of utilizing theretofore marginal land along the region's vast network of arterial routes. The supermarket, on the other hand, was the grocers' response, stimulated by the pursuit of higher-volume sales, especially during the lean years of the depression.

An underlying purpose of the book is to delineate in precise and concrete terms how a variety of factors can interact to generate and shape change. Thus I avoid focusing solely on the development of these new kinds of space and instead examine a wide range of matters pertaining to each type. The emphasis lies not with spatial innovation alone, but also with the complex circumstances of development of which it was a part. As an example, the drive-in market's contribution lay not just in the priority it gave to off-street space for automobiles, but also in fostering the concept of one-stop shopping for everyday goods, schooling merchants in the intricacies of working together in a single operation, and demonstrating the advantages of locations on the periphery of, or removed from, established retail districts. In its national diffusion, the drive-in concept was often closely tied to these other factors. Each type I examine also influenced at least one of the others. The super service station provided a model for the drive-in, but itself had drawn inspiration from earlier public markets. The drive-in laid an essential foundation for its usurper, the supermarket.

All these developments, of course, emanated from the pragmatic world of business; yet more elusive cultural and social issues also played a consequential role. For example, despite its bread-and-butter origins, the drive-in market was embraced by the city's avant-garde architects as a means by which building and machine could be related aesthetically and spatially. Planners saw the drive-in as a form that allowed neighborhood businesses to assume greater visual coherence while consigning them to neatly contained boundaries. Popular taste, however, held the parking lot in low esteem and readily accepted its relegation to a less prominent place at the supermarket. Early supermarket interiors were proclaimed a triumph of female taste, and, since the majority of shoppers were female, the type came to have a pronounced impact on retail space nationally. In the final analysis, the supermarket showed that what the predominantly female consumer society wanted in the marketplace was not extravagant decor and service but freedom and convenience.

My focus on Los Angeles addresses key events in the inceptive stage of what became a national transformation, but thereafter the story rapidly grows more complex. The end of this book is little more than an out-

line to suggest some aspects of the multifaceted nature of commercial change since World War II. With few exceptions, the details of that story have remained unexplored.[4] They beg further study, for, just like the super station, the drive-in, and the supermarket in Los Angeles, they can tell us much about the twentieth-century landscape and the values that have shaped it.

THE DRIVE-IN, THE SUPERMARKET,
AND THE TRANSFORMATION OF COMMERCIAL SPACE
IN LOS ANGELES, 1914–1941

I

MONKEY-WRENCH MERCHANDISING

By the late 1920s, gasoline stations in Los Angeles enjoyed a national reputation. No other metropolitan area, it seemed, had so many stations that
were large, convenient, and sometimes ornate where one could purchase
a wide range of goods and services for the car. A writer for *Printer's Ink
Monthly,* a leading organ for the advertising field, remarked that "when you
first drive up . . . , it is not difficult to imagine that you are being taken
care of by guardian angels."[1] But the author was of two minds about retail
outlets where consumer contact was with the technician rather than with
sales personnel—a relationship he dubbed "monkey-wrench merchandising." Many professed technicians were incompetent, he asserted; others
were unscrupulous; still others were incapable of speaking a language customers could comprehend. On the other hand, the technician could be far
more effective in this contact role than could someone savvy in merchandising alone. The technician knows the product as the salesperson never can;
the technician also may be much more concerned with quality than with
rapid turnover of goods.

     Like many others of the period, the account misjudged both the
California phenomenon it used as a prime example and the fundamental
changes that were beginning to occur in mass distribution. The gasoline
station was presented as a case of consumer abuse. The motorist might be
pampered while getting the tank filled, but other service facilities were

usually leased . . . to any farmer who has the few hundred dollars necessary. When one
farmer's savings are gone, another is generally ready, eager and willing. . . . The filling sta-

tion proprietor . . . sublets these shops for what he can get out of them. After a series of tenants have scrambled a series of motorists' batteries and so forth, the effect is seen in falling sales. . . . The motorist who has been stung in the service shops avoids that station. Then the proprietor . . . may go out of business, and somebody takes his place. And so on.[2]

Some California gasoline stations no doubt suffered from poor management, but so bleak an overall picture is not substantiated by the record. Had service been that poor, these facilities would never have proliferated the way they did during the 1920s, first in Los Angeles, then throughout the state and in many other parts of the country. Nor would the concept have substantially affected the way in which major oil and tire companies approached retailing. The technicians employed at a super service station, as these outlets were called, often came to the job with considerable experience. Their skills were profiled by the local press in the same way as those of leading personnel of new food, drug, variety, and even department stores.[3] The super station was the product of persons immersed in the world of motor cars. As a phenomenon, it represented the strengths, not the weaknesses, of monkey-wrench merchandising. Equally important, the type demonstrated new ways in which related businesses could operate effectively in an integrated fashion. Through this form of merchandising, an entirely different approach was taken to arranging retail facilities, one that accommodated motorists on the premises. Thanks to the technician, the easy movement of cars determined the entire configuration. A process thus was introduced that would eventually revolutionize the planning of retail facilities. Nothing like it had happened before.

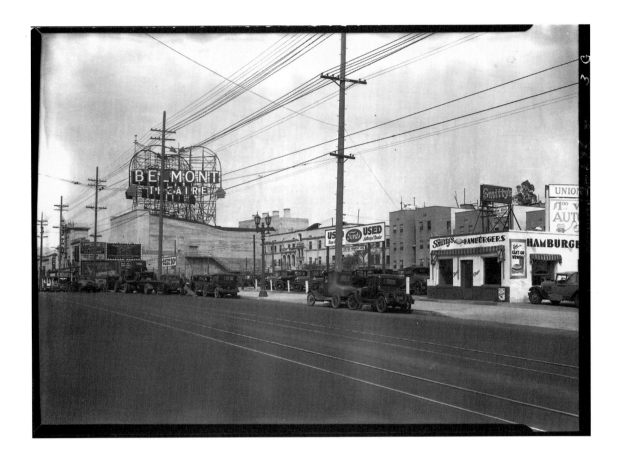

SPACE

In Los Angeles, as in other cities, concern for architecturally accommodating the automobile was slow to gain momentum, even after driving became a routine occurrence. Until the late 1920s, most of the solutions developed for off-street parking had no significant impact on the appearance of the buildings they served and little effect on the character of urban development. Parking lots were considered residue space. Unlike traditional open areas in cities and towns, these facilities were incidental voids. They were considered unsightly gaps in the urban matrix, exposing the unadorned side walls of adjacent buildings and enhancing the opportunities for outdoor advertisements (figure 1). The situation was no different for commercial districts in outlying areas. Through most of the 1920s, space specifically devoted to off-street parking was rare outside the urban core. Most such facilities served neighborhood movie houses, which drew more motorists than curbside parking could accommodate (figure 2). Even when conceived as an integral component of a business, the parking lot seldom affected the design of the building. The streetfront orientation of stores remained unaltered; walls facing lots were as plain as those never intended for public view.[4]

The other principal means of automobile storage was the parking garage, which, like the parking lot, was almost always located downtown during the 1920s. Some garages fully bespoke their utilitarian role, but most were embellished on the exterior, generating customer appeal by com-

1
Parque-n-Shoppe parking lot, Eighth and Los Angeles streets, Los Angeles. Photo "Dick" Whittington, 1930. (Whittington Collection, Department of Special Collections, University of Southern California.)

2
100 block, S. Vermont Avenue, Los Angeles; Belmont Theatre (1925–1926, no longer standing) and car lot at left. Photo "Dick" Whittington, 1931. (Whittington Collection, Department of Special Collections, University of Southern California.)

3
Auto Cleaning Company Garage,
816 S. Grand Avenue, Los Angeles,
1924. Photo author, 1997.

plementing the commercial buildings around them (figure 3).[5] Spatially, these facilities did not alter any aspect of the urban landscape; they simply added a new function to those housed in multistory business blocks. Similarly, garages in office buildings affected exterior design in a minimal way. Most were set below grade. Portals to those subterranean levels were sometimes no more than openings located toward or at the rear of the building. Even when conspicuously placed, they were treated much like other street-front bays save for the absence of enclosing partitions.

    While practical matters were dominant in shaping early automobile accommodation, a deeply rooted cultural concern for familiarity also affected the outcome. People react to changes in their physical setting in ways that are difficult to predict. For this reason among others, pronounced departures tend to be mitigated by features rooted in the past, particularly in the commercial sphere, where the development's success depends upon attracting people as tenants and customers. In both the city center and new outlying areas, the great majority of commercial buildings constructed through the 1920s adhered to the age-old tradition of fronting the street, abutting the sidewalk, occupying most (if not all) of the property frontage, and extending for much of the property's depth.[6] With few exceptions, buildings were not treated as freestanding objects, but as parts of a connective wall that distinguished private from public realms. The car was accommodated by channeling it through essentially conventional forms of open space. Public works programs of the early twentieth century widened and straightened thousands of municipal streets nationwide, and sometimes created street systems to encourage more diffuse forms of traffic flow. Nevertheless, the basic order was based on time-honored relationships between open public spaces and enclosed private spaces. However difficult the fit, the automobile conformed to these conditions far more than it modified them.

Allocating prime private space to the automobile and using this feature to generate the overall design of a commercial facility serving other purposes was an alien concept, even to many Angelenos, through the 1920s and later. However convenient, car lots were seen as a waste of space and money by retailers and as unattractive blotches on the face of the city by the proponents of civic improvement. The first significant change to this approach came in the workaday field of car service itself. The initial step came with the development of a brand-new building type—the filling station—which was conceived in the unstructured, unorthodox world of monkey-wrench merchandising.

FILLING STATIONS

The filling station had to perform simple tasks, but they were ones never before required of a building: dispensing gasoline and motor oil to mechanized vehicles. Both the elementary and novel nature of this function contributed to the early establishment of a design pattern that broke decisively from conventional uses of space. Property frontage was left open so that motorists could pull off the street and maneuver on the premises. This arrangement was born out of necessity. Of the possible alternatives, placing fuel pumps alongside the curb spawned a host of problems, including bottlenecks.[7] Constructing a building into which cars could enter for refueling incurred prohibitive costs unless the facility was also used for related functions, such as automobile service or parking—a factor that greatly limited the number of such examples. Situating pumps in alleys or rear service courts was never an option, as it would have made it difficult to attract customers.

The response to these circumstances was straightforward. Since the building needed to be no more than an enclosed kiosk, it was easily located back from the street so that cars could still be serviced at its front. The archetypal configuration of commercial architecture thus was transformed from a lot-filling, street-oriented establishment that clearly defined the boundary between public and private space, to one in which space was continuous, the separation of the two realms perceptually minimal, and the building proper a midspace object occupying only a fraction of the property. Despite its mundane purpose, modest size, and utilitarian appearance, the filling station was a revolutionary work that gave birth to the drive-in concept, whereby providing space for cars became the principal determinant of the setting, configuration, and sometimes even the internal layout of the facility.

Early examples of the type often manifested their new characteristics in a limited way. The standardized design for National Supply Stations, perhaps the first chain of such outlets in Los Angeles, represented the drive-in concept at a nascent stage when the initial units opened in 1913 (figure 4). The building was a utilitarian box fronted by a shed-roof porte-cochere sheltering a single pump. To get service, motorists were restricted to a single path leading from the street, much like a driveway. Yet the arrangement proved easily adaptable to larger, looser formats. Within a few years, numerous facilities could accommodate two or more cars at the pumps and had space for additional ones on the premises.

4
National Supply Stations, advertisement. (*Los Angeles Times,* 16 November 1913, VII-12.)

Matching convenience with the caliber of its product soon came to be associated with the filling station. The National Supply system was established by an alliance of prominent automobile dealers in Los Angeles and San Francisco to sell top-grade gasoline and motor oil at a low price. Their goal was to stem the widespread distribution of inferior products then supposedly plaguing the state.[8] Elsewhere, the filling station often was introduced to a region by a leading petroleum company as a marketing instrument for its own supplies. At a time when few safeguards existed to protect the purchaser of poor-quality goods of this kind, the filling station stood as a symbol of assurance.[9]

By the early 1920s, Los Angeles's mystique as a center for automobile-related innovations was sufficiently established that a number of people in the petroleum business believed the filling station had originated there in 1912. In fact, examples of drive-in facilities could be found in St. Louis and other cities several years earlier.[10] Southern California was nevertheless an important staging ground for new ideas due to the high incidence of automobile ownership there and the population's attachment to using those cars as much as possible. The region also was fast becoming a major center for the manufacture of petroleum and related products. The inclination to experiment was further encouraged by the mild climate, which obviated some of the costly building methods necessary in many parts of the United States. These circumstances contributed to an advance in the idea of a drive-in facility devoted to automotive service that greatly expanded both the scope of operation and the physical plant in which it was housed. The result was manifested in a grouping organized for the convenience of vehicular movement that soon came to be known as the super service station.

SUPER SERVICE STATIONS

The filling station was still a new phenomenon when a major expansion of the concept, combining numerous related functions in a single facility, was introduced in Los Angeles just prior to World War I. At that time, filling stations sold gas and oil; lubrication and cleaning were done separately elsewhere. A variety of shops specialized in different kinds of repairs or in the sale of tires or other accessories. The gathering of these enterprises in the super service station offered considerable convenience to consumers still trying to master the demands of maintaining an automobile. After 1918, as car ownership swelled, the concept quickly became a popular one. Dozens of super stations were constructed in southern California during the early 1920s and hundreds more could be found nationwide by the decade's end. Although the super service station has been all but ignored in recent histories, it had a profound impact on the practice of retailing automotive products. These facilities constituted an essential link between the filling station and the service stations that became ubiquitous by the mid-1930s.[11]

The earliest known super service station was built around 1914 by the Washburn-Walker Company on Western Avenue, some three miles from downtown, prior to that street's rapid transformation into an important business artery. The location lay close to affluent and prosperous middle-class households in what was then Los Angeles's fastest-growing residential area.[12] Called Service Town, the complex had a six-bay filling station with herms supporting its elaborate canopy. Behind lay a paved court, large enough to permit customers to make a full turn without reversing gears, surrounded by buildings for lubrication, body cleaning and polishing, crank-case cleaning, battery repairs, tire repairs, and accessories. Washburn-Walker offered a monthly car maintenance plan, including pickup and delivery of vehicles for people who did not wish to drive their own cars to the premises. The facility cost $35,000, a large sum at that time for any commercial establishment in an outlying area, but proved none too ambitious. Demand for services swelled to the point that the company soon erected a more modest second unit nearby to handle overflow traffic. Although the two Service Towns remained anomalies for several years, imitators began to appear after the war's end (figure 5). By 1922 the super service station idea gained acceptance to the point that it was being discussed as a trend.[13]

Customers appreciated the convenience of the super station. Early on, proprietors discovered that many motorists patronized the gas pumps because of the other services available and that these patrons were more inclined to have maintenance and repair work performed when it could be done at one place. The gas pumps were an essential frontispiece, as it were, to get motorists on the premises, but the greatest percentage of revenues came from the other components of the complex. The presence of each unit thus enhanced the appeal of the others. Package contracts for upkeep, personal attention to customer needs, and promotional campaigns became standard. The proprietor might run all the departments or lease some of them to specialists. Either way, the establishment was managed in a coordinated fashion. Automobile service thus entered the realm of modern retailing as an integrated business, that is, one with a number of distinct components run as a closely coordinated enterprise under single management.[14]

Super service stations flourished in southern California during the 1920s not just because of the amenities they offered motorists, but also because of intense competition among both oil companies and retailers.[15] Low wholesale prices, combined with the rapid growth in demand, led to an oversupply of gasoline outlets. Directories listed about 170 filling stations in 1920, almost 700 in 1925, and more than 1,500 in 1930 for the city of Los Angeles alone. The abundance of retailers kept profit margins low on the average. In addition, the now fairly uniform quality of most petroleum products lessened the competitive advantage of each concern. A choice location, an elaborate physical plant, and aggressive advertising could spawn increased sales, but also added significantly to overhead. Major oil companies and independent dealers alike thus resisted making more

than a modest investment in the filling station itself. However, if selling gas and oil alone provided few opportunities to increase profits, adding service, parts, and accessories allowed retailers to gain a competitive advantage, tapping into a vast potential market for sales.

The immediate source of inspiration for the first Service Town remains unknown. Automobile dealers had included service facilities for some years, but not until the early 1920s did most of them realize that refashioning their service facilities, in a manner derived from the department store's business structure, could make them a significant source of revenue.[16] At a time when most car dealers in Los Angeles and other cities were situated at the edge of the urban core, the super station proliferated because of its proximity to residential areas. The diffuse structure of the metropolis was, of course, a considerable advantage in this regard; super stations scattered along arteries throughout the region afforded more convenient service places for many people than did the concentrated nodes of automobile dealerships.

The idea of one-stop shopping as a profitable venture outside core business areas was fostered at an early stage of the super station's development by the success of several large retail, or "public," markets erected in Los Angeles as early as 1913.[17] Unlike their municipal forebears, these establishments were privately owned. Examples were built in many parts of the country during the early twentieth century, but the type seems to have enjoyed special popularity in California, in part due to that state's importance as a food distribution center and the absence of a tradition of municipal ownership. The growth of the public market owed much to

5

Shepard-Campbell Company service station, 2300 S. Figueroa Street, Los Angeles, ca. 1920; no longer standing. Photo early 1920s. (California Historical Society Collection, Department of Special Collections, University of Southern California.)

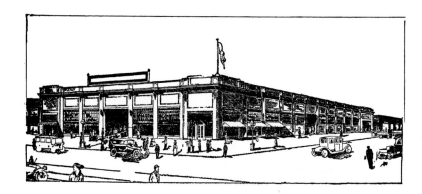

management policies. Proprietors emulated chain company executives in using the department store as a model, focusing on product quality, service, and price and advancing these attributes through aggressive promotional campaigns.[18] But in contrast to the typically small unit of the chain grocery store, the public market had a great array of goods, often including many specialized items. In early examples, each basic product type was sold by more than one concessionaire so that patrons could comparison-shop on the premises. The extent of the type's development in Los Angeles is suggested by the White Arcade, a pile encompassing over 32,000 square feet designed in 1914 for a close-in location at Main Street and Pico Boulevard, just south of downtown (figure 6). The layout was traditional to the type, with concessions oriented to a central circulation spine. The ambience, however, appears to have been fashioned after that of a department store, with the main space enframed by an arcade and culminating in a marble fountain and concert stage.[19]

The White Arcade and other public markets constructed in Los Angeles before World War I were located in or near the central business district.[20] Within a few years, the type began to proliferate in outlying areas. Decentralization fostered the type's appeal, for shoppers could now find all basic types of food products under one roof close to home. Advertisements emphasized that goods were offered at "downtown" prices, which were lower than those at the small neighborhood store; this was a particularly attractive draw when food costs soared during the postwar years. Decentralization also seems to have led to modifications in the business structure of local public markets, which were consolidated to include only one large department for each basic category of product (groceries, produce, meat/poultry/fish, baked goods were standard divisions). In this revised form, with four or five divisions, the operation could be managed more efficiently. Furthermore, the concessionaires often were chain organizations or branches of large regional companies that could contribute sound business practices and keep high prices at bay.[21]

Among the first wave of facilities constructed outside the city center, the Hollywood Public Market (1919–1920) was indicative of the trend (figure 7). Standing at the corner of Hollywood Boulevard and Wilcox Street in the heart of the district's burgeoning business center, the empo-

rium encompassed over 5,000 square feet of space, more than twice that of
most neighborhood food stores, and housed eight departments, an unusually high number.[22] When it opened, the Hollywood Public Market was
considered something of a novelty; however, by the closing months of
1922 at least thirteen other examples existed within a two-mile radius.
Most were about the same size, but the Beverly-Western Public Market
(1921–1922) was considerably bigger at 15,000 square feet (figure 8).[23]
The expansiveness and location of this outlet probably were designed to
secure drive-by customers as well as locally based trade; as it was situated
at what had become a major intersection of automobile routes. It also lay
conveniently between Western Avenue's two largest business centers in an
area that had markedly less congestion, since the immediate environs were
much less intensely developed. Similar siting techniques were used on a
number of subsequent public markets beyond the city proper. The big
Richardson's Market (1923) was constructed in the southern part of the
bedroom community of Alhambra along a major east-west highway not far
from an equally well traveled route connecting Pasadena and Long Beach

(figure 9).[24] Passing motorists may well have outnumbered local customers living in the rather thinly settled environs.

The attention paid to driving patterns in the location and in the business structure of the public market provided useful models for the super service station at a time when the latter was ceasing to be a novelty. By the early 1920s, the public market demonstrated that carefully selected sites in outlying areas could be advantageous for a sizable business catering to routine needs. On the other hand, no models existed for the layout of the super station, and thus it was not surprising that no prevailing pattern emerged during the type's inceptive phase. Most layouts were designed to provide ample maneuvering space and as a result had a sizable open yard around which the departments were located on one or more sides. Often the arrangement was a loose configuration of buildings and unsheltered fixtures possessing little coherence in design or suggestion of investment beyond that required to meet basic needs (figures 10, 11). The fact that many super stations started as modest facilities and grew over a period of years contributed to such results.[25]

Whether constructed incrementally or in a single campaign, some complexes followed the sample of Service Town, using a repertoire of embellishments to convey the impression of a large, prosperous, and respectable business. Among the most famous of these California establishments was the Muller Brothers station in Hollywood, which began as a small operation around 1919 and expanded to include twenty departments occupying five acres by the late 1920s (figure 12).[26] Like the original Service Town, the most prominent feature was an ornate, freestanding canopy sheltering rows of gasoline pumps and visually functioning as a gateway to the entire complex. This practice of architecturally addressing the street continued throughout the decade, in part to shade refueling motorists but also to make the facility relate to, and hence seem a respectable part of, established forms of outlying retail development (figure 13).

9
Richardson's Market, 208–236 E. Valley Boulevard, Alhambra, California, 1923, Byron D. Harper, architect; no longer standing. Photo ca. 1920s. (Security Pacific Historical Photograph Collection, Los Angeles Public Library.)

10

Foy's service station, 211 N. Figueroa Street, Los Angeles, ca. 1920s; no longer standing. Photo "Dick" Whittington, 1928. (Whittington Collection, Department of Special Collections, University of Southern California.)

11

Wilshire–La Brea service station, 5217–5259 Wilshire Boulevard, Los Angeles, 1920s; no longer standing. Photo "Dick" Whittington, 1928. (Whittington Collection, Department of Special Collections, University of Southern California.)

12

Muller Brothers service station, 6380 Sunset Boulevard, Los Angeles, begun ca. 1919; no longer standing. (*Filling Station,* June 1929, 23.)

The desire to conform to what were regarded as the salient qualities of the commercial landscape was shared by many of those involved
with creating a new architecture to accommodate the automobile. Much
as the fronts of downtown parking garages echoed those of office buildings,
so those of many facilities designed for the repair and storage of cars in outlying areas possessed attributes associated with nearby taxpayer blocks.
Some service garages also included store units along the street, minimizing
the visual impact of the automobile-oriented functions that lay behind
(figure 14). One of the most elaborate schemes was launched by the newly
formed Standard Motor Service Company in 1919 as the first unit in a proposed chain of facilities.[27] Located on Western Avenue not far from Service
Town, the plan entailed much the same scope of departments as well as a
large auto storage area on the second level. In their physical conception,
however, the two enterprises could not have stood further apart (figure 15).
Most of the Standard building was treated as utilitarian shelter, but was subordinated visually to a front section composed like a grand residence. A vehicular portal in the place of a front door provided the only architectural
clue to the building's actual purpose that was conspicuous from the street.

Counterpointing the forces of tradition and conformity was the
need to meet a new series of programmatic requirements at a reasonable
cost. Even without elaborate facades, fully enclosed garages were expensive
to build because of the large amount of unencumbered indoor space they

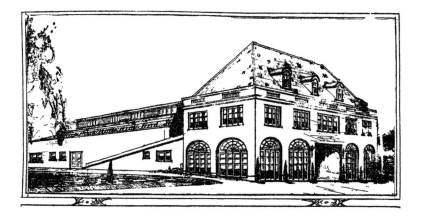

required. Having more than one level further necessitated using a costly steel or reinforced concrete structural system. With the super station, on the other hand, much of the space was left undeveloped save for grading and surfacing. The one or more buildings on the site covered short spans and could be erected employing substantially cheaper methods, just as with a modest taxpayer block. Furthermore, the demands of automobile storage and service were not always compatible. Achieving maximum profits from parked cars could impinge upon space needed for service, while servicing often spread dust and grime unwelcome to owners of stored vehicles. Service bays facing an open yard, which in turn had nothing other than a support function, seemed a far more efficient layout from the standpoint of both cost and use. The arrangement also carried associational benefits. While the garage was still seen as part of a man's world, the super station possessed a perceptual accessibility that was considered as appealing to women as to men.[28] Openness, as it turned out, proved more important than a decorous front when one had to remain behind the wheel to enter the premises. Given the rapidly increasing number of female motorists during the 1920s, this factor became important in advancing the super station's development.

Besides having a more inviting appearance than the service garage, the super station could convey its attributes to passing motorists so that the complex as a whole, not just a facade or signs, could serve as an effective advertisement. The streetfront canopy sheltering gas pumps might enhance the image of an operation in this respect. In 1922 Frank Muller remarked that, at his Hollywood outlet, "it is easily seen that quick and efficient delivery of car requirements are made with no delay to the customers."[29]

But another type of configuration, with an L-shaped building set toward the rear and enframing a large forecourt, proved optimal in allowing drivers to see at a glance the range of services offered. The L-shaped plan had no clear precedent; it seems to have emanated from a realization, or perhaps an instinctive sense, that fundamental differences in configuration would be necessary in designing a complex whose purpose could be understood at once by people traveling at significantly greater speeds than those of the streetcar or the pedestrian.[30] Experiments of this nature began at an early phase of the super service station's development. Perhaps the first example was built by the Auto Super-Service Company around 1921, which also may have inaugurated, or at least helped popularize, the generic use of the name (figure 16). Here gas and oil were dispensed next to a corner kiosk. Wide driveways to either side clearly revealed the extent of the complex. The layout still indicated some reluctance to yield too much of the streetfront to open space. Bracketing walls on both the kiosk and service center visually contained the court, and that court's center was occupied by a large building for the sale of accessories. Moreover, access to the service center was from the street on one end of the L, with the exit the opposite extremity.[31]

The L-shaped configuration was soon refined in the layout of other complexes. The Calmos Service Station in Hollywood (1923) represented what became a typical arrangement over the next half-dozen years (figure 17). The kiosk still punctuated the corner to serve as a beacon, but, like a filling station, was oriented to the street, making access to the pumps more direct. The service building behind was equally conspicuous, topped with ersatz minarets and domes, its bays opening directly onto the forecourt. The spatial order was straightforward and the components unified: the two buildings formed an integrated whole that clearly conveyed the movement of cars on the premises. A balance thus was struck between defining the operation through architecture and allowing open space as the predominant feature. Setting was an important factor in achieving that equilibrium. Corner locations were generally considered desirable for super service and filling stations because of the visual prominence they afforded as well as their potential to draw customers from two streets instead of just one. With the L-shaped plan, the corner lot became a virtual necessity, both for purposes of identification and for unencumbered vehicular movement.

By the mid-1920s, the super service station was becoming a common feature in the urban landscape of southern California. Layout, architectural treatment, and size continued to vary, but there were no significant deviations from the patterns established in the previous years. Large complexes sometimes included a cafe or even a few shops as added customer attractions (figure 18). Nevertheless, these marginally related functions were subordinate to the primary one of automobile care. The super station did not provide the nexus for more extensive building programs encompassing

16
Auto Super-Service Company service station, 1723–1725 S. Hope Street, Los Angeles, ca. 1920; no longer standing. (*Los Angeles Times,* 18 September 1921, V-9.)

Keep Down Up Keep

Vacation time imposes heavy burdens on your machine.

When you return from the mountains or seashore, leave the car with us for "SUPER-SERVICING."

Our new and scientific methods include oiling, greasing and washing the car, as well as cleaning by steam the motor and chassis.

Have you inspected the new and attractive Spanish type home of "SUPER-SERVICE"? We have 16,275 square feet of floor space and everything is equipped to give YOU real conscientious service. Our ladies' rest room is well appointed.

Drop in and get acquainted. Our prices are reasonable— our work is the best.

Gasoline and oil department open all night.

Auto Super-Service Company

Phone West 4964

17
Calmos Service Station, 4966–4982
Hollywood Boulevard, Los Angeles,
1923; altered. Photo "Dick" Whit-
tington, 1932. (Whittington
Collection, Department of Special
Collections, University of Southern
California.)

18
L. E. Preston Tire Company service
station, 657–659 N. Vermont Ave-
nue, Los Angeles, 1927–1928, John
A. Klarquist, designer/builder; no
longer standing. Photo "Dick"
Whittington, 1932. (Whittington
Collection, Department of Special
Collections, University of Southern
California.)

additional kinds of retail activities. Even a broader scope of automobile-
related ones was unusual. A "motor department store" developed in 1926
by Hollywood businessman E. F. Bogardus—which contained two auto
and two tire dealerships, along with outlets for accessories, electrical parts
and batteries, and lubrication, as well as for gasoline and oil—was an anomaly in the region.[32]

Much the same consistency was evident in the diffusion of the super service concept to other parts of the United States, a process that took
place from the mid-1920s through the decade's end. Generally, the repertoire of layouts and services followed southern California models.[33] The
most pronounced departure lay in image, which varied according to differences in climate and regional preferences in architecture (figure 19). In
places where examples were not as ubiquitous as in southern California,

entrepreneurs sometimes capitalized on novelty to create very ambitious complexes that attained a degree of local prominence seldom found in Los Angeles. In some cases, too, the super service station was combined with other functions, probably more as an expedient to increase revenue than as an integrated retail complex. A large station in the commercial center of Manhattan, Kansas, for example, included such disparate additional facilities as a flower shop, cafe, taxi company offices, and bus depot.[34] Such complexes remained the exception, however. Few functions proved compatible with the messiness of automobile service and repair, and few entrepreneurs who pursued this realm of monkey-wrench merchandising appear to have had much interest in markedly different lines of business.

AUTO LAUNDRIES

The one consequential addition to the super station's repertoire that emerged during the 1920s was the mechanized car wash, or auto laundry, as it was called. At that time, these facilities were closely tied to car maintenance and, in principle at least, were a logical extension of the super station's services. The type did not originate in southern California but some of the most significant contributions to its development occurred there, including the integration of related functions. The plethora of unpaved roads, in addition to the car's exposed mechanical parts and frequent casing leakage, made regular cleaning important to keep automobiles in good working condition. Commercial ventures devoted exclusively to this process were established in the Midwest as early as 1914, but methods other than hand scrubbing were still a novelty at the beginning of the next decade. Even with the introduction of air and water sprays, most auto laundries consisted of one or more stationary car racks, which positioned vehicles so that their undercarriages, sides, and tops could be washed. Often a minimal enclosure was erected to protect the equipment. By the mid-1920s, auto laundries of this elementary kind began to be built as

19
Ramsdell Brothers service station, Carnegie Avenue and E. Seventy-first Street, Cleveland, Ohio, ca. 1924–1925; no longer standing. (*Filling Station,* 25 December 1925, 42.)

appendages to filling stations in some parts of the United States; many others were erected as separate operations.[35]

Experiments with larger facilities were made as early as 1922 when a garage at St. Paul, Minnesota, erected an adjacent "wash bowl" where motorists could drive their cars around in a flooded basin to remove dirt from the underbody before leaving them for cleaning at the adjacent racks. At least one similar complex was built, this time in Chicago, but the idea was short-lived, perhaps owing to the fact that, as an open-air operation, it was unusable for much of the year in northern climates.[36]

A more sophisticated process was developed in 1923 by a Los Angeles enterprise, Wimsett System Auto Laundries, which constructed two outlets where cars moved on a circular platform while being cleaned in a processional, multistaged operation similar to an assembly line. Each facility was housed in a building that looked like an elaborate super service outlet and included a lunch room, an accessories dealer, and a filling station so that customers could perform several errands at one place (figure 20). Washing took from fifteen to twenty minutes, polishing about the same amount of time. The cost was high, with a minimum charge of $2.00.[37] With these facilities, the auto laundry was transformed from a utilitarian shed into a neighborhood landmark and destination for motorists in much the same way that the most pretentious super stations were recasting the mundane activities of gasoline purchase and automobile repair.

Over the next five years a number of competitors entered the business, constructing even more lavish plants. Speed was a primary objective. The quicker the service, the greater its appeal; the higher the volume, the lower the price. Pacific Auto Laundries boasted a ten-minute wash and a forty-minute cycle for washing, polishing, and cleaning the engine. Ever more elaborate equipment, including mechanical conveyors, was devised to reduce turnaround time.[38] Probably the largest and most influential undertaking was El Patio Auto Laundry (1926–1927) built on South Vermont Avenue by a local realtor, B. K. Gillespie (figure 21). The building was less pretentious than some, but departed from precedent by including a wide range of other automobile services. Gillespie adopted the super station idea in its entirety, although he refused to employ the label, claiming that "the average so-called 'super service station' of California is . . . modest in contrast" to the "acre of service" found at his establishment. Besides nine departments for car repair and maintenance, this "service community" included a restaurant, beauty parlor, and clothes laundry that customers could use while waiting for their cars. Unlike the gas pumps of the super station, the enormous car wash formed the centerpiece of the whole operation and generated the greatest revenue.[39]

Within two years of El Patio's opening, E. H. Kron, a dealer in car accessories, and Will Hays, head of the Motion Picture Association, approached Gillespie with a proposal to form a national chain of units patterned after the Los Angeles facility. Gillespie agreed, other businessmen joined the venture, and by the latter months of 1928 the Gillespie Automobile Laundry System had a string of operations on the west coast (San Diego, Long Beach, Pasadena, Oakland, and Portland) as well as others in Denver, Tulsa, St. Louis, and Atlanta. Twenty-eight additional units were under construction and a network of two hundred was envisioned. The biggest of these "super" auto laundries, such as those in Denver and Tulsa, were impressive not only in their size but in their elaborate appearance (figure 22).[40] These buildings were in effect the ultimate super service stations, with few counterparts in southern California and far grander than most automobile-related facilities in their own communities. The Gillespie System set a new standard for such places nationwide, which was emulated, but probably never excelled, by competing companies.[41]

21
El Patio Auto Laundry, 260 S. Vermont Avenue, Los Angeles, 1926–1927, M. Eugene Durfee, architect; no longer standing. Photo "Dick" Whittington, 1930. (Whittington Collection, Department of Special Collections, University of Southern California.)

Gillespie also had found an effective mix of functions for his auto laundry; but most attempts to expand into neighborhood retail functions failed to develop beyond singular experiments. By far the most lavish project of this kind in southern California was a complex for the Western Auto Wash Company. Designed in 1927 by Morgan, Walls & Clements, the most prominent Los Angeles architectural firm to create distinctive commercial buildings in outlying areas, the laundry building was festooned with Spanish classical details but composed as if it were an ancient Greek stoa, with a line of cars rather than pedestrians entering its portals (figure 23).[42] Despite its decorous exterior, the facility sat far back from the street and soon was obscured from view by two even more ornate retail blocks housing a market, drug store, and other emporia catering to everyday needs (figure 24). Before or after cleaning, automobiles could pull up

directly to the store buildings, whose rear elevations were treated as elabo-
rately as their streetfronts. A filling station was also part of the ensemble
(figures 25, 26). This arrangement encouraged motorists to combine errands and perhaps to have the car washed as often as they purchased food.
However, for patrons who weren't following that pattern of consumption,
the layout was unwieldy. Cars winding their way through the premises to
be cleaned would inevitably cause traffic problems for shoppers wishing to
go only to the stores. This mixture of functions may have been chosen to
make the auto laundry seem more respectable, especially to women. That
objective was harbored by B. W. Sinclair, owner of the Gillespie franchise
for San Diego, who added streetfront stores to his facility so that "all the
unsightly features heretofore associated with auto laundries [will be] entirely eliminated."[43]

Through Gillespie's own example, the auto laundry developed
into a full-scale service center for cars. On the other hand, with few exceptions—such as the Muller Brothers complex in Hollywood—the super station never expanded to include a full-scale auto laundry operation.[44] Auto
laundries occupied a considerable amount of space and were difficult to
add to existing plants. Furthermore, the cost of such a facility was at least
$50,000, surpassing all but the most expensive super stations. Even if they
had the space and the financial means, most super station operators could
not add auto laundries because Gillespie and others who held patents on

22
Western Gillespie System service station, 1402–1426 S. Boston Avenue,
Tulsa, Oklahoma, ca. 1928; demolished 1983. (*National Petroleum News*,
20 March 1929, 118–119.)

23
Western Auto Wash, 920 S. Western
Avenue, Los Angeles, 1927, Mor-
gan, Walls & Clements, architects;
no longer standing. Photo "Dick"
Whittington, 1927. (Whittington
Collection, Department of Special
Collections, University of Southern
California.)

24
Ninth and Western business center,
918–922 S. Western Avenue, 1927–
1928, Morgan, Walls & Clements,
architects; no longer standing. Photo
"Dick" Whittington, 1929. (Huntington Library.)

their respective "systems" were not eager to share them widely. Success for the auto laundry required a high-volume trade in a limited market. In selling franchises, Gillespie took pains to ensure that locations were so far removed from one another that no potential for competition could exist among them. The small cadre of others who promoted their own systems no doubt harbored the same concern. The market was also limited, due to the substantial cost of washing; as a result, most of these complexes were located near well-to-do residential areas.

Behind such immediate obstacles to integration lay a basic difference in circumstances through which each type developed. The super station was conceived and operated by persons whose careers were closely tied to the automobile. Many individuals came to the field with experience in the manufacture or sales of cars or of related products. Others had worked at filling stations. Even when not previously employed in an automobile-related trade, most super stations owners were immersed in running their businesses, which often bore their names.[45] Auto laundries, on the other hand, tended to be built as investments by men such as Gillespie whose expertise lay in other realms. At least in southern California, car washing was an externally generated phenomenon, the work of persons who, among their diverse ventures, underwrote costly mechanical inventions and equally costly installations with the hope of creating a lucrative new industry.

Both the size and nature of the investment that so rapidly propelled the auto laundry into the limelight worked with even greater speed to arrest its development during the depression. Improvements to the process had lowered prices somewhat—Gillespie charged $1.50 for washing—but the service no doubt seemed ever more a luxury. Equally important, major improvements in both road surfaces and car manufacture rendered the car wash more cosmetic than utilitarian. Under the circumstances, the large, elaborate auto laundry of the 1920s remained an exceptional phenomenon. Even in Los Angeles, probably no more than two dozen such complexes were constructed. The idea did not reemerge as commercially attractive until the prosperous post–World War II years when, once more, southern California appears to have played a pivotal role.[46]

TRANSITION

Size and the owners' objectives also had a decisive impact on the fate of the super service station. In southern California and in other regions, most super stations were developed by independent retailers. The success of these operations soon attracted the interest of major tire and oil companies, whose eventual involvement had a significant impact on both the form of buildings and the nature of services they provided. As early as 1921, a costly super station was erected in Hollywood by the Pacific Rubber Company.[47] Comparable ventures seem to have been few during the next

25
Ninth and Western business center, rear view. Photo "Dick" Whittington, 1929. (Whittington Collection, Department of Special Collections, University of Southern California.)

26
Ninth and Western business center, elevated rear view. Photo "Dick" Whittington, 1929. (Whittington Collection, Department of Special Collections, University of Southern California.)

several years, but national tire company sponsorship of super stations emerged as a major trend by the end of the decade. The three largest manufacturers—Firestone, Goodyear, and B. F. Goodrich—all of which had plants in Los Angeles, took the lead in developing full-service outlets, owing to the success of early experiments and to ongoing problems with retaining good dealers at their conventional outlets.[48] By the late 1920s these companies began constructing facilities modeled on those of the independents, but bearing a distinct corporate imprint and with an authorized dealer running all departments except, perhaps, the filling station (figures 27, 28). During the 1930s, as independent owners played a less consequential role in the automobile service business, tire companies continued to build large service centers, and it is primarily through their participation that super service stations continued to be built into the mid-twentieth century.[49]

Major oil companies showed much greater reluctance to enter the super service field, even though a number of them took leases on the filling station component at an early stage in the type's development. Throughout the 1920s the petroleum producers' involvement in the retail field centered on selling their own products, relying heavily on brand recognition for sales.[50] Super stations cost more to build, and running them required more time and effort than most salaried employees in the petroleum business were willing to invest.[51] Yet by the late 1920s, oil companies

27
Goodyear Service, Inc. service station, 181–185 S. La Brea Avenue, Los Angeles, 1930, Allen Ruoff, architect; altered. Photo "Dick" Whittington, 1932. (Whittington Collection, Department of Special Collections, University of Southern California.)

sought to bolster retail profits beyond those possible from a filling station and to capture a share of the super station trade. The initial strategy focused on adding those services for which the demand was greatest—most commonly greasing, lubrication, minor repairs, and the sale of tires, batteries, and a few accessories.[52] Southern California was an ideal place for experimenting with this idea because the mild climate enabled many such functions to be performed outdoors or with minimal shelter, thus keeping the cost of the physical plant well below that of the typical super station (figure 29).

Once the financial soundness of providing a limited range of services was proven, oil companies began to create a new type of building tailored to that program. The result was a compact, freestanding, fully enclosed structure that generally contained one or two service bays adjacent to the office. This building type was relatively inexpensive to construct, designed with standardized components and graphics, and well suited to all parts of the country. At first these outlets were often called super service stations to take advantage of a term that had gained widespread appeal, but by the mid-1930s, when the type emerged as the industry standard, they became known simply as service stations (figure 30).[53]

Capitalizing on the super service station idea while at the same time transforming it enabled major petroleum companies to consolidate their leading position in the sale of basic automotive products and services.

28
Goodrich Silvertown, Inc. service station, 3318 W. Washington Boulevard, Los Angeles, ca. 1920s; no longer standing. Photo "Dick" Whittington, 1930. (Whittington Collection, Department of Special Collections, University of Southern California.)

Both the role of the independent dealer and the super station declined during the 1930s. Relatively few examples were erected, save by tire companies, in southern California or elsewhere after the initial years of the depression. The decline was driven not as much by cost as by the major oil companies' discovery that sizable buildings were not a central determinant of profits. Numerous comparatively small service stations, scattered throughout an area, often could best serve most customers' needs most of the time.[54] These circumstances enabled the type rapidly to become a ubiquitous fixture nationwide.

The refinement of monkey-wrench merchandising in the automotive service field to form the most effective bridge between the large corporation and the consumer thus in time led to leaner, more compact outlets

29
Standard Oil Company station, Los Angeles. Photo Albert Frey, 1932. (Courtesy Albert Frey.)

30
Texaco service station, Type C, 1937, Walter Dorwin Teague, designer. Location unknown, but probably on west coast. Photo ca. 1937. (Courtesy Texaco, Inc.)

rather than larger, more organizationally complex ones. The super service station formed an important transitional stage in the sequence, but its most significant legacy lay in demonstrating how cars could effectively determine the setting and configuration of facilities catering to the motorist. The phenomenon also underscored the potential of integrated business development catering to routine needs on a small scale. Both characteristics served as direct models for the drive-in market, which began to develop in southern California while the super station was still in its infancy, and which served as a catalyst for changes that eventually had a profound impact on retail development in the United States.

II

STORES THE ROAD
PASSES THROUGH

The idea must have seemed a rather odd one. In June 1923, C. L. Peckham—head of an insurance adjustment firm in Glendale, a rapidly growing middle-class residential community just northeast of Los
Angeles—announced plans for developing a commercial property that
broke from convention in its design, tenant structure, and siting. The project would cost $65,000, considerably more than most speculative real es-
tate ventures sited along the metropolitan area's web of arterial routes.
Peckham had persuaded three associates, several other businessmen, and a
physician to join him in a syndicate to realize the plan. He was confident it
would provide a model solution to problems experienced by many investors who sought to profit from the abundance of as yet undeveloped boulevard frontage in the region.

      In the abstract, at least, the plan had many virtues. Merchants
would be attracted by low rental rates, made possible because the property
was cheap. Although the lot was large, with a frontage of 200 feet and a
depth of 175, a major tenant did not have to be secured in order to maximize use of the land; small stores could line the perimeter on three sides.
Even those stores placed at the rear of the lot would enjoy visual prominence since all units would open onto an expansive court. People would
come to these stores, twenty-three in all, because the ensemble offered
a full range of food items and provided for additional everyday needs as
well—a range then seldom found in a single establishment, especially one

outside downtown. Equally enticing, shoppers could drive right up to the stores they wished to patronize and park in the 15,000-square-foot court. The space would be covered with white crushed granite—"similar to that used by the Standard and other oil stations"—and it would be illuminated after dark by spotlights. Restrooms were on the premises and a covered walkway would protect customers from the elements as they circulated from store to store.[1]

The scheme looked quite unlike the streetfront buildings that lined the arteries of outlying areas in cities coast to coast and were usually regarded as necessary, but unattractive, features of the urban landscape. Peckham's store group had a different configuration and would stand out as a landmark. Designed by an up-and-coming Pasadena architect, Frederick Kennedy, the exterior motifs were derived from postmedieval English vernacular sources and, together with the U-shaped form, suggested a handsome stable compound on some grand estate (figure 31). The image was reassuring—quaint, ornamental, intricate in detail—and would be viewed as an asset to nearby residential tracts then being developed. The complex was given a name befitting that image: Ye Market Place.

Peckham reputedly initiated the project because of his frustration at having to drive around a block two or three times in order to find a parking space while running errands. He had moved to Glendale at the turn of the twentieth century when it had been a small town. The subsequent exponential growth of the community and of traffic congestion had, among many other things, made once simple tasks difficult. One did not have to be a longstanding resident to find such conditions annoying, since many motorists had recently moved from smaller communities in the central United States were driving posed no such irritations, and many others had recently purchased automobiles only to find that the machine meant to facilitate affairs caused inconveniences of its own. Peckham sensed that many people would find his alternative appealing.

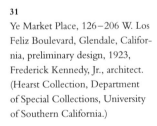

31
Ye Market Place, 126–206 W. Los Feliz Boulevard, Glendale, California, preliminary design, 1923, Frederick Kennedy, Jr., architect. (Hearst Collection, Department of Special Collections, University of Southern California.)

Peckham also understood that conventional wisdom did not apply to choosing a location for his motorist-oriented store. The site was neither near the center of Glendale nor in a neighborhood commercial node along a streetcar line. Instead, it lay well to the south of concentrated settlement, fronting Los Feliz Boulevard, which formed a new, direct link to Hollywood and a primary route between northern and southern portions of the metropolis, bypassing downtown Los Angeles. The property also lay between Brand Boulevard and Central Avenue, the two major north-south arteries of Glendale, and near the San Fernando Road, then the principal connector between Los Angeles, the newly annexed San Fernando Valley, and points further north. Long considered marginal land, the acreage around the three proximate intersections of these thoroughfares was just becoming recognized as promising for commercial development. Tracts within a half-mile radius were being transformed by residential construction, testifying to Glendale's appeal as a bedroom community. But the area was not a neighborhood in the traditional sense. Subdivisions were scattered and few houses lay close to where these routes converged. Rather it was the potential trade from passing motorists that elicited the attention of investors. Twenty thousand cars daily traversed this portion of the San Fernando Road alone. Since 1921 a former Hollywood realtor, L. H. Wilson, had been arduously boosting San Fernando frontage lots for commercial purposes, prophesying that the area would become a major business district. About a year later, the sizable Gateway Market opened at San Fernando and Brand; other businesses were starting to follow.[2]

If Wilson may have dreamed that his bailiwick was destined to grow into another Hollywood Boulevard or Western Avenue, Peckham probably had different concerns. He chose a site not in what realtors considered a nascent business center, but a short distance away where land values were not inflating so rapidly—a site that nonetheless was easily reached by car and was seen by thousands of drivers in the course of their daily movements. The profits secured from giving shoppers something they wanted could be handsome enough; the fact that by so doing one could also turn a languishing property into a lucrative asset made the prospect all the more tempting. The real estate potential perhaps motivated Peckham as much as did his shopping frustrations.

The project may have seemed *too* unconventional at first, for twelve months elapsed before construction began. Perhaps financing was a problem. Whatever the cause, the realized edifice was not nearly as fanciful as that originally presented. Kennedy's design was abandoned in favor of one prepared by the Hollywood construction firm of Malcolm Smith. Without modifying the layout, the new scheme was unembellished, making vague, and much less expensive, allusions to arcaded Spanish colonial buildings (figure 32). But if the result had an inelegant, bare-bones character, the scheme still demonstrated how this new configuration could yield an exterior composition that was at once practical and distinct from the vast majority of retail outlets.

32

Ye Market Place, as realized, 1924,
Malcolm Smith, designer/builder;
no longer standing. Photo ca. 1920s.
(Security Pacific Historical Photo-
graph Collection, Los Angeles
Public Library.)

The project's business structure underwent more substantial modifications. Instead of the original twenty-three twenty-by-thirty-foot units,
most merchants occupied a more-or-less continuous space, which was also
open to the arcade and the parking lot beyond. The layout was predicated
upon a consensus among the merchants not just to coexist under one roof
but to integrate advertising, store hours, and other aspects of their operations. Two of the participants were long-established concerns. Young's Market Company, one of the largest food retailers in the metropolitan area, had
its first Glendale outlet in the complex, selling meat, poultry, and fish.
E. A. Morrison, Grocer, had its thirty-fourth store adjoining Young's.
Other firms sold baked goods, delicatessen items, produce, flowers, and
kitchen equipment. There was also a lunch counter, and later a filling station was added.

The array of goods no less than the novel layout enabled Ye Market Place to open with great fanfare. On Saturday, 24 October 1924, an
estimated forty thousand people coming in eleven thousand cars bearing li-
censes from thirty-four states attended the twelve-hour ceremonies.[3] The
odd idea was beginning to seem like a good idea, and within a few years it
emerged as commonplace throughout the region. Most of the distinctive
features developed at Ye Market Place became standard for a new type,
soon to be called the drive-in market. By 1928, these facilities were being
constructed in Los Angeles at the rate of about a dozen a month; three
years later, more than two hundred would exist in southern California. Collectively, drive-in markets played a pivotal role in transforming the methods
by which consumer products were distributed beyond the realm of
monkey-wrench merchandising. To many observers, these establishments

represented a wholly new approach to retail development. Willard Morgan, the most prolific chronicler of the drive-in market's rise to prominence, described them as "stores the road passes through."[4]

OPERATION

The drive-in market was not quite the unprecedented breakthrough portrayed by some advocates. Just as the public market had influenced the super service station, so now the super station provided the model for coordinating related businesses at a single establishment whose layout was tailored to the parking needs of customers. The L-shaped form, which proved among the most popular for the super station, became the standard configuration for the drive-in market. Furthermore, the specific retail complexion of the drive-in, with a single concessionaire purveying each basic kind of food product, was adopted from local examples of the public market.[5] The drive-in's significance lay in combining these precedents. As a result, consumers became accustomed to a very different kind of shopping pattern from the norm, one based on mobility. The most routine of household needs could be satisfied by purchasing more goods, more conveniently, under circumstances that seemed more removed from the traditional public realm, and in places further afield from home.

The process of amalgamation was not as simple as it might appear in hindsight, however. Like many novel undertakings, the drive-in market went through a gestation period during which it had a small following. Only three examples are known to have been built in 1925, and five the following year. Ye Market Place proved successful enough, but observers were no doubt unsure whether the idea might work as well elsewhere. Even more important was the uncertainty about the intrinsic merits of the building's size and layout. Considerable variation occurred initially in both these spheres, and experiments dominated the development of drive-in markets for some three years. One of Ye Market Place's first successors was little more than a roadside stand in an urban setting, with only a car width's separation between the sidewalk and its front. Other examples suggested a taxpayer block set back from the thoroughfare. At least one design repeated Ye Market Place's form, but at about twice the size, with a cross street bisecting the ensemble. Yet another scheme had numerous stores in addition to the market, all forming a long range parallel to the artery from which it drew its trade. In some cases, the form could be quite compact. One early drive-in adhered to a conventional taxpayer block design in having apartments on its second floor.[6]

Not until the closing months of 1927 did projects begin to be initiated in sufficient number for the type to cease being a novelty and begin its meteoric ascent as a prominent trend in local retailing.[7] The number of parties willing to make the substantial monetary commitment remained small until there were enough successful examples to demonstrate that the concept was sound. Once that critical mass was attained, the drive-in market became widely viewed as among the region's best commercial real estate investments of comparatively modest scale.

In its formative stage and its subsequent diffusion, the drive-in market was principally advanced by persons like Peckham, who were interested in gaining a profitable return on their land, rather than by those employed in the distribution of food. Many who built drive-ins were engaged in real estate activities, either as developers or in offices handling brokerage, management, and other services. About an equal number of investors assumed a passive role, hiring a real estate firm to undertake the project on their behalf. Whichever the case, the real estate industry was the major force behind selecting a site (or deciding how best to use a site already in hand), determining the facility's basic characteristics, choosing the designer and contractor, and securing tenants. The real estate field was both an instigator and guide, the catalyst and the perpetrator of the phenomenon.[8] The success of the drive-in came from a series of clever, intuitive responses to shoppers' mounting anxiety over traffic congestion in outlying areas, to many food retailers' desire to improve their trade in an increasingly competitive climate, and to southern Californians' insatiable appetite for real estate as a means of increasing their assets.

Many consumers acquired a preference for the drive-in market over chain and other neighborhood food stores because of its convenience. The opportunity to pull off the street, park adjacent to the store, and have purchases placed in the car by an attendant was regarded as an enormous advantage. At some drive-in markets, customers could even remain in the driver's seat and give their order to a clerk, although this practice does not appear to have been widespread owing to the bottlenecks it could generate. Furthermore, conventional wisdom held that most customers preferred to leave their cars while shopping. To facilitate the process, some markets had an employee aid in vehicular circulation and watch parked cars.

For a store catering to such elementary needs as food, the impact of the automobile was especially great. Customers were believed more likely to shop at places that best conformed to their driving habits. "Distance is a negligible consideration," observed the head of an advertising agency specializing in food accounts; "the automobile is a convenient shopping basket." Even if a new food store was situated several blocks away from one already established in a neighborhood business center, shoppers might be willing to drive there or even further afield if the emporium offered better services. Available parking space close by the store was a major concern in this regard. Contemporary accounts emphasized that women especially did not like having to search for curbside space, which at busy times of the day could be some distance from the store, and that they disliked toting heavy packages back to their car even more. Increasing traffic in outlying areas brought restrictions to curbside parking, the most stringent of which tended to coincide with peak shopping periods when congestion also was at its worst. No-parking zones were established around the primary intersection of many a commercial node, the stores at these once choice corners suffering accordingly. Even when curbside space could be found, the unwieldy nature of cars and their gear shifts made parallel parking a dreaded maneuver for numerous motorists.[9]

Drive-in proprietors also discovered that, just as the automobile was a social equalizer, so the amenities of their establishments could attract a broader patronage than most neighborhood food stores. Alexander Haddad, one of the pioneers in the drive-in's development, explained:

Many rich Hollywood women have stopped here [his Beverl'y Open Air Market] to buy and remarked that they like the drive-in market because they do not have to call up a delivery boy and thus pay double for their groceries. A well-dressed woman would not be seen carrying an armful of bundles several blocks, but the same woman will come into the drive-in markets day after day and make her purchases directly from her car. She is able to see and select her food products, and as a result buys more than ordinarily.

The combination of privacy afforded by driving to the premises, convenience of the site layout, and ease of making selections personally had great appeal. Haddad noted:

The average woman does not like to change her dress and fix up just for a short food-buying trip to the corner grocery, where she must get out of her car and make her purchases. During the morning hours many of the neighborhood women slip on a kimono and drive to my market without bothering even to change their slippers to substantial shoes as would be required for any other purchasing trip. The orders are taken directly while she sits comfortably in her car. This service appeals to the busy woman who is continually looking for . . . time-saving method[s] and appliances.[10]

Even when leaving their cars, patrons found the drive-in market a relatively informal experience. Removed from the street, they could stay in a semi-private, controlled environment, making transactions with clerks quickly if needed (figure 33). For the first time, everyday shopping seemed an activity somewhat sheltered from the public domain. The appeal was not just for women, as Peckham realized. Men reportedly were more inclined to stop at the drive-in than at a streetfront store because so doing entailed only a short diversion on their way home from work or during other trips.[11]

Equally important to the drive-in market's popularity was the convenience it afforded by offering a more or less full range of food items under one roof. By the late 1920s public markets and a few chain outlets carried much the same array; however, the pedestrian orientation of most such stores inhibited purchasing more than could be carried home in a trip. Driving did not change matters much unless one was able to find curbside space close by, which was increasingly difficult. But when the car was parked on private property virtually adjacent to the stalls, the advantages of one-stop shopping became much greater. Purchases could be transferred easily to vehicles by either the customer or a clerk, taking as many trips as needed. Furthermore, leaving purchased goods in the car (many of which were still open) was not a source of worry. Ease of access to goods led consumers not only to purchase them in greater quantity, but to buy items for which they would not have made a special trip and to make impulse purchases. Prices averaged slightly higher than at chain stores, but the difference proved inconsequential. Customers were quite willing to pay the

added cost for the amenities of off-street parking, fast service, and selection; they also were willing to drive greater distances to get them. A well-run drive-in could draw from a larger geographic area than a neighborhood store, markedly altering trade patterns in the process.[12]

One of the foremost requirements of a drive-in market was to possess a strong group of tenants. Each retailer not only had to be reputable in his own right, but had to work well with the others, for the success of the operation depended upon its being run as a unified entity. As with the super service station, one weak department could undermine the entire business. The main difference between the structure of the two was that the drive-in did not generally have a manager. Often the grocer assumed coordination responsibilities; nevertheless, each concessionaire enjoyed more or less equal status. This arrangement, combined with a unified merchandising plan, made the spirit of cooperation the more essential among all parties.[13]

Finding the right tenants might have proven difficult in many instances had not a large number of food retailers been anxious to pursue an alternative to their current business situations. Sometimes the location of their stores posed problems as a result of increasing car use. Many sites adequate for securing a decent pedestrian trade were now being bypassed by motorists owing either to congestion or rapid traffic flow. Even more pressing was the competition independents and some small chain operations were experiencing from major chain grocery companies, which established hundreds of units throughout the metropolitan area by the latter part of the decade.[14] At a time when chains seemingly threatened to monopolize the field unless concerted action was taken to arrest their growth, many retailers saw the drive-in as a means of survival. In addition to off-street parking, tenants could capitalize on some lessons learned from the chains, including greater attention to consumer habits, product turnover, display, and advertising. The loosely integrated organization of the drive-in carried further advantages. Operating expenses were shared, pricing policies coordinated, uniform hours kept, and identity consolidated. At the same time, customers could enjoy direct contact with merchants, a relationship that was a long-standing strength of the independently operated neighborhood store.[15]

The revenues generated by a well-run drive-in market were attractive to merchants and owners alike. A study conducted at the height of the type's popularity indicated that income from a drive-in ran about four times that from a conventional food store in a comparable location. Most leases were structured on a percentage basis, then a relatively new practice, so that both parties enjoyed direct benefits from profits. For self-employed food retailers, the overall statistics were especially encouraging. The failure rate among individuals operating a conventional neighborhood store in the region was claimed to be over ninety percent during the 1920s, while the rate for those who ran a department at a drive-in market was about forty percent.[16] Many people selling food in southern California knew little about the business. In planning a drive-in market, however, brokers could be picky in assembling their tenants because of the advantages of participating in such an enterprise. Numerous concessionaires came to the drive-in with years of experience and a solid reputation. Often, too, independents were bolstered by the presence of a well-known local chain in groceries (E. A. Morrison, Fitzsimmons), baked goods (Van de Kamp), or even produce (Ito Brothers).[17] Like the super service station, the drive-in represented a higher standard of merchandising than the norm.

Other factors also contributed to the drive-in market's popularity. Hot or rainy days discouraged pedestrian shoppers, but had little effect on motorists. The drive-ins' volume of trade enabled them to operate for longer periods. Most food stores were open eight or nine hours, their employees working on a single shift. On the other hand, drive-in markets typically operated two shifts, extending from around 7:00 AM to midnight. This schedule, in turn, attracted additional customers, including those who worked late or who preferred to shop in the evening.[18]

FORM

In its form, use of space, and relationship to the urban context, the drive-in market was a pronounced departure from commercial facilities other than the super service station. The standard accumulation of buildings along the spine of a commercial center and the attendant plethora of signs tended to minimize the distinction between stores. Unless carefully planned as an ensemble, these precincts formed a visual melange the cacophonous impact of the whole overwhelming whatever distinct features might be found on each part. From the vantage point of an automobile, moving at speeds appreciably greater than those of a streetcar or a pedestrian, that effect was intensified, even in blocks where harmonious facade design was attempted (figure 34).[19] Most food emporia differed little from their neighbors in terms of size, configuration, and visual role in the landscape. Only the open front, which had become characteristic of many produce stores as well as groceries in the region by the 1920s, distinguished these outlets from those selling other types of goods (figure 35).[20]

In contrast, the drive-in market's building mostly occupied land toward the rear of the lot, traditionally considered the least desirable. The primary space was the forecourt, which was reserved for automobiles. Inside space averaged about three times that of a conventional store, but it could appear larger still due to the building's long front and siting away from the street. This configuration made the building stand out as an individual entity, conspicuous even when its architectural treatment was comparatively modest (figure 36).

The spatial order of most drive-in markets was not just one of a store block pushed back from the street. Diagrammatically, it was analogous to attaching several units in such a block end to end, bending the link more or less at midpoint, and opening most of the internal long side to the forecourt (figure 37). Because the conspicuousness of the open front and

34
Commercial district, perhaps in South Pasadena. Photo "Dick" Whittington, 1930. (Whittington Collection, Department of Special Collections, University of Southern California.)

the absence of congestion were primary concerns, deliveries were barred
from the forecourt whenever circumstances permitted. Given the ability
to control this space, merchants could ensure that goods were brought
through alley entrances, which had long been shunned by delivery personnel. Other inducements bolstered this change. Both the corner site and
long building elevation at the rear facilitated vehicular access. Sometimes,

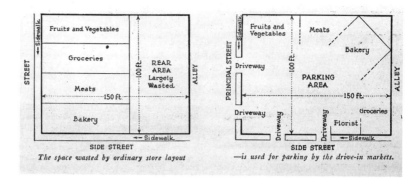

The space wasted by ordinary store layout — is used for parking by the drive-in markets.

37
Diagrammatic comparison of drive-in market and conventional food store plans. (*Magazine of Business,* July 1929, 42.)

38
Redwood Market, 7601–7609 Beverly Boulevard, Los Angeles, 1927, Harry Beall, designer/builder; no longer standing. Rear view. Photo Albert Frey, 1932. (Courtesy Albert Frey.)

39
Mac Mar Market, 4721 Whittier Boulevard, Los Angeles, ca. 1928; altered. Interior. Photo "Dick" Whittington, 1929. (Whittington Collection, Department of Special Collections, University of Southern California.)

too, space was available for parking delivery trucks so that the right-of-way could remain free (figure 38). Probably more than any other building type of the decade, the drive-in market gave order to a segregation of shopper and service routes that merchants had sought for years.

Differences in spatial arrangement also were pronounced inside. The narrow and deep layout of most stores necessitated using a substantial part of their selling area for circulation and limited the ways in which goods could be arranged. Space tended to seem cavernous and confined even when the dimensions were generous by standards of the day and the store illuminated by modern electric fixtures and skylights (figure 39). The internal organization of drive-in markets, on the other hand, entailed treating each department as an integral component of the whole, which, together with the long open front, made the space appear freer and more variable (figure 40). Circulation was parallel and close to the light, airy frontal zone. Service spaces could be kept to a minimum and combined among the coordinated departments. The layout of each department as well as its relationship to the others was devised to maximize contact between customer and product through displays that were at once compact and continuous from one department to the next. An efficient layout was also important from the standpoint of service, minimizing the distance moved in assisting customers and the staff needed to perform that function. The results seemed to achieve the best of two worlds: each department occupied a relatively small area, facilitating fast, labor-saving service, while the unified treatment of the whole engagingly conveyed the extent of goods and

40
Billie Bird Markets, Store # 12, 2311–2321 W. Main Street, Alhambra, California, 1929; altered. Interior. Photo "Dick" Whittington, 1933. (Whittington Collection, Department of Special Collections, University of Southern California.)

41

Western Avenue, looking north near
Wilshire Boulevard intersection.
Photo C. C. Pierce, 1924. (Califor-
nia Historical Society Collection,
Department of Special Collections,
University of Southern California.)

services offered. Little room was allocated to storage, since products were
selected for rapid turnover.

Outside no less than in, the drive-in market was experientially
different from most other retail establishments. From the motorist's perspective, typical outlying business districts were like a corridor whose
center was a wide but not clearly divided path with a stream of steadily,
sometimes erratically, moving vehicles (figure 41). The buildings that defined the edges were separated from this current, psychologically as well as
physically, by rows of parked cars. Access to stores was from an altogether
distinct zone that often was not easily reached. As a concession to drivers,
new outlying areas of many communities in the south-central and south-
western states had sufficiently wide arteries to enable right-angle or diagonal parking directly off the street.[21] Perhaps because of the intensity of
land speculation, this practice failed to gain favor in southern California during the 1920s. Only in places where the public right-of-way had yet to be
fully utilized could motorists claim the residue space for temporary use
(figure 42).

The drive-in market helped to create a new relationship between
motorist and store, with the forecourt serving as an entry. At the super service station, this space was the principal one customers penetrated, leaving
their cars near the appropriate service bay. At the drive-in market, however, the forecourt was an intermediate zone, the place from which people

could go inside the building at any number of points (figure 43). This integration of movement—from street, to lot, to building—was a departure both in the path taken and in the strong visual ties between its parts. Never before had motorists' access to interior space been so much the basis for the configuration of a complex.

Luring the motorist off the street was not as simple a task as it might seem, however, particularly as competition among drive-in markets rose toward the decade's end. To a greater degree than the planners of many super service stations, drive-in owners chose sites in relation to traffic patterns. In both cases, of course, the location had to be along a well-traveled artery, but the drive-in's requirements were more demanding.

42
9000 block Sunset Boulevard, West Hollywood. View looking west, Sunset Hills Market (1928) at right. Photo "Dick" Whittington, 1932. (Whittington Collection, Department of Special Collections, University of Southern California.)

43
Pioneer Market, Paramount Boulevard and Jackson Street, Paramount, California, before 1930; no longer standing. Photo ca. 1934. (Security Pacific Historical Photograph Collection, Los Angeles Public Library.)

Beyond substantial traffic flow throughout the day, the key locational factor was heavy use during the peak shopping period in the late afternoon. Most sites thus were on the homeward-bound side of commuter routes, with the building oriented to evening rush-hour traffic. Even though many customers were women who did not work, it was believed that they were reluctant to cross over streams of traffic to enter the forecourt, so that the homeward-bound orientation would be the most advantageous from their perspective as well.[22] Exceptions existed, mostly in places where traffic flow was less one-directional at any given time or in more remote precincts where traffic was probably never very great.

Placement on a corner site was regarded as essential, primarily so that the market could be as conspicuous as possible to approaching motorists. Major intersections were generally avoided, however, except in areas without much concentrated settlement, where owners may have felt it necessary to divert motorists from two well-traveled routes in order to sustain business. Elsewhere, the presence of extensive cross traffic or of stop lights was considered detrimental, because the number of vehicles moving in different directions and the changing of traffic signals distracted motorists' attention from streetside businesses.[23] A lightly traveled cross street served to enhance the perception of openness and easy access to the forecourt. The L-shaped plan became the norm because it was the most effective in making the facility conspicuous, spatially tying the interior to the forecourt and orienting the ensemble to the public rights-of-way beyond.

Siting was related to form in other respects as well, not least of which was the size and configuration of the lot. Ideally, that lot would be a rectangle, its depth not appreciably less than its width, so that the front and its displays were prominently on view from the street and ample room existed for parking. When the property was shallow or otherwise irregular, the effect on the building mass tended to be minimized by architecturally emphasizing the relationship between the long, linear forecourt and building front. One of the most effective solutions under these circumstances was the arc-shaped plan that transformed the two arms of the L into a continuous facade (figure 44). In other cases, the L was bent to conform to the site so as to underscore the length of the front from the principal approach path.

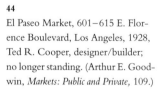

44
El Paseo Market, 601–615 E. Florence Boulevard, Los Angeles, 1928, Ted R. Cooper, designer/builder; no longer standing. (Arthur E. Goodwin, *Markets: Public and Private,* 109.)

45
Hercules Motor-In Market, 1241–
1249 W. Washington Boulevard, Los
Angeles, ca. 1928. Photo author,
1989.

While the great majority of drive-in markets were variations on the L plan, some were merely rectangular blocks. The rectangular form made sense when the property was a narrow gore, where any arrangement other than having the market extend across the rear from one street to the other would negate the visual impact of its front and of the forecourt from the motorists' vantage point (figure 45). On the other hand, the U-shaped form, introduced at Ye Market Place, proved undesirable in most instances. Obliquely referring to the Glendale complex, Willard Morgan explained in no uncertain terms:

Such a market looks particularly blank while moving at a moderate speed along the main highway. The stores located farthest back from the street cannot display their goods to selling advantage because their displays cannot be seen. The stores occupying the sides are not selling their displays to advantage because of the confusion of columns and arches which distract from the motorist's view.[24]

Several compositional devices were developed in response to the drive-in market's siting requirements. The facade of the standard taxpayer block was composed in an additive manner, with more or less identical bays stretching end to end and no one portion receiving appreciably greater emphasis than the others.[25] Some drive-in markets adhered to this pattern, but more characteristically the front was varied, to function, in Morgan's words, as a "living billboard" that could attract the eye of the passing motorist and register a favorable impression in an instant.[26] By 1928, two partis had become standard, one emphasizing the ends, the other the central portion where the two arms joined. The pervasive use of these conventions suggests they were explicitly marshaled to enhance the market's attraction to the eye and underscore its function as a unified entity.

46
Tower Market, 1400–1410 Whittier
Boulevard, Montebello, California,
1929, A. G. Erickson, designer/
builder; altered. Photo ca. 1929. (Se-
curity Pacific Historical Photograph
Collection, Los Angeles Public
Library.)

The end bays could be minimally differentiated by slight projec-
tions in the wall plane, and perhaps in the roof line as well. When enclosed
store units were part of the program, they were situated at one or both
ends, allowing for distinctions in the treatment of openings. Sometimes
one end would be further punctuated by a second-story office or loft space
or by a purely decorative element (see figure 44). The two end bays were
seldom made identical; one generally received greater emphasis and was situated adjacent to the major artery to enhance the building's conspicuousness. The principal device used to give focus to the central section was a
turret or tower, which could range from one of modest dimensions (see
figure 36) to a soaring beacon visible some distance away (figure 46). In
these cases, the wings tended to remain simple, without changes in composition at their ends.

Irrespective of the parti, the aim seems to have been to capitalize
on the building's form to create a dynamic composition of assembled
masses that would stand out amid the open space of the forecourt and intersecting streets, especially when seen at an oblique angle from a passing car.
In most cases, advertising was kept to a minimum, underscoring the unified nature of the operation. Drive-in markets typically had a steel overhead sign bearing the establishment's name and smaller, discreet ones
identifying the departments (but not the merchants) over the open bays
(figure 47). Unified signage, subordinated to the building itself, distinguished these complexes from most taxpayer blocks where, no matter how
meticulous the architectural treatment, tenants soon encumbered the exterior with inharmonious signboards (figure 48). Not all drive-ins, however,
stood out as a clear comprehensible whole. In a few cases, the variety of
components was excessive, creating a visually jumbled array (figure 49).

The size of drive-in markets had much the same consistency as
their form. The standard for lots on which these buildings were erected in

47
Pico Drive-In Market, 3621–3633
Pico Boulevard, Los Angeles, 1929,
Walter Hagedohm, architect; no
longer standing. Photo ca. 1935.
(Courtesy Progressive Grocer.)

48
Commercial building, 3601–3613
W. Third Street, Los Angeles, ca.
1927, attributed to Morgan, Walls &
Clements, architects; altered. Photo
"Dick" Whittington, 1930. (Whit-
tington Collection, Department of
Special Collections, University of
Southern California.)

49
El Benito Market, 300–310 W.
Colorado Boulevard, Glendale,
California, 1928, A. B. Christ Co.,
designer/builder; no longer stand-
ing. (Glendale Public Library.)

the metropolitan area was between 9,000 and 14,000 square feet. Frontage in most cases ranged from 100 to 170 feet, property depth from 70 to 140 feet. Moreover, the two dimensions seldom differed by a wide margin, so that the typical lot was a not-too-elongated rectangle. The length of the market front could vary considerably, but most buildings had a depth of twenty-five to thirty-five feet, with that of the enclosed shop units slightly greater.[27]

The drive-in markets' limited size was directly related to the nature of their operation. Four food departments was considered a minimum if the establishment was to function as a true market. Most examples contained four to six but seldom more, since an underlying aim of the operation was to concentrate on products in frequent demand. Groceries, fruits and vegetables, meats, baked goods, and delicatessen items formed the usual divisions. The scope of departments and the products each carried had to be sufficiently great to make shopping there more convenient than at competing stores, but not so large as to dilute the compact display and rapid turnover of goods.

The size of each department depended on the nature of goods it carried and the space required to display and sell them; yet these differences did not seem great at most drive-in markets, nor did they vary much from one establishment to another (figure 50). Too much space consumed by one merchant could diminish the visual draw of his colleagues' spaces and undermine the whole concept of a unified selling area that would induce customers to move freely between departments. It was equally important to keep the size of each department such that it could be run by one individual at a time, thus avoiding high personnel costs (figure 51). Most departments occupied roughly the same amount of floor area as that to which the public had access in a small, efficiently run neighborhood food store, and often the space was less owing to shared circulation paths.[28] Thus, whereas a sense of spatial expansiveness was a basic objective, a large space was not.

50
El Adobe Market, 5201–5209 Hollywood Boulevard, Los Angeles, 1928, Arthur Kelly, architect, Joe Estep, associate; altered. Ground floor plan. (*Architectural Record,* June 1929, 604.)

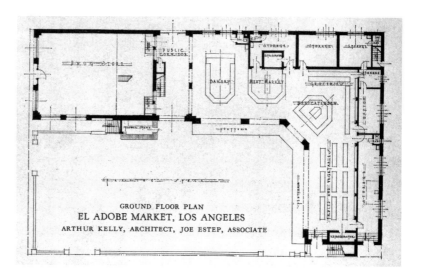

GROUND FLOOR PLAN
EL ADOBE MARKET, LOS ANGELES
ARTHUR KELLY, ARCHITECT, JOE ESTEP, ASSOCIATE

Many drive-in markets included one or two additional units selling unrelated goods and services for which there was a steady demand. Flower shops, drug stores, cafes, and laundry call stations were the most common types. These functions required fully enclosed space that was almost always located at the ends of the building so as not to interfere with the market area. While similar experiments had been tried at some super service stations, the drive-in market was the first type characteristic to outlying areas where complementary stores were incorporated on a widespread basis.

The appeal of including stores stemmed from the potential to increase overall sales. This merchandising strategy echoed that of the market itself: customers would be inclined to purchase items beyond those that precipitated the trip when other kinds of goods were available on the premises. Both the market and the abutting stores could benefit from this relationship. The idea no doubt appealed to food merchants as it could bolster their trade. Other business owners responded positively, since motorists' driving habits often affected their sales as well. A drug store proprietor in one drive-in market admitted that he could not have succeeded in that neighborhood had his business been housed in a conventional streetfront unit; vehicular traffic was too great, pedestrian traffic too little. The opportunity to lease space at a drive-in market was key to his decision to locate in the area. The same reasons lay behind the organizational structure of Moderncraft Laundry, established in 1930 with a network of eleven sta-

51
Alpha Beta Market #28, 416–424
E. Philadelphia Street, Whittier,
California, 1930, David Bushnell,
architect; destroyed by fire ca. 1963.
Interior, showing meat department
and its manager, Edward Schmidt.
Photo early 1930s. (Courtesy Edward Schmidt.)

tions where customers could deposit and retrieve their clothing, all housed in drive-in market store units.[29] From the investor's standpoint, these additional outlets at a drive-in carried another advantage. The ratio of area required by the market proper relative to that of the forecourt often left an "excess" space at one or both building ends. Small convenience-oriented stores would not cause forecourt congestion, but could add measurably to revenues.

The other component common to these complexes was a filling station, which was almost always situated on the corner of the lot adjacent to the intersection (figure 52). This facility's relationship to the ensemble was the same as at super service stations: it stimulated additional trade but was not the primary generator of income. Customers enjoyed the convenience of purchasing gas and oil while on a trip to the market; leaving one's car at the filling station while running short errands elsewhere on the premises apparently was not unusual.[30] As with other merchants, filling station operators found the association with the drive-in market profitable, particularly since the competition in their own field was so intense.

More often than not, the filling station represented a minimal investment, constructed of prefabricated steel components, ubiquitous for the type, but very different in character from most of the markets (figure 53). Beyond monetary savings, this treatment permitted the market building to remain visually dominant. In cases where other functions were situated in more elaborate corner kiosks, the purpose of the complex as a whole could be somewhat obscured from the driver's vantage point (figure 54).

Additional automobile care facilities were seldom included at drive-in markets. Little inducement seems to have existed for combining them, in part because a large amount of space and investment were required in order to offer a full range of goods and services in both spheres. Often, too, super stations were already operating in the vicinity. Perhaps the most important factor was that the two functions tended to be incompatible. Shopping and leaving the car for service were activities not likely to be done on the same trip. Super stations generated noise and dirt, a situa-

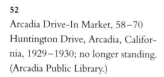

52
Arcadia Drive-In Market, 58–70 Huntington Drive, Arcadia, California, 1929–1930; no longer standing. (Arcadia Public Library.)

53
Filling station kiosk at unidentified drive-in market, Los Angeles area. Photo Albert Frey, 1932. (Courtesy Albert Frey.)

tion far from conducive to purchasing food in the open air. Also, cars parked at the station would inhibit the flow of those coming to the market.

While the ground area occupied by the drive-in market remained limited, attempts occasionally were made to augment revenues by adding a second story. The utilization of this full level for offices at El Adobe Market (1928) on Hollywood Boulevard was unusual, since the cars of those additional patrons could bring congestion to the forecourt (figure 55).[31] In most other two-level projects, only a small portion of the upper area was developed as offices. Generally this space was reserved for the building's owner or one of the tenants, so that access could be controlled and the parking space would be minimally impinged on. The Clock Market in Beverly Hills (1929) included a seven-room apartment for the proprietor of the drug store directly below, but the presence of dwelling units was rare. The planners of drive-ins seem to have been aware that the range of compatible functions was narrow.

If the form and size of drive-in markets remained generally consistent, there was much greater latitude in the development of imagery. Expression ranged from ornate historicism to strident modernity. Work could be exotic and evocative of a Hollywood set or thoroughly utilitarian in character. Budget certainly affected the outcome, yet the attitudes and tastes of those who created them were at least as significant. Some owners, caring more about a good return on their investment than about appearance, probably believed that the drive-in market should be as matter-of-fact a building as most neighborhood stores traditionally had been. No doubt some real estate brokers in charge of developing projects also considered image in the most pragmatic terms. But others sought to make their building a landmark, conspicuously different from its neighbors in more than size and configuration. The importance of a distinctive image was soon recognized, for the very fact that the drive-in market was a new type ran counter to the practice of relying on formulaic designs. A broad spectrum of individuals—from builders with small practices to some of the region's biggest architectural firms, from designers committed to the tenets of eclecticism to prominent members of the modernist avant-garde—contributed to the varied character of the results.[32] In this respect, the tendency to experiment persisted as long as drive-in markets were built.

Some drive-ins, particularly those in lower-middle-class and prosperous working-class neighborhoods or in areas where residential development was sparse, provided little more than basic shelter (figure 56). The building front was a long version of small, often freestanding, wood-frame stores, hundreds of which lined arteries in unprestigious parts of the metropolitan region. Many more drive-ins were costlier, with embellishments of the sort common to the simplest taxpayer blocks of the period. Yet others used historical references, Hispanic sources being especially popular. The

54
Drive-in market, 9600–9608 Brighton Way, Beverly Hills, 1928, Gable & Wyant, architects; no longer standing. Photo "Dick" Whittington, 1929. (Whittington Collection, Department of Special Collections, University of Southern California.)

55
El Adobe Market. Photo "Dick" Whittington, 1931. (Whittington Collection, Department of Special Collections, University of Southern California.)

56
Main & 41st Street Market, 4101–4113 S. Main Street, Los Angeles, 1928–1929. Photo author, 1986.

drive-in's forecourt, with an open-front building and food displays as a backdrop, seemed a fitting modern counterpart to the traditional plaza.[33] The market function remained ubiquitous in the plazas of Hispanic communities, which constituted an increasingly popular image among Anglo Californians. Los Angeles's plaza continued to host market activities into the early twentieth century. This associational link between tradition and machine-age amenity was sometimes made more explicit by placing a fountain, a wishing well, or even an old cart as a decorative feature in the forecourt, despite the reduction of parking space that resulted (figure 57).

Composing the front as an arcade proved a more effective way to meet programmatic needs while cultivating a regional identity. In contrast to most traditional applications, here the arcade did not shelter a passage but merely separated indoors from out.[34] With the bays open during business hours, the effect could remain true to its historical origins without encumbering displays or the direct path of customers. Among the most polished examples was Morgan, Walls & Clements's Plaza Market (1928), where a rich repertoire of details was composed in a fresh, spirited manner, at once evocative of the past and bespeaking its orientation to the motorist (figure 58).

Arcuated bays had a drawback, however, in that their relatively close spacing could block clear views of the interior when seen from an angle and thus impair the perception of the market as an open, continuous space. Wider bays, common to streetfront stores, were often preferred, and the tendency soon emerged to extend the bays yet further.[35] This latter treatment also lent itself well to Hispanic allusions. Often the ties were vague: canopied entries, broad stucco wall surfaces, and low-slung tile roofs—perhaps punctuated by a more referential tower or comparably embellishing focal point (figure 59).

57
Hattem's Market, 4267–4277 S. Western Avenue, Los Angeles, 1927, Walter Hagedohm, architect; demolished. Detail of foundation. Photo ca. late 1920s. (Courtesy Maurice Hattem.)

Beyond Spanish references, the historical vocabulary used for drive-in markets was quite limited though sometimes unorthodox. The fanciful design of the Mandarin Market in Hollywood (1928–1929) no doubt was intended to capitalize on the popularity of Sid Graumann's Chinese Theater, which had opened less than two years earlier and had become an icon of the region (figure 60). The Persian Market (1929) stood on what was then the main route to Venice, one of the area's prime beach resorts boasting an elaborate commercial center suggestive of its Adriatic namesake and a festive "Moorish" bathhouse facing the ocean (figure 61).[36] Such exotic embellishments must have made a memorable impression on the motorist, but the degree to which they could be employed effectively was limited. If one "Chinese" market stood out as a landmark, each additional

58
Plaza Market, 4651–4663 Pico Boulevard, Los Angeles, 1928, Morgan, Walls & Clements, architects; no longer standing. (*Architectural Forum,* June 1929, 901.)

59
Aurora Drive-In Market, 6302–6320 N. San Fernando Road, Glendale, California, 1930, Alfred F. Priest, architect; altered. Photo ca. 1931. (Security Pacific Historical Photograph Collection, Los Angeles Public Library.)

60
Mandarin Market, 1234–1248 Vine
Street, Los Angeles, 1928–1929,
M. L. Gogerty, architect; no longer
standing. Photo late 1920s/early
1930s. (California Historical Society
Collection, Department of Special
Collections, University of Southern
California.)

61
Persian Market, 12137–12139 Washington Place, Los Angeles, 1929,
George M. Thomas, architect; no
longer standing. (*Los Angeles Times,*
16 June 1929, V-2.)

one would reduce that impact unless all the outlets formed a chain. In a
few cases more than one drive-in market was constructed by a single
owner, but no true chain of these establishments ever materialized, preclud-
ing the rationale for a strong corporate imprint on a network of facilities.[37]
Furthermore, exotica was closely associated with the character of roadside
stands and other places of diversion from which most market owners sought
to distance themselves. The concern for presenting a respectable image,
combined with the versatility and perceived appropriateness of Hispanic references, appear to have curtailed forays into less conventional modes.

On the other hand, modernism was well received in the commercial realm. Art deco was widely used for drive-in markets and, as with
Spanish imagery, enabled lively embellishment on otherwise simple buildings without great expense (figure 62). Most of the ornament was integral
to the wall surface, formed by molds in the pouring of concrete or the application of stucco.[38] The departure from historicism was primarily one of
ornament. Even when the massing was varied, a sense of visual order

tended to remain strong. The break from tradition was matched by businesslike reserve.

Not all art deco examples were so restrained. At the Tower Market in Beverly Hills (1928–1929), motifs from the 1925 Paris decorative arts exposition were adapted in a manner that rendered the complex like no other of its type (figure 63). The building was little more than a stuccoed frame fronted by decidedly unstructural pylons similar to those at the fair's Porte d'Honneur. This heraldic counterpoint reached a climax at the corner filling station, which formed the base for a vertical sign, several stories high, that was a near copy of L. H. Boileau's Porte d'Orsay.[39] The building's dual role as a large, uninterrupted selling space and a celebration of convenient retailing for the motorist was expressed with élan, if not with the originality that most observers probably assumed. Willard Morgan, however, reported that the scheme was a dismal failure. The interior seemed shabby compared to its theatrical front, and the thick, closely spaced pylons obscured a clear view of the displays. Amid the visual pyrotechnics, the one sign announcing the complex's name and function seemed comparatively modest. Within a few months of its opening, the facility was forced to close and undergo an extensive remodeling.[40] Coming at the height of the drive-in market's popularity, the fiasco afforded a

62
Avenue Market, 3053–3075 Telegraph Avenue, Berkeley, California, ca. 1930; altered. (*Architect & Engineer,* July 1954, 18.)

63
Tower Market, 8670–8680 Wilshire Boulevard, Beverly Hills, 1928–1929, Roderick Spencer, J. J. Landon, and Harrison Clarke, associated architects; no longer standing. (*Filling Station,* June 1930, 34.)

64
Mesa-Vernon Market, 4330–4344
Crenshaw Boulevard, Los Angeles,
1928, George J. Adams, architect; de-
stroyed by fire 1992. Photo "Dick"
Whittington, 1929. (Whittington
Collection, Department of Special
Collections, University of Southern
California.)

conspicuous demonstration that novel design in itself by no means ensured
success in attracting a motorist trade.

The effectiveness of imagery in the marketplace was not tied to
the use of eclectic or modernist vocabularies or to restrained or theatrical
treatments per se, but rather to how a given set of expressive qualities reinforced the building's programmatic needs. To some modernists, the requirements of the drive-in market made it seem an opportune proving ground
for new avenues of expression. The immediate results were well accepted,
widely publicized, and, it appears, influential on later retail work in the region. These markets were inspired by some of the more radical strains of
modernism abroad as well as in southern California, but were not tied to
specific models.

Such an approach began at a fairly early stage in the drive-in's
development. The Mesa-Vernon Market, the plans for which were completed in May 1928, possessed a bold, abstract simplicity of a kind then
seldom found in realized projects in southern California or elsewhere in
the United States (figure 64).[41] Long-span wood trusses permitted unusually wide bays so that the openings to the forecourt and street appeared
almost continuous. The lateral flow of space and the sheer length of area
spanned were articulated by wooden grills, the one ornamental component
of the scheme, above which the stuccoed wall surfaces acted as a foil, but
also as a decisive cap to give the building its pristine, horizontal geometry.

An equally unusual approach was taken with the design of the
Palm Market (1928–1929) located near the ill-fated Tower in Beverly Hills
(figure 65).[42] Again, horizontality was paramount on the front, here without compositional variation, although the bay spacing tended to render the
effect somewhat repetitive and static. The openings were not as prominent
as the wall, its great expanse bereft of decoration, but were given a textural
richness by untroweled mortar joints—making the surface appear somewhat like adobe—and open concrete-block grills above. The exterior thus

read as a neutral screen and an immense, abstract sign against which several palm trees stood in slightly surreal isolation.

The idea of the drive-in market as a billboard appealed to no one more than Richard Neutra, the Viennese émigré who moved to Los Angeles in 1925 and soon gained an international reputation as a leading architect of the avant-garde. Neutra prepared several designs for drive-in markets that were probably self-initiated as a means to refine his ideas of a machine-age aesthetics and perhaps to secure clients in a potentially lucrative sphere.[43] For the "Los Angeles Drive-In Market" (no doubt a generic name), Neutra composed the front as a rhythmic steel frame with minimal separation of the open bays (figure 66). The canopy was integral to the structure, the beams extending to support fixed glazed panels, permitting additional daylight to enter the premises on overcast days. Neutra also broke with convention in giving the building a semicircular form, designed to provide an easy turning curve for cars so that they could move from department to department while drivers made purchases without leaving their

65
Palm Market, 8300–8328 Wilshire Boulevard, Beverly Hills, 1928–1929, J. Byron Severence, architect; no longer standing. Photo Albert Frey, 1932. (Courtesy Albert Frey.)

66
"Los Angeles Drive-In Market," ca. 1928, Richard Neutra, architect; project. (*Chain Store Review,* September 1928, 29.)

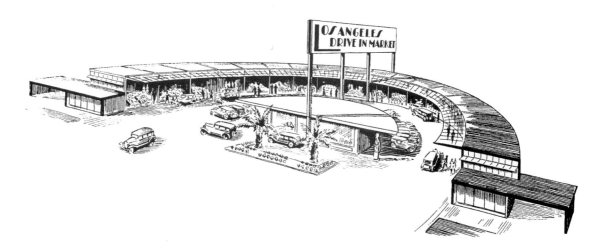

seats. Parking space lay outside this path adjacent to the centrally placed filling station.

Developing a form based on moving automobiles represented the essence of the drive-in concept in theory, but the solution was far from realistic. The arrangement would have made it impossible for unsuspecting motorists to spot the forecourt until they were passing the entry point. An overhead sign stretching from the front to the rear of the property was devised to attract potential consumers at a distance, yet it would have been insufficient to alert them to the abruptness of the turn they would be forced to negotiate. Since the passage was one-directional, motorists would have had no second chance to turn. Another basic flaw was that, with cars moving parallel to the market bays, only a few seated customers could have been served at one time and only if they knew all they wanted to purchase and knew the sequence of the departments. At this stage, Neutra did not seem to understand the value of the corner lot or how the automobile should in other ways determine the building's layout. Expression came at the expense of practicality.

A second scheme, probably designed later, revealed a clearer comprehension of the drive-in market's requirements. In this more conventional plan, Neutra introduced a number of stunning features to enhance the building's visual appeal. The front was to be two stories high, completely open, surmounted by a thin parapet with large illuminated signs (figure 67). This section projected far from displays, giving the building a

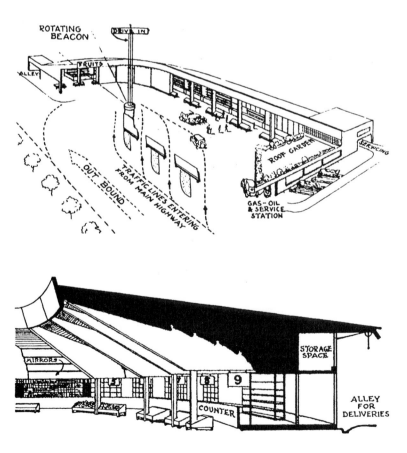

more active relationship with the street and providing shelter to parked motorists below. Between the supporting cantilevered trusses, probably of
wood, were to be a series of mirrors, each tilted at a slightly different angle
to form a cove and provide multiple reflections of the scene below, so that
from the street the impression would be of a signboard suspended above an
ethereal interplay of machines, people, and products. At night, the effect
would have been even more dramatic, with a rotating beacon casting poly-
chromatic light across the signs and recessed fixtures illuminating the mir-
ror plates. Here Neutra theatrically dematerialized architecture, allowing
graphics, ever-changing light patterns, and the stuff sold at the place to en-
gage in a spirited, kinetic display.

Neutra's unrealized second project may well have influenced the
design of the Yucca-Vine Market in Hollywood (1930) by his somewhat
younger colleague, Lloyd Wright, who also was emerging as a leader in the
local avant-garde (figure 68).[44] Wright, who seldom missed an opportunity
to create startling effects with his expressionistic use of form, decoration,
and materials, was faced with a constricted midblock site and a low budget.
He adopted the idea of minimally enclosed market space and a cantilevered
roof to attract the eye of customers on the periphery. In other respects, the
scheme was quite different from Neutra's. Perhaps taking a cue from several recent projects by his celebrated father, Wright developed a taut but
perceptually casual geometry of oblique angles for both the plan and the elevations.[45] The market front was uninterrupted save for thin V-shaped steel
struts that seemed more like decorative flourishes beneath the bulky roof
(which was in fact no more than a series of sharply pitched beams enve-
loped in corrugated, galvanized iron). The same cheap material was used
for the rear walls and display baseboards—all of it sprayed with aluminum
paint. In a masterful play of illusion, the building appeared at once massive
and minimal: Great chunky blocks were rendered as flimsy planes sup-

67
Drive-in market, probably for Los
Angeles area, ca. 1929, Richard Neu-
tra, architect; project. (*American
Builder,* July 1929, 60.)

68
Yucca-Vine Market, 6319–6331
Yucca Street, Los Angeles, 1930,
Lloyd Wright, architect; no longer
standing. Photo early 1930s. (Special
Collections, University of Califor-
nia, Los Angeles.)

ported more by some unexplained force than by an intelligible system. Day or night, the effect was difficult to ignore.

The Yucca-Vine Market was merely a prelude to the expressive pyrotechnics devised for an unexecuted scheme to have been located between Wilshire and Santa Monica boulevards on a narrow gore lot marking the western entrance to the Beverly Hills business district (figure 69).[46] With extensive street frontage on its two main sides, the building was designed as little more than a covered display area. Departments were separated by thick pier groups supporting a roof garden and a sign tower that would have made the most flamboyant advertising devices in the metropolitan area seem tame by comparison. Projecting toward the intersection at an arresting sixty-degree angle, this structure held a giant banner near the end and, below, an even larger rotating sign shaped like a snowflake and outlined with neon tubing. This would have been an enormously conspicuous building that was scarcely a building at all, a grand gesture functioning as a portal to one of the region's most prestigious communities, yet based solely on commercial interest.

Little precedent existed for work such as the Mesa-Vernon and Palm markets or those by Neutra and Wright, in large part because comparable conditions were unusual elsewhere. Aside from automobile service facilities, the drive-in concept was seldom applied to buildings of any type in other parts of the United States before 1930. Furthermore, outside southern California, avant-garde forms of modernism were extremely rare save for designs by a few mavericks such as Frank Lloyd Wright and Eliel Saarinen.

By 1930 modernism in Europe was, of course, more prevalent, more diverse in nature, and often more radical in concept and expression. For almost a decade, adventurous designs had been created in the retail sphere incorporating large glazed areas, bold graphics, new applications of materials and structure, and dramatic lighting effects, with results that seemed wholly different from those of the immediate as well as the more distant past. Yet since the patterns of urban development remained much more traditional in nature, most of the work in this vein consisted of large retail stores and shop fronts on the ground floor of office buildings in dense urban centers or of small clusters of stores attached to housing blocks.[47] Freestanding one- and two-story retail facilities in outlying areas were neither numerous nor an important facet of commercial design. Some parallels existed in work of other types such as exposition pavilions and open-air shelters for public transit systems.[48] Yet in all these cases, the correspondence lay in a general approach to design rather than in specific solutions.

The drive-in markets of southern California thus afforded a unique opportunity at that time to apply modernist concepts of use as a basis for expression to complexes that were not only arranged to accommodate the automobile, but were part of an urban order where movement by car was a primary generating force. Thus it is little wonder that a European modernist such as Neutra relished the possibilities of applying his vision of a *neue Sachlichkeit* to the drive-in market just as he did to the skyscraper.[49] Swiss-born and trained Albert Frey, after working for Le Corbusier in 1929, came to New York and soon thereafter made a pilgrimage by car to southern California to see the work of Neutra, R. M. Schindler, and others who then formed the greatest concentration of avant-garde architects in the nation. Along the way, Frey looked at skyscrapers and industrial structures such as grain elevators, which were by then well-known icons for modernists in Europe.[50] But once in California he was surprised by the proliferation of the drive-in markets and automobile service facilities. With this work, the ideas he and his European colleagues had talked about were manifested in abundance as part of the everyday urban fabric.[51] From this perspective, the typical drive-in market or the prefabricated steel service station, like the grain elevator, were not exceptional designs in themselves, but were function-generated buildings that provided an essential premise for developing a new architecture (figure 70).

Although avant-garde designs for drive-in markets were anomalies when built, they appear to have influenced—or at least anticipated widespread trends in—retail architecture. The Mesa-Vernon and Palm markets were among the most widely published examples of the type.[52] Their broad, unadorned masses, relying on form, displays, signs, and a few embellishments, became a standard repertoire for retail buildings between the late 1930s and 1950s. Neutra's first drive-in market scheme, published in the *Architectural Record* and *Nation's Business* in 1929, appears to have gained an appreciative audience during the 1930s among some young practitioners and students. Its minimalist vocabulary of framing, glass, and giant overhead sign became a standard for hundreds of retail complexes after World War II.[53] Wright's expressionistic approach set the stage for many drive-in facilities in southern California and elsewhere from the late 1930s through the 1950s.[54] Avant-garde experiments with the drive-in market

remained focused on expression; they did not alter its basic program or layout, which were already well established through trial and error at the grassroots level. The modernist contribution lay in testing the limits of new vocabularies predicated on space and movement no less than on form.

LOCATION

While proponents of a new architecture saw the drive-in market as a valuable means by which to advance their cause, the collective impact of examples of every kind was significantly altering patterns of commercial development, laying the groundwork for a new spatial order in the urban landscape. By 1931 a motorist could drive along most major arteries in well-settled portions of the metropolitan area and see at least one drive-in market. However, examples did not exist everywhere. Some care usually went into selecting the areas where a project was located, for it represented a substantial investment. Base construction cost commonly ran $10,000 to $20,000; the total outlay averaged around $30,000 to $50,000.[55] Moreover, because the drive-in's design was so specific to its purpose, conversion to some other use would be costly were the venture to fail. The target audience had to have the mobility as well as the income to sustain the operation. As a result, some of the greatest concentrations of drive-in markets occurred in the most affluent parts of the metropolitan area, including Hollywood, Beverly Hills, and Pasadena. Solid middle-class areas such as the Southwest district, Glendale, Santa Monica, and Long Beach had more or less equal rates of incidence. Drive-in markets also could be found in prosperous working-class communities such as Montebello, Maywood, and South Gate. On the other hand, almost none were built in low-income areas such as those to the immediate south and east of downtown.

Within the precincts chosen, traffic patterns were key to determining how the drive-in market related to other commercial activities. Often the site was on the fringe of a retail node, however modest its size (figure 71). The land was cheaper than in a centralized location, justifying the use of frontage space for off-street parking. Equally important, the property was removed from the congestion caused by intersecting thoroughfares and the taxpayer blocks clustered around it. Vehicular access to the drive-in thus was improved; at the same time, businesses there could capitalize on the trade attracted by the nearby node. This approach to siting, introduced at Ye Market Place and several other pioneering examples, helped to set a new pattern for the location of retail establishments in outlying areas and began to emerge nationally by the end of the next decade.

In other cases, the drive-in market was situated much like many filling and super service stations as well as a few public markets, some distance from any nodal concentration of commerce, drawing trade from through-traffic as well as from nearby residential blocks (figure 72). Often the drive-in was among the first retail facilities in such places, its presence helping to attract other businesses. Elsewhere, drive-ins were constructed before much development of any kind took place in the vicinity (figure 73). To a certain degree these latter emporia functioned in an analogous way to roadside stands, which proliferated along rural highways in southern California and many other parts of the country during the 1920s (figure 74).[56] Both types primarily depended upon passing motorists for their trade. However, a significant difference existed, for the drive-in was oriented not to recreational vehicular paths, but to routine ones of area residents. If enough people living within about a one-mile radius drove by the site on a regular basis, a respectable business could be sustained and, just as in more densely settled districts, other retail outlets might be attracted to the vicinity. The drive-in market thus helped to pioneer business locations within an urban context rather than standing as an outpost that would long remain isolated in more or less open surroundings. The initial separation of the market from the communities it served nevertheless was a novel practice at that time, one that must have seemed odd to observers who did not comprehend the new dynamics of movement created by widespread automobile use.

When the drive-in market was a catalyst for commercial development, the resulting aggregation often lacked the centralized structure of a neighborhood business district, having no clear hierarchy of sites or functions. At a pivotal point in the metropolitan area's growth, when business owners were beginning to understand the implications of a mass motoring populace, the drive-in market demonstrated how even a place catering to mundane shopping needs could be an attraction in itself. At the beginning of the decade, progress in commercial development was measured almost entirely by the growth of concentrated business centers. Several years later, the drive-in market was instrumental in spawning an alternative tendency whereby destinations also could lie at sites scattered on a linear path to meet everyday needs along the miles of thoroughfares that traversed greater Los Angeles. The result was a new structure for retail development rather than a dilution of existing patterns.

71

Shopping district at Pico and Redondo boulevards, Los Angeles.
Aerial view showing Nu-way
Open-Air Market, 1929, C. Roderick Spencer, J. J. Landon, and
Harrison Clarke, associated architects; no longer standing. Photo
Spence, 1934. (Photo Archives, Department of Geography, University
of California, Los Angeles.)

Wilshire Boulevard, Beverly Hills, aerial view looking east toward intersection of San Vincente Boulevard, showing Clock Market (at left of tall building in midground) and Palm Market (at lower right corner of San Vincente intersection). Photo Spence, 1936. (Photo Archives, Department of Geography, University of California, Los Angeles.)

73
Las Palmas Market, 11300–11308
W. Pico Boulevard, Los Angeles,
1930, Alexander Mattson, designer;
altered. Photo "Dick" Whittington,
1930. (Whittington Collection,
Department of Special Collections,
University of Southern California.)

74
Pier Avenue Market, Redondo
Beach, California, ca. 1920s; no
longer standing. Photo "Dick" Whittington, 1934. (Huntington Library.)

It is unclear how extensively market conditions were studied during the course of deciding where to locate a drive-in. Systematic site analysis for retail projects remained at a nascent stage. The pioneering methods
oriented to outlying areas were developed by the chain companies during
the 1920s; however, those techniques were predicated on a nodal form of
business growth.[57] No model existed to guide the less tightly knit structure
of the drive-in market's location. A considerable amount of pertinent data
nonetheless could be gathered as the basis for an informed choice. A survey
of traffic patterns was published in 1924 delineating the streets that had
emerged as primary automobile routes. Subsequently updated tallies of
traffic flow in a given place were not uncommon.[58] Data compiled by municipal offices, by public transportation, utility, and other business concerns
as well as insights gained through personal observation and exchanges with

realtors and merchants provided an abundance of information about the extent and nature of residential development in most parts of the region.[59]

The degree to which statistics influenced a decision more than empirical judgement no doubt varied from case to case, yet the overall consistency in the drive-in market's locational patterns suggests that some care generally went into planning and that the process soon became conventionalized. Given the newness of such concerns and the paucity of applicable precedents, firsthand study of successful ventures in all likelihood played a central role in considering locale no less than other characteristics of the drive-in market. But whatever the methods employed, the type's development underscored the importance of planning based on factors other than such traditional ones as pedestrian traffic or streetcar transfer points.

Drive-in markets were almost always developed as individual entities rather than as part of some larger commercial project.[60] In a few cases, however, they were conceived as integral support facilities to planned residential tracts and were seen by some parties as instruments for containing commerce that would advance the cause of comprehensive planning. Leimert Park was the most significant example to include a drive-in market, the Mesa-Vernon. Occupying a 238-acre site, the scheme drew inspiration from some of the most prestigious undertakings in the nation, but was oriented to a middle-class audience of modest means. The developer, Walter Leimert, sought to demonstrate that a comprehensive approach to planning and design could enhance the market appeal and hence the profitability of moderate-income developments. In 1926 he hired the Olmsted Brothers to prepare the master plan and subsequently commissioned some of the region's leading architects of houses to design model units. Leimert created restrictive covenants for all properties and established a community association to ensure a high standard of future improvements and maintenance.[61]

Leimert considered the retail sector an essential component of the undertaking. The company's on-site office was designed for conversion to a drive-in market once lot sales were completed. Soon the need for more extensive facilities became apparent. The Mesa-Vernon Market was the initial component of a contained shopping district designed to provide a full spectrum of services to residents; it was one of the few such ventures to be realized in the metropolitan area before World War II (figure 75).[62]

Leimert was quick to recognize that, among commercial buildings in outlying areas, the drive-in market could be a poignant symbol of good planning. It was hardly an accident that he invited two of the state's most prominent figures in that field, Gordon Whitnall and Charles Cheney, to the Mesa-Vernon Market, or that he used the occasion officially to inaugurate the Leimert Business Center. He further knew how welcome the services provided by the drive-in would be among the tract's residents and that the facility could in fact stimulate property sales.[63] The drive-in market was explicitly portrayed as a neighborhood asset in a promotional booklet published by the Los Angeles Chamber of Commerce during the late 1920s, which featured one example on the same page as endearing scenes of upper-middle-class residences—a coupling unthinkable for the standard taxpayer block (figure 76).

Today · All eyes are on
LEIMERT BUSINESS CENTER

LEIMERT BUSINESS CENTER one of the greatest future shopping-sub-centers of Los Angeles! Another LaBrea and Wilshire in the making! A place where businesses, ESTABLISHED NOW, will reap a large harvest of profit! A spot where investments made now, will mean future fortunes! Think of it! . . . A scientific analysis made by experts states that, with proper development, Leimert Business Center will be the future PRINCIPAL SHOPPING PLACE of 85,000

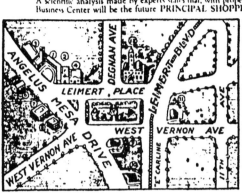

people. That development has started! It is gaining momentum daily! Seventeen businesses now located. Where important traffic streets come together from seven directions will soon be the great shopping place study this situation. Merchants examine this future of the southwest. Investors, study this situation. Merchants, examine this future great center. The greatest business sub-center of Los Angeles is on Hollywood Boulevard. The second now is on Wilshire at La Brea. We believe that the Leimert Business Center will unquestionably be at least the THIRD greatest shopping sub-center of Los Angeles.

1. Mesa Vernon Market, opening today. 2. New Branch, Pacific National Bank, under construction. 3. Four stores, already leased, construction beginning. 4. Three stores in hands of architect. 5. Florist. 6. Ice cream Shop. 7. Restaurant. 8. Pan Stores. 9. Shell Station. 10. Union Station. 11. Rehfield Super Service, construction beginning. 12. Site reserved for Theatre.

OPENING of
Mesa-Vernon Market
Saturday and Sunday, November 17 & 18

Leimert Park does things right! By developing the right kind of homes amid ideal surroundings, Leimert Park enjoys the greatest building activity in the city today. And now Leimert Business Center marks its opening with the finest drive-in market ever built!

The picture below shows the Mesa-Vernon Market which opens TODAY, completely leased and every tenant ready to break all sales records. Special events have been planned that will bring tens of thousands of visitors during the week end — a Gala Opening.

THE tenants of the Market include foremost dealers, such as J. E. HANSON at the Bakery; H. A. STIMPSON at the Grocery; M. LINDENBAUM at the Drug Store, FRED H. KRAMER in the Meat Dept; and ENDOW & SUZUKI handling Fruits and Vegetables. In the professional suite are Dr. F. C. DIVER and H. B. SIMONS, D. D. S.

The stores are offering a number of items at actual cost for the Gala Opening event.

Buildings designed by Geo. J. Adams, Hollywood Architect

Dedication of Leimert Plaza
and the Fountain

City and County officials will participate in Ceremonies timed for 8 o'clock Saturday evening, Nov. 17th, when LEIMERT PLAZA and the beautiful Fountain are dedicated to public use. In addition to the officials, the concerns listed on the right will be represented, all of whom have been of splendid assistance in making for the present success in the development of Leimert Park

The Los Angeles Investment Co., developers of View Park, are providing additional festivities for the occasion.

Altogether, the opening of Leimert Business Center and the Mesa-Vernon Market will be an occasion long remembered in Los Angeles. Ample Parking space provides for the thousands of cars that will come from every section of the city.

We wish to acknowledge the hearty Co-operation of
The Security Title Insurance & Guarantee Co.
The Ralph G. Wolf & Co.
The L. W. Blinn Lumber Co.
Billingsley Mortgage Co.
Pacific National Bank
Weber Showcase & Fixture Co.
Shell Oil Co.
Barber Bros.
"Buddy's" Nursery
Herbert K. Barber, Commercial and Overhead Doors

HOW TO GO:
Drive West on Santa Barbara Avenue or West Vernon Avenue, 8 blocks beyond Western Avenue. Follow the signs to Angeles Mesa Drive

Walter H. Leimert Co. Inc.
Developers of Leimert Park & Leimert Business Center
3001 W. Vernon Ave., Ph. VErmont 1174
The title to all property in Leimert Park is guaranteed and insured by Security Title Insurance and Guarantee Co.

FORTUNES in the Making!
In pricing lots, we have not attempted to anticipate the tremendous future of the business area. Here is a genuine opportunity for PROFITS!

Patios and Pools Lend Enchantment

Open-Air Markets in the Neighborhood Supply Fresh Fruits and Vegetables

75
Advertisement for Leimert Business Center and opening of Mesa-Vernon Market, 1928. (*Los Angeles Times,* 17 November 1928, I-5.)

76
Illustrations accompanying an essay on "Home Life," showing Vineyard Market, 952–962 Vine Street, Los Angeles, 1926–1927, A. Burnside Sturges, architect. (Los Angeles Chamber of Commerce, *Los Angeles To-Day, City and County* [ca. 1930], 8.)

    The drive-in market demonstrated how routine shopping outlets could effectively be integrated apart from existing commercial nodes in a single facility whose design and location were determined by its clientele's parking needs. Yet by 1930, these buildings were fast losing their currency as a preferred outlet for food. Within a few years, the drive-in helped transform the basic configuration of the shopping center; however, that process occurred in cities far removed from southern California. Locally, the drive-in soon became seen as a thing of the past, replaced by another new kind of emporium, the supermarket, which gave few overt signs that its predecessor existed.

III

THE LOS ANGELES SUPER

It is little wonder that consumers relegated the drive-in market to antique status, given the nature of the stores that supplanted them. In 1938, the experience of shopping at one of the new supermarkets was still unknown to many people across the nation; it was so memorable to many others that a detailed narrative was presented in the *Saturday Evening Post*. Using a hypothetical family, the author followed the Muzaks, who

discovered their first supermarket one Saturday night when a traffic jam slowed up their fourth-hand automobile. The three Muzak children saw a glare of light down the street and simultaneously shouted, "Fire!" Poppa Muzak maneuvered the car out of traffic and parked. They elbowed through the sidewalk crowds, to stand finally with mouths agape. The glare came from red and white floodlights illuminating a square one-story white building of modernistic design. Its seventy-five foot plate-glass front was covered with banners announcing: "Supermarket Grand Opening." Strings of pennants fluttered on the streamlined roof; and multicolored neon signs flamed from the triangular tower.

The show did not stop there:

The interior was a blaze of brilliant white light. Down one side of the building glittered the sparkling glass and white enamel of the longest meat case Momma Muzak had ever seen. Across the front of the store spread a monster display of fresh fruits and vegetables. . . . The huge building was completely filled with pile after pile of foods—acres of it, it seemed to momma. . . . The store was jammed with a thousand customers.

Big-eyed, the little Muzaks led the way through clicking green metal turnstiles, and things began happening to them—free chocolate-coated ice-cream bars for the children, cigarettes for Poppa Muzak, a cut flower for momma.

But the biggest surprise was the cost of merchandise.

"Look, poppa," [Mrs. Muzak] cried. "My coffee! Only thirteen cents! Never did I buy it cheaper than nineteen cents at Schmaltz's. Maybe I should get a pound."

Poppa waved his cigarette expansively. "Maybe two pounds you should get. Or three."

When the Muzaks had finished looking around the store, "they had bought enough food to last . . . a week or more." Since then,

Every Friday or Saturday poppa [drives] momma three miles to the new supermarket. Often, they [take] Mrs. Grensci, who lives in the flat above them and [has] no automobile. Overnight, the supermarket divorced them from Schmaltz's independent grocery and the corner chain store.[1]

The Muzaks lived in northern New Jersey, where supermarkets had already caused conspicuous changes in shopping patterns and no small degree of consternation among independent grocers and chain store executives over the past several years. Yet many parties in the food business still questioned the supermarket's long-term viability. Some observers considered it a by-product of the depression, a creature destined for extinction with the return of economic prosperity. Often, too, assessments cast the supermarket as a poor business proposition. The rock-bottom prices upon which many outlets based their appeal allegedly made them unstable operations at best. Chain companies, which had invested so heavily in perfecting customer services, were certain that shoppers would soon tire of having to walk down aisle after aisle among mammoth displays selecting goods without the assistance of clerks.[2]

Despite the doomsayers, the supermarket was well on its way to becoming a major phenomenon in food retailing, one that an official at the U.S. Census of Business believed to be "the fastest-growing, basically sound development in the history of retail distribution."[3] The supermarket in fact helped to revolutionize the distribution system by firmly establishing low price as a transcendent factor in mass consumption appeal, by expanding the scope of self-service shopping, and by selling food and other convenience goods at a much larger volume than previously thought possible. These buildings also accelerated the trend of business development away from established nodes, with location predicated on easy access for substantial numbers of motorists.

Just what constituted a supermarket was debated during the 1930s as much as its significance to retailing. Frequently, a specified minimum annual sales figure was cited as the key determining characteristic, but sales alone hardly distinguished the supermarket—either as a business operation or as a shopping experience—from its predecessors.[4] Conceptually, the supermarket was structured to meet the demands of a large trade. Sustaining that trade was essential to the life of the business, and was achieved by offering products of dependable quality and in wide variety at low prices—prices often lower than those of major chain stores. The pricing schedule meant a low profit margin on any given item; only through high-volume sales could the supermarket function as a financially sound operation. To reduce overhead, staffing was kept to a minimum and self-service used to the fullest extent possible. These demands necessitated a completely integrated business structure. The building itself had to be larger than most, if not all, other food stores of previous years. Since the super-market depended on motorists for much of its clientele, a tangent parking lot of substantial size became a standard feature at an early date. At first, many supermarkets were utilitarian in character, but by the mid-1930s creating an environment consumers found attractive became a primary concern. No one of these aspects was new; it was their combination that made the supermarket so pronounced a departure in the retail field.

What was a revelation for the Muzaks of America had become commonplace for southern Californians by the mid-1930s. The Los Angeles super, as it was known in the industry, had flourished in the region for nearly a decade. No other part of the United States came close to matching the proliferation of these emporia that occurred there before World War II. The supermarket was not wholly invented in Los Angeles as were the super service station and the drive-in market; facilities that were key prototypes for the supermarket emerged independently in several cities during the 1920s. Yet a greater contribution was made to the development process in the Los Angeles metropolitan area than in any other part of the country. Not only were examples far more numerous there, but the region was the most active proving ground for new ideas and for applying those ideas on a large scale.[5] What had become the industry's highest standard for supermarket design and operation at the end of the interwar decades was to a substantial degree set by Los Angeles precedents. Well before that time, anyone questioning the type's significance for the future need only have examined how the Los Angeles super already had gained preeminence in the local field, quickly outstripping its competition, including the still new and beguilingly convenient drive-in.

TRANSITION

Four years after the drive-in market began its rapid ascent, the type suffered an equally swift eclipse. The number of drive-in markets planned for the Los Angeles area in 1931 amounted to about one-third of that undertaken the previous year, the rate of new projects taking its sharpest drop toward the summer's end. Only three drive-in markets are known to have been built in 1932. So pronounced a change might easily be related to the concurrent economic downturn. At the beginning of 1931 business activity in the region was rated at 30 percent below "normal," and the value of building permits issued in Los Angeles during 1930 dropped about 20 percent from those issued in 1929. The region's business activity experienced a further 20 percent decline the following year, while the value of Los Angeles building permits decreased by more than an additional 44 percent. Conditions were even worse in 1933 and 1934, with declines in the city's building permit values greater than 57 percent and 12 percent, respectively.[6]

But it was not the downturn in building that brought the demise of the drive-in market. Dollars spent on constructing supermarkets during the early 1930s may well have equaled, if not exceeded, those spent on food stores of all kinds during the years immediately previous.[7] What did change was the intensity of competition resulting from hard times. In the process, low prices became an ever more consequential factor in the operation of food stores; those with the best selection of goods at the lowest cost found themselves in the strongest position. The most effective means of sustaining lower price schedules was to increase the volume of goods sold. Merchants could achieve that objective by increasing their trade radius and getting customers to purchase more. Widespread automobile use made possible the former, so long as selection and price were sufficiently appealing. The car also allowed customers to transport larger quantities of food home. Equally important to fostering volume purchases was the electric refrigerator, which could hold many more perishable foodstuffs than most household ice boxes. Introduced on the retail market in 1925, the electric refrigerator gained acceptance among affluent and middle-class families alike, far beyond manufacturers' initial expectations. During the late 1920s and the 1930s, sales skyrocketed and prices dropped correspondingly.[8] Owning a refrigerator thus facilitated consumers purchasing food at lower prices and on fewer occasions. Under the circumstances, driving some distance to the store once or twice a week did not seem burdensome.

Numerous food retailers were skeptical at first about changing their business methods, for conventional wisdom held that a large physical plant carried unduly high risks. The bigger the facility, the more difficult it was to sustain an adequate trade. If the enterprise failed, moreover, the investment lost was much greater than with a standard store unit in a taxpayer block, which could readily be converted to other uses. Raising the capital to start such an operation—to construct the building, equip it with expensive fixtures, and stock it with what seemed an enormous inventory—likewise posed obstacles. Yet once the imperative for volume sales became clear, merchants soon realized that restructuring their operations, however costly and fraught with risks, was necessary if they were to remain competitive. Once established, the tendency to build supermarkets in Los Angeles progressed, in the words of one observer, with "almost cyclonic momentum": between 1930 and 1932 hardly a week passed without a new unit opening. Four years later, it was estimated that over 180 supermarkets were operating in the area, and that they commanded 35 to 40 percent of the retail food business, posing the greatest threat ever to chain store companies.[9]

The drive-in market helped pave the way for these developments. Through the proliferation of drive-ins, southern Californians quickly became accustomed to the conveniences of one-stop shopping. Equally important, consumers had gotten in the habit not just of driving to the store, but of choosing one store among many based on the strengths of its location, goods, and pricing. However, the drive-in was structured to fit the traditional routine of shopping on a more or less daily basis and purchasing a modest quantity of goods on any given trip. Higher-volume sales necessitated a larger selling area, a larger on-site storage facility, and, since the car was a central agent in the process, a larger parking lot as well. Size was not the only issue. The drive-in's configuration came to be seen as fundamentally unsuited to the shifting demands of the field. Flexible space now was considered of primary importance, so that the quantity of goods of any given type could be adjusted according to available supplies and market demand. The linear arrangement of the drive-in was far less conducive to this fluidity than the unobstructed, rectangular space, about twice as deep as it was wide, that came to typify the supermarket. Merchants also discovered that many customers resisted moving in a long, linear path from one department to the next. Instead, the tendency was to purchase a single type of product and ignore the rest, "turning my store," in the words of one exasperated drive-in operator, "into a curbside business like a barbecue stand." To remedy the situation, this particular building was expanded to occupy the forecourt, and its operator reported that once customers could see more items, sales trebled.[10]

In general, the drive-in's forecourt now was often seen as too small, its configuration a creator of bottlenecks. Moreover, this space occupied what was still regarded as the most valuable part of the property. Given the choice of retaining off-street parking or expanding sales and storage areas, some merchants chose the latter. With the forecourt arrangement, too, open-front displays, now increasingly seen as a vital means of attracting customers, were often hidden from view by parked cars; and those cars were now viewed as detracting from the appearance of the building. Compared to the small streetfront stores of the 1920s, drive-in markets had a conspicuous presence in the urban landscape, even with the visual "mess" of parked cars. But compared to the large and often exuberant facades of supermarkets, the entire fronts of which were given over to sidewalk displays, drive-ins seemed less prepossessing. The supermarket reclaimed the street. Frontality regained the importance it had had before the advent of the drive-in concept; but now this arrangement was devised to attract the eye of the passing motorist more than that of the pedestrian.[11]

Such a rapid replacement of a popular new type also was due to differences in the parties responsible for each phenomenon. The drive-in was the creation of real estate investors and their agents, who sought ways to make the metropolitan area's abundant boulevard frontage profitable. As long as the drive-in afforded retailers a competitive advantage over conventional streetfront stores, they were eager to participate in such projects. When conditions changed, however, the food industry had no special allegiance to the type. The supermarket, on the other hand, was an internally generated response—the invention of persons in the retail and wholesale food trades, and specifically tailored to their new merchandising needs. Even when real estate interests were involved, they worked closely with an experienced merchant in choosing the site and developing the design of the building. The drive-in did not face immediate extinction with the supermarket's rise; while many closed during the 1930s, many others continued to operate as sound businesses. Nevertheless, the supermarket became the unquestioned outlet of choice among retailers, whose lead the real estate interests now followed.

Finally, the shift could take place so rapidly because the Los Angeles super had strong local precedents. Expansive public markets had been built in outlying parts of the metropolitan area since the early 1920s. One of the region's largest food retailers, Ralphs Grocery Company, had erected enormous stores that enjoyed unusual success and embodied all the characteristics of the supermarket, as it would come to be known nationally by the eve of World War II. Before the depression, when price was not so important a factor, the big Ralphs stores demonstrated the value of having a wide range of desirable goods that customers could select easily themselves in a setting the Muzaks would have considered remarkable indeed.

RALPHS

Ralphs led the supermarket field in southern California from the time its first large, self-service stores were opened in 1928 through the post–World War II era. The company had by far the biggest network of supermarkets in that or any other region. These facilities embodied numerous innovations in their design and operation that eventually had a national impact. Ralphs also ranked among the oldest food establishments in the state, and at least some of the innovative techniques the company developed for the supermarket were rooted in practices established decades earlier. George A. Ralphs founded the enterprise in 1873 at Sixth and Spring streets, a location then several blocks below the commercial core but well placed to serve the fledgling residential areas that fanned to the south.[12] At an early date, Ralphs formulated an operational structure, based on volume purchases and sales as well as on competitive prices, that gained the company prominence among the city's retail food businesses. To keep abreast of metropolitan growth, Ralphs instituted citywide delivery service in 1896. The store itself moved into larger quarters five years later and again in 1913 (figure 77). Although the business remained close to its original site, the nature of the location had changed dramatically. By 1910, the store lay in the heart of the rapidly growing business district. Ralphs increasingly catered to an elite trade that sought a wide range of fancy goods as well as stock items. The third building fully embodied this shift, its ornate interior filled with genteel displays and staffed with pampering attendants (figure 78). Here space was organized in a linear fashion characteristic of sizable downtown clothing and other specialty stores, with counters separating customers from goods and purchases wholly dependent upon interaction with salesclerks at designated stations. Ralphs's development at this stage epitomized a trend in food retailing, then evident in a number of large cities, that markedly distinguished the commercial services available in the urban core from those in outlying areas.[13]

Ralphs broke from convention, however, in also becoming a pioneer in decentralization. Its first branch unit opened in 1911 at Pico Boulevard and Normandie Avenue long before other major downtown Los

77
Ralphs Grocery Company store,
514 S. Spring Street, Los Angeles,
ca. 1902; no longer standing. Photo
ca. 1902. (Courtesy Ralphs Grocery
Company.)

78
Ralphs Grocery Company store,
635 S. Spring Street, Los Angeles,
ca. 1913; no longer standing. Interior. Photo ca. 1910s. (Courtesy
Ralphs Grocery Company.)

Angeles storeowners undertook such ventures. Located amid the fast-growing Southwest district, which was a major focus of middle-class residential development, the new facility was then considered large for an outlying retail operation of any kind, especially one not sited in a business node (figure 79). From the beginning of its branch development, Ralphs located its stores as destinations that would not depend on neighboring commercial enterprises to bolster trade. Rather than catering to a walk-in clientele living within a radius of a few blocks, the outlet functioned as a staging area for an increasingly broad-based distribution system. Most of the store's business was through orders that were delivered, and hence much of the building contained storage space from which goods might efficiently be taken to householders.

A second, and considerably more opulent, branch was constructed in the Southwest district four years later (figure 80). Appearances were a significant factor in the design of this outlet; no small amount of money was invested in a showy front, quite atypical of the matter-of-fact treatment then still common to commercial buildings in outlying areas. Situated on Vermont Avenue at Thirty-fifth Street, near some of the city's most affluent neighborhoods, the building no doubt was conceived to appeal to an elite trade by being an attraction in itself as well as by purveying choice goods. Considerably more space seems to have been allocated to the sales area than at the initial branch, so that patrons could find many, if not perhaps all, of the products displayed at the parent store. For the first time in Los Angeles, a branch outlet conveyed the sense of both elegance and choice then associated almost entirely with downtown shopping.

79
Ralphs Grocery Company store, 2791–2793 W. Pico Boulevard, Los Angeles, 1911; altered. Photo ca. 1910s. (Courtesy Ralphs Grocery Company.)

80
Ralphs Grocery Company store,
3500–3558 S. Vermont Avenue, Los
Angeles, 1915; no longer standing.
Photo ca. 1910s. (Courtesy Ralphs
Grocery Company.)

Over the next decade, Ralphs opened seven additional branches, making the company one of the largest food retailers in the metropolitan area, comparable in volume of goods sold to scores of small neighborhood groceries operated in the metropolitan area by a large chain such as Safeway.[14] Slowly and in increments, Ralphs's internal organization came to function more like that of a chain than of a centralized business with satellites. The Spring Street facility remained the flagship store, but it became ever less pivotal to the operation as a whole. By this point, if not before, branches offered a full range of goods, making them equals rather than appendages to the parent store. Reflecting the rise in stature of these offspring, the new unit on Seventh Street, near the western edge of downtown, became home to Ralphs's business office in 1923.

The new branches were sizable by standards of the time, containing around 6,000 square feet of selling area and a roughly equal amount of space for storage and delivery functions.[15] Both in arrangement and character, the selling areas were markedly different from that of the Spring Street store (figure 81). In the branches, space was organized laterally, with wide aisles between counters. Fruits, vegetables, and some other goods were displayed so that customers could inspect them at will before purchase, as at a public market. Moreover, the palatial trappings were replaced by a more informal setting in which merchandise more than architecture held the limelight. George Ralphs's nephews, Walter W. and Elmer L. Ralphs, who had run the company since the mid-1900s, and his son, Albert George Ralphs, who had recently joined them, appear never to have

81
Ralphs Grocery Company store, 723
W. Seventh Street, Los Angeles,
1923; no longer standing. Interior.
Photo ca. 1923. (Courtesy Ralphs
Grocery Company.)

doubted that a big store could sustain a profitable trade. At the same time,
their fiscal policy was prudent. Expansion was financed through surplus capital. In contrast to most food stores in the region and elsewhere during the
interwar decades, Ralphs's buildings and the land on which they stood
were owned outright. Equally unusual, the company owned and operated
all departments on the premises.[16] The ambitiousness of the enterprise was
matched by complete control over its every aspect.

      The territory into which Ralphs expanded was for the most part
occupied by middle-income households. The new branches formed an arc
from Hollywood to the Southwest district; north of downtown, stores
were in the Highland Park district and Glendale. The elaborateness of the
Vermont Avenue branch was seldom emulated; the new buildings looked
more like ordinary taxpayer blocks. However, a decisive turn was taken
with the design of one outlet, erected in 1926 as both a retail facility and
the production center for Ralphs's bakery department. Designed by Morgan, Walls & Clements in a freewheeling, Spanish-inspired mode that had
become a trademark of this firm, rising amid the vast landscape of modest
bungalows in the Southwest district, the pile was trumpeted by the *Hollywood Daily Citizen* as "a palace with walls like an oriental rug" (figure 82).[17]
The exterior was in fact as elaborate as any commercial building then
found on Hollywood Boulevard or any other street beyond the city center.
Here Ralphs reinstituted for a mass market the practice of creating a landmark to symbolize the reputation of the firm, the strength of its business,
and the quality of its goods—a building that, like the company, stood out
from the norm. Erecting elegant facilities became a central component of
Ralphs's next expansion campaign, which began less than a year later and
resulted in some of the first true supermarkets in the United States.

      Two additional changes in merchandising strategy were key to
Ralphs's development of the supermarket. The first was self-service, al-

ready a feature in many chain groceries, which the firm began as an experiment in 1925 and standardized for the grocery departments of all its units within four years. The other change was eliminating deliveries, again a common chain practice, which Ralphs began to implement throughout its system in 1928 and completed two years later.[18] Store managers discovered that when customers could select their own goods, they not only tended to buy more but were less inclined to have them delivered, since they had driven to the premises. Nevertheless, the abruptness of the shift carried risks. The chains' success with cash-and-carry, as it was called, was based on customers making only a small number of purchases on each visit and hand-carrying these goods home. Ralphs, on the other hand, had to maintain a considerably higher sales volume per trip. To achieve this goal—to get large numbers of people to choose its stores over many others and to make a substantial number of cash purchases while there—the company focused on providing a selection of quality goods at reasonable prices that had few rivals. Ralphs claimed to have the greatest array in the metropolitan area of nationally advertised brands as well as respected local brands. Equally important were the store's conveniences, which at once imparted a sense of freedom and made the clientele feel pampered. New buildings were considered vital to meet these objectives. Concurrent with eliminating deliveries, Ralphs began to open new stores that were far larger and more lavish than most food emporia in Los Angeles or elsewhere in the nation. After building nine enormous new stores in less than half a decade, Ralphs had nearly trebled its selling capacity.[19]

After the "palatial" bakery, Ralphs commissioned Morgan, Walls & Clements to design a prototype for its supermarkets, which was also one of the first large retail facilities on Wilshire Boulevard's Miracle Mile, a fast-growing locus of trade for western sections of the metropolis.[20] The exterior again drew from Spanish sources, a mode then in the height of fashion, using a free interplay of baroque and medieval details to create a sense of exoticism on a relatively grand scale (figure 83). As at some earlier Ralphs outlets, additional space was included for lease to discrete commer-

82
Ralphs Grocery Company bakery, 3617 W. Washington Boulevard, Los Angeles, 1926, Morgan, Walls & Clements, architects; altered. Photo ca. 1930s. (Courtesy Ralphs Grocery Company.)

cial enterprises, a technique the company used to offset some of its investment and maintenance costs. But here the program also was developed to maximize the conspicuousness of the pile. The second-floor space, leased to a popular chain restaurant, was massed to suggest the base of an enormous tower. The whole treatment was in fact as suggestive of the elite origins of its vocabulary—in buildings for the church and the nobility—as of its commercial purposes. With such physical and symbolic pretensions, Ralphs was seeking a preemptive presence for its new stores.[21]

Subsequent work was designed in the same manner but by another architect, Russell Collins, who gave greater emphasis to the food emporium proper without lessening the sense of theatricality.[22] Among these buildings, the Pasadena store (1929) had the most lavish facade, its tower serving solely as a beacon (figure 84).[23] This was the last occasion leasable space was included, here reduced to two small shops. However, the effect was made grand by incorporating a portal, much like those to the production lots of motion picture studios, that led to off-street parking for forty cars—the first time Ralphs incorporated this amenity. Thereafter, car lots became a standard fixture for new stores, their boundaries unshielded and their capacity progressively larger. Later modifications also included adding access to the store direct from the lot and greatly increasing glazed areas on the side elevations to brighten the interior (figure 85). From the outside, the most important change was that the facility was now treated as a free-

83
Ralphs Grocery Company store, 5615–5633 Wilshire Boulevard, Los Angeles, 1928, Morgan, Walls & Clements, architects; demolished 1989. Photo "Dick" Whittington, 1929. (Whittington Collection, Department of Special Collections, University of Southern California.)

84
Ralphs Grocery Company store, 171–181 N. Lake Street, Pasadena, 1929, Russell Collins, architect; demolished. Photo ca. 1930s. (Courtesy Ralphs Grocery Company.)

85
Ralphs Grocery Company store, 2024 E. Tenth Street, Long Beach, California, 1931, W. Horace Austin, architect; no longer standing. Photo 1930s. (Courtesy Ralphs Grocery Company.)

standing object, conspicuous not just as a decorated facade but as a massive block defined by open space, claiming its own territory in the urban landscape unchallenged by neighbors. Perhaps inspired by the example of Bullock's Wilshire department store, Ralphs designers toward the end of the building campaign embellished the sides as much as the front, without undermining the traditional importance of the front. At the same time, these outlets took a cue from the drive-in market in the degree to which parking space was a prominent part of the ensemble and was perceptually tied to the shopping space within.

The size of these stores—about 10,000 square feet each for sales and storage areas—made their siting an especially important factor. Yet beyond easy access by car from a large number of middle- and sometimes upper-middle-income households, no single pattern predominated in their location. Planned shopping districts held appeal. Not only was Ralphs among the first major stores to build on the Miracle Mile, it was an early comer to Westwood Village. Two other stores were sited close enough to the big commercial centers of Hollywood and Pasadena to benefit from their trade and yet remain apart from their traffic congestion. One store was located in the much smaller core of Alhambra, then a rapidly growing, prosperous bedroom community.[24] The four others—on Pico Boulevard southeast of Beverly Hills, on Vermont Avenue near the southern fringe of the Southwest district, at Huntington Park, and at Long Beach—were in more isolated locations, places passed by thousands of cars daily, but without concentrated commercial activity.[25] As models for siting this latter

86
Ralphs Grocery Company store, 6121 W. Pico Boulevard, Los Angeles, 1931, Russell Collins, architect; no longer standing. Photo "Dick" Whittington, 1933. (Whittington Collection, Department of Special Collections, University of Southern California.)

group, Ralphs had its own early branches as well as the more recent success of those drive-in markets that created new destinations for the motorist. Now, however, the building was on a scale that bespoke its intended commercial hegemony in no uncertain terms (figure 86).

Inside, the visual drama was of a different order. The retail space was two to three stories high, clear-spanned by the use of the still novel lamella system of vault framing—an arched net composed of small wooden members—and illuminated by skylights and huge windows on two or three sides (figure 87).[26] Ceilings were polychromed in stencil work to complement the colors of fresh produce and packaged goods. The expansiveness underscored the organization of the selling area, which was not perceptually divided into discrete departments but treated as a unified space. Aisles were formed by long and comparatively low, multitiered shelves, arranged in parallel groups that fostered easy movement from one end to the other. Most goods were thus displayed openly for customers to inspect and choose. This shelving arrangement was a prototype for the gondola—long tiers of unbroken, open shelving extending from a vertical supporting frame—which would become a standard fixture in supermarkets a decade later.

The character of these spaces differed from those of the big public markets, where the arrangement was more compartmentalized, the ambience more utilitarian, and the appointments sometimes quite elementary (figure 88). The new stores were also more elegant than the previous generation of Ralphs branches. For women especially, these buildings were de-

87
Ralphs Grocery Company store, 6121 W. Pico Boulevard. Interior. Photo "Dick" Whittington, 1931. (Whittington Collection, Department of Special Collections, University of Southern California.)

88
Richardson's Market, Alhambra, California. Interior. Photo ca. 1930s. (Alhambra Public Library.)

signed to give a routine shopping place some of the drama of the stylish emporia downtown, while avoiding any of the palatial trappings associated with many of those outlets, including Ralphs's Spring Street store. The setting seemed at once dramatic and equalizing. Harriet Burdsal, home economics columnist for the *Hollywood Daily Citizen,* described the Wilshire Boulevard store as "beautiful beyond expectations," fancifully likening the interior to a "marketplace of Rome, where Phoenicians came to peddle their bright silks and bits of treasure from afar," and commented elsewhere that the company's stores provided "ample proof of our [i.e., women's] esthetic might."[27] Here Ralphs created a new kind of space that was lofty, imposing, yet nonhierarchical and conducive to perambulation, allowing consumers to choose their own paths of movement as well as their own goods. In no previous instance had so large a retail space seemed so perceptually open and so liberating.

The selection of goods displayed at Ralphs supermarkets matched the expansiveness of their quarters. Ralphs aggressively claimed to stock numerous items infrequently used as well as those in constant demand, making oblique comparison to the chain companies' fixation with rapid turnover at the expense of variety. Prices were competitive with those of the chains, although Ralphs did not participate in the reduction wars in which many other early supermarket operators later indulged. The quality of products sold was more important than rock-bottom prices in Ralphs's merchandising plan. Complete owner control of the operation engendered a sense of confidence among customers. Ralphs's reputation for dependability was also fostered by its longstanding success. Having been in business for over fifty years, the company became identified with the growth and progress of the city itself.[28]

Efficiency and convenience were just as central to Ralphs's operating policy. With the "quick service system," customers could pick up a shopping basket at the entry and serve themselves from the grocery section. By 1931, self-service also was introduced as an option at the produce department, making Ralphs one of the first establishments to do so. But even when most of the selling area was self-service, a premium continued to be placed on employees paying close attention to customer needs. Attendants were available to help locate items and, if requested, to bring full baskets to the cashier. Ralphs most touted its range of up to eight checkout stands located near the exit so that only one payment could cover all purchases—an unusual, perhaps unique arrangement when it was implemented in the late 1920s.[29] At drive-in and other markets with concessions, purchases had to be made department by department. Since Ralphs owned all of its departments, having one place for payments was not only feasible but economically advantageous for the company, once the orientation to self-service was made. The system saved customers considerable time both in the transaction and in having goods packaged. Furthermore, this sequence encouraged perambulation, which included return visits to aisles for additional purchases. No provision was more important to liberating sales space physically and perceptually.

At Ralphs, the retail area of the large market became fully integrated. Ornamental opulence on the exterior was equaled by the attributes of space, selection, and service—including self-service—inside. Burdsal remarked that the "tendency toward permanency in architecture corresponds with the tendency toward quality in every item of merchandise on the Ralphs shelves." After inspecting the Wilshire Boulevard store, she concluded, "It's getting to be such a pleasant proceeding, going to the market, that [m]any women who have not been enthusiastic about housekeeping must succumb before long to the spell of it."[30]

In formulating its unorthodox approach, Ralphs may well have been influenced by the film industry's drive to increase trade by erecting movie palaces in outlying as well as central urban precincts, a process that began in earnest during the 1920s and reached its peak at about the time Ralphs's expansion program began.[31] Like the movie palace, these supermarkets were big, seemed elegant to their middle-class clientele, and catered to that trade's wishes without great cost. Similarly, Ralphs devised its stores as attractions, providing experiential amenities that relatively few other commercial enterprises in outlying areas could match. As with the movie palace, too, the investment required was huge. Base construction cost alone ran between $70,000 and $85,000 for most of the new markets; the price of land and fixtures could more than double that amount. Not the least of Ralphs's contributions to the retail field was its early demonstration that the depressed economy did not herald an end to such lavish outlay for facilities, but rather demanded new campaigns to compete for diminishing sources of revenue.

Ralphs's first supermarkets made the operation unique among food retailers not just in Los Angeles, but throughout the United States. The companies that came the closest, both in size and structure, were the Houston-based J. Weingarten and Henke & Pillot, themselves exceptional firms that seem to have had no counterparts elsewhere prior to the depression. Both companies were similar to Ralphs in starting with large city center emporia where their operational policies were established before branch development. The two Houston firms also became the locally dominant

89
Henke & Pillot South End Store,
2806–2820 Travis Street, Houston,
Texas, 1923; altered. Photo 1940s.
(Courtesy Progressive Grocer.)

force in food retailing, each through a network of sizable, owner-operated
stores that sold a full range of high-quality goods at low prices and were
strategically located across outlying areas of the city. Founded in 1901,
Weingarten opened a new downtown store thirteen years later; in its size
and configuration, it became a model for the company's later supermarkets.
Self-service was initiated in the grocery department soon thereafter.
Branch units began to be erected after World War I, culminating in a
1929–1932 expansion campaign that gave Weingarten a total of ten stores
from 7,500 to 20,000 square feet in size.[32]

     Henke & Pillot was an older operation, established in 1872, and
focused on building fewer but far larger markets when it started to expand.
Its first branch store (1923) contained over 30,000 square feet, probably the
most ambitious of its kind in the country at that time (figure 89). Equally
important, the building was situated one block away from Main Street, the
thoroughfare along which other retail outlets congregated. Henke & Pillot
widened the street fronting its huge facility and laid out a broad approach
and side streets—all to accommodate diagonal curbside parking for approximately 300 automobiles. Three years later, Henke & Pillot opened an even
larger facility (40,000 square feet) with adjacent off-street parking for some
450 cars to one side; this was one of the largest lots serving a single store

anywhere in the nation at that time (figure 90). The sea of space made the store seem modest by comparison, an arrangement as unusual as the building itself. A third branch followed in 1931, somewhat smaller in its dimensions but otherwise patterned along much the same lines.[33]

Off-street parking was also an important component of the Weingarten stores. Units built between 1929 and 1932 each had a lot at least equal to the ground area occupied by the building. Unlike Henke & Pillot stores, the principal facade of each Weingarten unit was oriented to the parking area, irrespective of whether this relationship allowed the front to remain parallel with, or at right angles to, the street. In establishing strong ties between the building and parking lot, Weingarten appears to have followed the example of Houston's third major food retailer, A–B–C Stores, a younger, smaller operation no less prone to experiment. As early as 1927, an A–B–C unit, designed also to serve as the company's offices, had been set far back from the street, its big forecourt a latter-day plaza and the building itself vaguely reminiscent of the recently "restored" Palace of the Governors in Santa Fe (figure 91).[34]

The time frame in which the large Houston stores were built and the specific attributes of their design and operation suggest that work in southern California had no influence. Like Ralphs, the two largest companies' expansion programs were shaped by earlier in-house practices. The

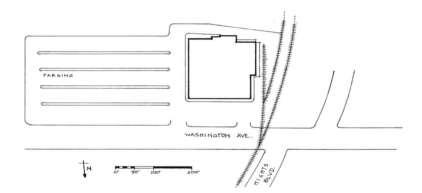

90
Henke & Pillot West End Store, 3000 Washington Avenue, Houston, 1926; altered. Site plan. Drawn by Brenden Meyer based on drawing in *Houston Post,* 7 December 1926, 8.

91
A–B–C market, 2120 Main Street, Houston, 1927, William War Watkin, architect; no longer standing. (*Civics for Houston,* January 1929, 6.)

large size of Henke & Pillot units, their locations away from established business centers, and the space accorded to customer parking occurred in combination before anything comparable on the west coast. Even the parking area appears to have stemmed from local patterns. Like the setting of Henke & Pillot's initial branch, many towns in the region had streets in the commercial core that were wide enough to permit diagonal parking, with traffic sufficiently light to permit customers to stop in front of their destination. This relationship was maintained at several of the early Weingarten branches—and at hundreds of commercial properties developed in the south central states during the late 1920s and 1930s—by setting the store far enough back from the street to enable a row of parked cars in the intervening space.

The much larger forecourt at the A-B-C and later Weingarten stores was analogous to the Hispanic plaza and even more akin to its subsequent Anglo counterpart, the courthouse square. At numerous Texas county seats, the space between the landscaped area in which the courthouse stood and the surrounding blocks that comprised the commercial center was so wide that it could accommodate four ranges of parked vehicles, two curbside and two in between. The need for so much space was felt principally on market days well before the advent of the automobile, and the practice of parking in the middle as well as along the sides of these streets has continued through the twentieth century. For the many Houstonians who had lived in towns and rural areas, the supermarket forecourt probably did not seem like a new element at all, but rather a traditional one modified by the exigencies of its urban setting.[35] On the other hand, the parking arrangement of the second and third Henke & Pillot stores was not unlike that of recent factories, where tangent, fieldlike spaces were set aside for workers' cars. Since both these Houston outlets were located in industrial precincts and near prosperous working-class neighborhoods, this spatial correspondence was not out of place, even if it was unusual for a retail outlet.

The utilitarian analogy evident in Henke & Pillot's program was especially obvious in the buildings themselves, which looked much like wholesale or warehouse facilities of the period. Most Weingarten and A-B-C stores were not much more assuming, their fronts rendered similarly to those of unadorned taxpayer blocks. Inside, the setting also was matter-of-fact, the large sales area resembling that of a public market.[36] Self-service was limited. Space was clearly divided into zones by department, and purchases were made at each of these stations. The single range of checkout stands, which made a freer, more integrated flow of space possible, remained a thing of the future for the Houston stores. Likewise, some years would pass before any of these companies adopted the idea of imparting a sense of elegance to the supermarket, indoors or out. While Ralphs was not alone in the field, no other company could match the extent to which its operation presaged that of leading supermarkets a decade later.

92
Young's Market, 1610 W. Seventh
Street, Los Angeles, 1912, Charles F.
Plummer, architect. Photo author,
1987.

EXPERIMENTS

When Ralphs inaugurated its expansion program in 1928, attitudes among
competitors differed widely as to the soundest merchandising approach.
Not only was the drive-in market at the height of its popularity, but chain
store executives and many independent merchants remained skeptical of in-
vesting so much money in any one facility lest the location prove unprofit-
able. Others who did accept the idea of a store created for volume sales
adhered to practices more traditional within the trade. The pioneering business to erect a very large and elegant food store in an outlying area of Los
Angeles was Young's Market Company, which moved from its downtown
headquarters to a much grander building on West Seventh Street some ten
blocks to the west in 1924 (figure 92), near the exclusive enclaves from
which so much of its trade came. Young's was unusual also in the extent
of its operation, which by then encompassed a chain of forty-six small outlets—specializing in meats, coffee, and fancy and baked goods—through-

out the metropolitan area. Locally, the business ranked among the most impressive of its type, grossing some $8,000,000 in 1924, but its organizational structure remained highly centralized. Young's new "palace of art" functioned as the showcase and also the nerve center of the entire operation. At the turn of the century Young's and Ralphs's downtown stores were patterned in much the same mold, but Ralphs's agenda had become very different by the late 1920s.[37] No hierarchy existed among Ralphs's big stores scattered throughout the metropolitan area. The downtown facility had for some time served as just another unit. By 1937, its location became so marginal that the store was closed, the first Ralphs outlet to experience that fate.[38]

Despite their prominence in the trade, neither Ralphs nor Young's provided the immediate base upon which the Los Angeles super began to proliferate during the 1930s. Through 1931, the principal force in the expanding scale of food stores in the region was the public market. After the initial post–World War I years, few large outlets of this kind were constructed until the late 1920s, when a number of new examples comparable in size to Ralphs's first supermarkets were constructed. Experienced retailers spearheaded most of these projects because they, like the Ralphs, believed that volume sales were essential to future success and that a wide variety of goods, combined with reasonable prices and easy access by car, were the key means of achieving that objective.

As in the early 1920s, the basic operational structure of the public market remained one concession for each type of food product.[39] Yet within this framework, considerable variety existed. Some concessions were quite specialized—fish and poultry departments, for example, as well as one for meat, or a department devoted strictly to tobacco products—while others were more broad-based, so that the number of departments could vary from five to twenty at facilities of more or less equal size. Sometimes complementary functions were included. Departments carrying the range of goods found at chain drug stores were among the most common; beauty shops, post offices, and other routine services were part of the ensemble on occasion. Approaches to running the facility varied as well. Independent concessionaires could be contracted to operate all the departments. For his Union Public Markets in Glendale (1929) and east Hollywood (1930), Andrew Westra, a twenty-five-year veteran of food wholesaling and import businesses, followed this pattern, securing prominent retailers such as Young's and concentrating his own energies on management and promotion. The Homecroft Public Market (1930) in the Southwest district was built by four food retailers who ran three of the five major departments themselves, coordinating the operation without a separate manager. Hattem's Shopping Center (1931), also in the Southwest district, was one of the few operations comparable to Ralphs in being entirely owner-operated.[40] Hattem also followed Ralphs's example in having several discrete stores in an ancillary part of the complex.

Large public markets of the late 1920s and early 1930s tended to be more visually prominent than their predecessors. Few approached the ornate treatment of a Ralphs store; most, however, were conceived to function in the same way: as landmarks capable of attracting motorists' attention at a distance. The Great Southwest Market (1928) at Vermont and Slauson avenues had a twin-towered facade punctuating elevations composed as grandly scaled arcades (figure 93). The 1929 Metropolitan Market nearby was even fancier, its streetfronts bedecked with theatrical distortions of quattrocento motifs.[41] Hattem's Shopping Center was perhaps the most overtly fashioned as a beacon, with a tiered corner tower housing the owner's offices and pied-à-terre (figure 94). But no consensus existed on the ex-

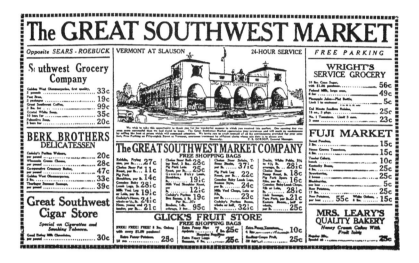

93
Great Southwest Market, 5800
S. Vermont Avenue, Los Angeles,
1928, Walter Hagedohm, architect;
destroyed by fire 1992. (*Los Angeles
Evening Herald,* 15 June 1928, B-15.)

94
Hattem's Shopping Center, 8021–
8035 S. Vermont Avenue, Los
Angeles, 1930–1931, Walter Hagedohm, architect; altered. Photo
"Dick" Whittington, 1931. (Huntington Library.)

tent to which the exterior should be embellished; the Homecroft was more subdued and the Union Public Market in Hollywood was frankly utilitarian in character (figures 95, 96).

Inside, these emporia still evoked some of the workaday character of the nineteenth-century market hall. However, significant changes were beginning to occur, very possibly influenced by Ralphs. Hattem's Shopping Center had one of the most elaborate interiors, its features suggesting an opulence associated with stylish apparel shops of recent vintage (figures 97, 98). As with the new Ralphs stores, Hattem's facility attained a balance between elegance and efficiency. Similarly, too, a sense of openness was pervasive. Unlike in most earlier markets of substantial size, the selling area was uninterrupted by structural supports. This arrangement was becoming an important feature for the type generally, and was often emphasized in promotional accounts. Yet at Hattem's and elsewhere the arrangement of goods remained traditional, with each department its own, self-contained unit and many goods accessible only through the hands of sales staff (figure 99).

Large public markets learned from Ralphs and the drive-in market to allocate generous space for off-street parking, which was now usually located to the side or rear of the building. The capacity of these lots appears to have ranged from a minimum of about twenty cars (typical of drive-in lots) to around two or even three times that number (equivalent to the lot of a new Ralphs). In some cases attendants helped customers in finding a space and toting purchases to their automobiles. Patrons could

95
Homecroft Market, 6221–6227 S. Vermont Avenue, Los Angeles, 1930, Walter Hagedohm, architect; no longer standing. Photo "Dick" Whittington, 1930. (Whittington Collection, Department of Special Collections, University of Southern California.)

enter the building directly from the car lot at the Great Southwest, where access was from all four sides, and at Hattem's, where access was from three. Most examples were situated on corner properties so that at least two elevations, with much of their wall planes open to the sidewalk, formed the public face.

The conspicuousness of large public markets was enhanced by their location apart from concentrated business development. In some cases the choice of site was reinforced by other destinations nearby. The Great Southwest lay across Slauson Avenue from a Sears store that had opened a year earlier; the Grand Central Market in Glendale (1929) rose near that community's recently completed airport.[42] Yet elsewhere facilities stood more or less in isolation. The sole competing focus of retail activity near Hattem's came from a Ralphs several blocks to the north, which was completed that same year.

PROLIFERATION

The cost of a large public market, which could represent a total investment of $200,000 or more, precluded construction of many examples. Most food merchants could not raise the capital for such a venture, and those who did seldom could afford to do so more than once.[43] But the basic concept of these facilities provided the springboard from which the Los Angeles super became a ubiquitous part of the metropolitan landscape during the early depression years. The process began by combining features such as the conspicuous exterior and clear-span selling space of the large public market with the form of the more modest "small" public markets, averaging 4,000 to 7,000 square feet, which had flourished throughout the 1920s. From the street, examples of the latter group looked like neighbor-

96
Union Public Market, 4315–4327 Beverly Boulevard, Los Angeles, 1930, Balch & Stanbury, architects; altered. Photo Albert Frey, 1932. (Courtesy Albert Frey.)

hood grocery stores, while operationally they were similar to a drive-in, with four or five concessions carrying modest quantities of all basic kinds of food products (figure 100). These facilities attracted little attention in trade literature compared with the drive-in or, later, the supermarket.[44] Yet the type had proven its worth to the extent that many retailers, expressing caution at a time of economic uncertainty and intensifying competition, drew upon it as a point of departure in expanding their businesses.

      The change from public market to supermarket was evolutionary to the point that no clear line of separation can be drawn between the two. By 1930, examples could be found that were in some respects simply expanded versions of the small public market, averaging 6,000 to 8,000 square feet.[45] Besides the change in size, uninterrupted selling space became characteristic, conspicuously expressed outside by a long, open front enframing produce displays (figure 101). Most examples retained the minimum number of departments, with few products other than food available. Like their modest forebears, they were typically sited on midblock lots and often surrounded by other stores as part of commercial nodes. Some provided off-street parking; many did not. Stores of this kind—which by the mid-1930s were commonly called supermarkets—represented a cautious, pragmatic move, without any decisive breaks from convention. Indeed, the supermarket probably gained so strong and swift a foothold within the local trade because it met the immediate demands of increased volume while not seeming an abrupt change. Most of this work was undertaken by small,

97

Hattem's Shopping Center, interior of market at opening. Photo "Dick" Whittington, 1931. (Courtesy Maurice Hattem.)

98

Hattem's Shopping Center, stairs to mezzanine. Photo "Dick" Whittington, 1931. (Whittington Collection, Department of Special Collections, University of Southern California.)

area-based chain companies and by groups of independent retailers who pooled their resources in cooperative ventures.[46]

On the other hand, major chains based outside the region resisted even an incremental shift to larger buildings. Safeway, which had considerable sums invested in the several hundred neighborhood stores it operated throughout the region, was the most conservative. During the early 1920s,

Safeway did start to carry a full range of food products; however, its new stores remained under 4,000 square feet. By 1937 a standardized design was developed in the form of a small supermarket with a side lot usually graded for off-street parking, but not until four years later did units exceed 6,000 square feet.[47] When the Great Atlantic & Pacific Tea Company entered the Los Angeles market around 1930, its new stores were the same size as Safeway's. Soon the company found that its national reputation was insufficient to attract an adequate trade unless some attention was paid to local conditions. By the mid-1930s, A&P was constructing small supermarkets that were 6,000 to 8,000 square feet (figure 102).[48] When run well as part of a vast network, outlets of this size could be profitable enough, as Safeway's practices revealed. Bigness did not ensure success, but it did seem to provide a competitive advantage. By 1936, it was estimated that the percentage of business done by major chain food stores in the metropolitan area had fallen from 42 percent to under 20 percent since the late 1920s, a decrease attributed almost entirely to the rise of the supermarket.[49]

Well before A&P decided to build modest-sized supers, independent retailers were embarking on considerably more ambitious projects in the hope of augmenting their trade. The increase in scale, with buildings that approached the dimensions of a Ralphs store, began as early as 1931 and gained momentum over the next several years despite the turbulent economy.[50] The open-front display area remained the primary visual focus of these designs, which, with facades approaching 100 feet in length, added to their distinct presence in the urban landscape (figure 103). The building surface tended to be little more than a billboard—a linear stretch of light-

99
Hattem's Shopping Center, interior. Photo "Dick" Whittington, 1931. (Whittington Collection, Department of Special Collections, University of Southern California.)

100
Martin's–South Park Public Market, 4418–4420 Avalon Boulevard, Los Angeles, ca. mid-1920s; altered. Photo ca. 1926. (Security Pacific Historical Photograph Collection, Los Angeles Public Library.)

101
Roberts Public Markets store, Los Angeles area, ca. late 1920s/early 1930s. Photo ca. 1940. (California Historical Society Collection, Department of Special Collections, University of Southern California.)

colored stucco supporting large-scale signs, but few integral details. This barebones approach may well have been influenced by the depression; such buildings could be erected for about half the cost per square foot of the fanciest Ralphs stores.[51] By emphasizing product display, retailers expressed their long-standing prejudice that merchandise, prices, and service were more important than architectural embellishment. That view persisted among a number of supermarket operators throughout the decade. On the other hand, a taste for stores with greater individual identity arose in certain quarters. Ralphs's success, especially, demonstrated that consumers enjoyed shopping in an environment that did not seem mundane. By 1933, some competitors were again seeking to create elaborate facilities.

The favoring of architecturally decorative buildings entailed no basic modification to the open-front parti, but it did result in a distinct change of appearance. On some examples, the enframing wall was treated as sculpture in the streamlined forms made popular by the 1933 Century of Progress Exposition in Chicago. The open area was no more conspicuous than the zone above it, which was rendered as an enormous, abstract frieze, with decoration set in relief and large-scale signs. Pylons, or even towers, which had proven so effective a device at drive-in markets, often enframed the composition at one or both ends (figure 104). The prime examples in this vein were by Morgan, Walls & Clements, who were earning a reputation as the region's preeminent designers of supermarkets. Having made a specialty of commercial work in outlying areas during the previous decade, the firm also gained an impressive record in the design of food stores, including several drive-ins, public markets, and the prototypical Ralphs super-

102
Atlantic & Pacific Tea Company store, 1853 N. Vermont Avenue, Los Angeles, 1935; no longer standing. Photo ca. 1935. (Wady Medamar Collection, B'hend & Kaufmann Archives, Pasadena.)

103
La Brea Food Spot, 435 N. La Brea Avenue, Los Angeles, ca. 1932; no longer standing. Photo ca. 1940. (California Historical Society Collection, Department of Special Collections, University of Southern California.)

104
Thriftimart store, 401 Wilshire Boulevard, Los Angeles, 1934, Morgan, Walls & Clements, architects; altered. Photo "Dick" Whittington, 1937. (Whittington Collection, Department of Special Collections, University of Southern California.)

market. What kept the office in the lead was its ability to translate lessons learned from experience to a new program and in a striking new architectural vocabulary. Like the historicizing Ralphs stores, these supermarkets were conspicuous and seemed elegant. Even more important, the firm gave the supermarket an appearance unlike that associated with any other building type. Retailers had defined the basic size and form of these buildings in response to the pragmatic concerns of their trade; Stiles Clements and his associates set the standard in giving this program an exuberant character that could be followed widely. Even run-of-the-mill examples might possess a bold, purposeful face that made them seem, in the public mind, paragons of modernity and hallmarks of the city itself (figure 105).[52]

That modernity was, of course, in a wholly popular vein. Unlike the drive-in, the supermarket appears to have elicited little interest among avant-garde architects, probably because its boxy mass and traditional streetfront orientation left little room for formal design innovations. A hypothetical scheme of 1931 by the German immigrant J. R. Davidson, then in the early stage of his independent career, was a rare exception (figure 106).[53] Davidson emphasized transparency—an open front with no visual frame, topped by an advertising panel, perhaps translucent, perhaps backlit—that would have been particularly effective at night. For the most part, however, Los Angeles's growing cadre of avant-garde modernists were becoming ever more divorced from the pragmatic sphere of commercial architecture.

That pragmatism remained driven by the persistence of convention as well as by the imperatives of change. Throughout the 1930s, most

105
Sav-On Food Mart, 601–609 N. Dillon Street, Los Angeles, 1939; altered. Photo "Dick" Whittington, 1939. (Whittington Collection, Department of Special Collections, University of Southern California.)

market operators continued to insist on the open front as a means of displaying produce (figure 107). This prejudice, in turn, necessitated keeping departmental divisions, each with its own staff and pay stations. Self-service often remained limited to canned and other prepackaged goods, which many operators believed were the only ones customers were inclined to purchase without the assistance of clerks. Set at the rear of the selling space and separated from other parts by checkout stands, these areas could foster

106
"Driv-in-Curb Market," 1931,
J. R. Davidson, architect; project.
(Special Collections, University
Art Museum, University of California, Santa Barbara.)

107
Atlantic & Pacific Tea Company,
1853 N. Vermont Avenue store, interior. (Wady Medamar Collection,
B'hend & Kaufmann Archives,
Pasadena.)

a perceptual sense of division in an otherwise unbroken space (figure 108). Even when the barriers were less pronounced, the use of different display equipment and of different circulation paths in each department contrasted conspicuously with the uniform arrangement of the new Ralphs stores (figure 109). Equally pronounced was the absence of loftiness, natural light, and architectural embellishment found in Ralphs's buildings.

The preference for frontality in supermarket layout also affected the exterior and site plan. By the mid-1930s, having a sizable parking lot to one side was a standard feature, yet the adjacent wall was rendered in a utilitarian manner. Unlike those at the new Ralphs stores, this elevation had only a minimal window and no direct entry to the store (figure 110). Thus, whereas the operation now occupied a significant amount of land—often twice the size of parcels on which many drive-in markets stood—and the building itself was generally freestanding, the spatial order remained traditional, as if the supermarket was but an inflated neighborhood store. The big parking lot was treated as residual space—vacant land awaiting the construction of another building.

Large, open-front supermarkets continued to proliferate in southern California until the United States entered World War II, and well before then had attracted widespread attention among food retailers, real estate interests, and architects nationwide. Walter Leimert, who had developed the Mesa-Vernon drive-in, wrote enthusiastically in 1939 that the supermarket was "one of the outstanding features of Los Angeles, immediately noticed for its size, its lighting and ornamentation, and its marvelously attractive front display[s]." The availability of so much undeveloped arterial frontage, which had fostered the development of drive-ins, likewise proved beneficial to the rapid spread of big supermarkets.[54] The grandest examples of the mid-1930s soon became sufficiently commonplace to render obsolete those preceding them by only a few years. The average size was estimated at 10,000 square feet in 1935, and 20,000 square feet by the decade's end. Parking for 150 cars was considered high in 1933; space for 300 was not unusual by 1939.[55] The overall cost of the project often reached $200,000, comparable to that of a large public market or of a Ralphs store of the late 1920s.

Both the cost and the size of the facility appear to have had a direct bearing on location. The larger the investment in the food store, the more likely its separation from established business centers. Inexpensive land and avoidance of traffic congestion became standard factors in siting, accelerating the tendency toward scattered-site business development. The supermarket's impact on this tendency stemmed not just from the large number built, but also from the crowds each could attract. Probably no other building type did more to foster fragmentation of shopping patterns outside the city center during the interwar decades. Despite its widespread application, however, the supermarket remained foremost a fixture of middle-class precincts. Only toward the end of the period did large units begin to be sited in predominantly blue-collar parts of the region.[56]

Increased size did not lead to changes in the supermarket's operational structure. More brands may have been added and goods stocked in greater quantity, but the division into five or six main departments remained standard. As with the large public market, some nonfood sections often were incorporated; after the repeal of prohibition, liquor became one of the most common of these. Discrete concessions also remained the norm, although the large scale of the supermarkets and the unrelenting competition between them underscored the arrangement's weaknesses. Concessionaires did not always cooperate when they needed to adjust quickly to changing circumstances so as to maintain high-volume sales. The advantages evident in Ralphs's complete ownership of the operation led to a gradual consolidation trend that was distinct, if not yet widespread, by 1941.[57]

To a large extent, the pressure to improve performance—after, as well as during, the depression—came from the rapidly increasing number of large, well-equipped supermarkets. When only one or a few such outlets existed in a district, their trade could be very substantial. Consumers in the Los Angeles area sometimes drove as far as twenty-five miles to a supermarket. With each successive opening, however, the market share of any given outlet was likely to decrease.[58] By 1941, areas such as Hollywood and the Southwest district were saturated with supermarkets. Householders did not have to drive far before encountering at least one such enterprise. The competition among them was so fierce that sometimes clusters of two or more emerged, not because proximity enhanced business, but rather because newcomers sought to draw trade away from existing outlets through such means as undercutting prices, greater publicity, and even, perhaps, a flashier building (figure 111).

Cutthroat competition led to a success rate among supermarkets that was markedly less than their growth rate. Out of an estimated 350 Los Angeles supers built by 1939, only about 40 percent were yielding the handsome profits that had lured so many merchants into the fray. Ten percent had closed. Among the remaining 50 percent, half were operating at reduced rents, so that their tenants were "able to earn a marginal wage"; the other half retained their original rent schedules, pushing tenants to "the verge of bankruptcy." The situation afforded a textbook example, in the mind of one seasoned appraiser, of the "old adage that 'inordinate profits breed ruinous competition'."[59] Yet the situation was not so ominous as to stifle further development. Whatever its weaknesses, the supermarket was now widely regarded among southern California food retailers as the best kind of facility. Many merchants also saw expansion rather than retrenchment as the way to advance their lot.

Besides consolidating departmental ownership, some supermarket operators established a network of stores as a strategy to improve competitiveness. Among the first merchants to take this course were concessionaires Miller Allen and John Huck, who, between 1932 and 1936, purchased three large public markets and one drive-in whose owners were

108
Atlantic & Pacific Tea Company,
1853 N. Vermont Avenue store,
self-service section. (Wady Medamar
Collection, B'hend & Kaufmann
Archives, Pasadena.)

109
La Brea Food Spot (later Caler's Market), interior. Photo "Dick" Whittington, 1941. (Whittington Collection, Department of Special Collections, University of Southern California.)

experiencing financial difficulties. Three of the outlets—all of which were now called supermarkets—lay in the Southwest district, giving the firm a conspicuous presence in that lucrative trading area. In some other cases, a troubled business in a good location became an expeditious means for an aggressive retailer to broaden his base.[60] However, most companies expanded by constructing new stores tailored to their specifications. Young's began inaugurating a chain of supermarkets in 1933. To avoid undermining its many older units still in operation, the big stores bore a different name, Thriftimart, while boasting embellishments commensurate with the parent company's prestigious reputation (figure 112; see also figure 104).[61]

Others who had started local chains of small neighborhood stores prior to the depression entered the arena as well. Sam Seelig, who had sold his 263 units to Safeway in 1925, came out of retirement seven years later to run a supermarket in Hollywood, and opened two more of his own in 1937. One of Seelig's old competitors, Charles von der Ahe, worked quickly to replace small Von's stores of the 1910s and 1920s with supermarkets (see figure 110). By 1941, he owned a chain of twelve supers, the largest in the metropolitan area save for Ralphs.[62] Widespread name recognition and uniform policies affecting prices, brands carried, and layout were among the attributes promoted by supermarket chains no less than chains of smaller food stores. One of the most successful firms of the period, however, followed an opposite strategy. Ben Surval, a veteran wholesaler who had built one of the first supermarkets in Hollywood, was joined by grocers Al and Morris Wisstein to erect others, each with its own name and complexion tailored to the particular characteristics of the trading area.[63]

Whatever the approach, expansion was still gradual and modest in scope. Very few businesses had more than three large supermarkets until after World War II, when local chain development became rapid. The stan-

110
Von's Olympic store, 1020 S. Fairfax Avenue, Los Angeles, ca. 1934; no longer standing. Street elevation, showing former open front, probably enclosed after World War II. Photo "Dick" Whittington, 1953. (Whittington Collection, Department of Special Collections, University of Southern California.)

111
Business development around Pico and La Cienega boulevards, Los Angeles, showing Ralphs store of 1931 (right) and Farmer's Public Central Market, store #2, 1935–1936, W. Douglas Lee, architect (center). Photo Spence, 1939. (Photo Archives, Department of Geography, University of California, Los Angeles.)

112
Thriftimart store, 4301–4315 Degnan Boulevard, Los Angeles, 1935, Morgan, Walls & Clements, architects; destroyed by fire 1992. Photo "Dick" Whittington, 1939. (Whittington Collection, Department of Special Collections, University of Southern California.)

dard for that pace was set by Ralphs, which continued to grow on a large scale during the 1930s, adding twelve new supermarkets to its arsenal in a seven-year period.[64]

RALPHS, II

Ralphs also continued as the principal innovator in the field, not least through its buildings. When the company began its second supermarket construction campaign in 1935, it continued to resist the conventional mold, capitalizing instead on the visual prominence a large store could attain when treated as a freestanding, three-dimensional object. The possibilities of such treatment were enhanced by the use of corner lots and an arresting repertoire of streamlined elements. All these new stores were designed under the aegis of Stiles Clements, whose office was reorganized under his leadership in 1937 and who proved ever adroit at perceiving shifts in taste, manifesting them in ways that made it seem as though he had precipitated the change. For Ralphs, Clements now created a new trademark image that was less overtly ornamental and more suggestive of an elegant machine, without the streetfront emphasis of most supermarkets.[65] Broad horizontal bands of glazed and concrete surfaces stretched across the elevations, with no strong hierarchical distinction between front and sides (figure 113). Indeed, new units no longer possessed a front in the traditional sense. In at least several designs, warehouse spaces lay adjacent to the street corner, while the principal elevation was oriented to the car lot (figures 114, 115). The space allocated to automobiles got progressively larger— up to three times the area occupied by the building, an unusually high ratio at that time. The store still possessed a strong presence from the street. That elevation was rendered much like the adjacent one facing the parked cars, the two sides compositionally unified by a sculptural pylon at the juncture. Nevertheless, each store was planned to be seen from all sides so that it would not just stand out as a landmark for motorists approaching some

113
Ralphs Grocery Company store, 9331 Wilshire Boulevard, Beverly Hills, 1937, Morgan, Walls & Clements, architects; no longer standing. (*Super Market Merchandising,* September 1937, 6.)

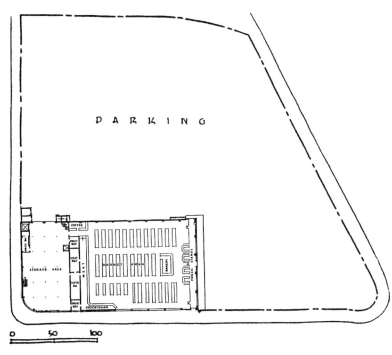

114
Ralphs Grocery Company store, 3635 Crenshaw Boulevard, Los Angeles, 1939–1940, Office of Stiles Clements, architect; no longer standing. (California Historical Society Collection, Department of Special Collections, University of Southern California.)

115
Ralphs Grocery Company store, 8575 W. Third Street, Los Angeles, 1941, Office of Stiles Clements, architect; no longer standing. Site plan. (*Architectural Record,* October 1941, 73.)

blocks away but, at closer range, would seem accessible and inviting from the exterior no less than inside. The connection between space to accommodate automobiles and space for efficacious merchandising, characteristic of the drive-in market, was beginning to develop in new ways.

Clements's solution for Ralphs was by no means an obvious one, however. By preference or habit, most businessmen and their architects still thought of the streetfront as the building's showpiece, despite the concern now given to off-street parking. The drive-in market had departed from this pattern, but its integration of building and exterior space seems to have fallen from favor along with the type itself. The advantages of this relationship, however, were not lost on Clements, who adapted the idea to a new scale and a new design vocabulary. His plans for Ralphs stores still addressed the street, standing right at the property line. Yet the three-dimensional qualities of these schemes, where the whole arrangement as well as the expressive character of the building stemmed from the open space that surrounded it, were highly unusual for retail architecture of the period. Clements took the building-forecourt symbiosis of a drive-in market a step further, in a pragmatic but also lyrical response to merchandising needs.

The freedom with which Clements could manipulate the exterior composition was to a large degree due to his client's preference for enclosed stores. While most food merchants still viewed the open front as an icon of their trade, Ralphs had long recognized its functional drawbacks. Direct sunlight, hot and cool temperatures, wind, and dirt all decreased the shelf life of fresh produce. Combined with street noise, these elements also detracted from the overall quality of the environment inside.[66] Ralphs did not experiment with the open front when it came into vogue during the early decades of the century, a preference undoubtedly reinforced in the late 1920s since produce displays at the property line would have rendered a single range of checkout stands unworkable. But as the supermarket became ubiquitous and those displays attained an extravagance and appeal they had seldom enjoyed earlier, the Ralphs may well have understood that their new buildings had to be all the more carefully conceived to attract customers.

Among the most conspicuous amenities Ralphs offered was air conditioning, which was becoming important for many kinds of retail establishments but was impossible to use with an open-front arrangement. The basic qualities of space developed for the earlier Ralphs stores worked well for the new, streamlined ones. While not as ornamental as before, the sense of spaciousness and unity was enhanced by wider aisles and more compactly ordered displays (figure 116). Self-service now dominated the merchandising plan, although it still does not appear to have been extended to every department. As many as ten checkout stands were used. The selling areas were somewhat larger (up to 14,000 square feet), with storage space provided at about equal size so as to keep stock adequate. Continual modifications were made to improve both natural and artificial lighting.[67]

By the late 1930s, the capacity of Ralphs stores to attract customers was such that the construction of a new unit could have considerable
impact on its environs. Walter Ralphs claimed that the nature of residential
development in an area might be studied for as long as several years before
a decision was reached on locating a store there.[68] Sometimes expansion
penetrated well-settled precincts, as did the 1936 store on Santa Monica
Boulevard near Vermont Avenue. Standing in sharp contrast to its older
neighbors, the facility was conceived to draw a substantial clientele away
from a number of existing establishments (figure 117). But most of the
new supermarkets were sited in isolation on the urban periphery, staking
claim to a trade area that was often still coalescing. The company's prestige
enabled some units to be built in advance of nearby residential tracts. Even

118
Crenshaw Boulevard, Los Angeles,
looking from Exposition Boulevard,
Ralphs store (1939–1940) at right.
Photo "Dick" Whittington 1940.
(Whittington Collection, Depart-
ment of Special Collections,
University of Southern California.)

when under construction, a Ralphs store could enhance the appeal of such property among prospective homebuyers. The store also could function as a catalyst for commercial development. When the emporium at Crenshaw and Exposition boulevards opened in January 1940, work was already under way on a range of complementary stores in the adjacent block, establishments whose owners viewed the supermarket as the anchor for a modest-sized shopping district (figure 118).[69]

When Ralphs's thirty-first store opened on Ventura Boulevard in the San Fernando Valley less than two months before the bombing of Pearl Harbor, the company had left its mark throughout the metropolitan area, from North Hollywood to Long Beach, Santa Monica to Whittier. Seven stores were operating in the Southwest district, five along the Wilshire corridor, four in Hollywood. No other retail concern enjoyed such ubiquitousness with facilities designed for volume sales. After World War II, other southern California food merchants would adopt many of Ralphs's attributes, such as operating on a large scale with multiple units; full ownership of departments; enclosed, air-conditioned buildings; and a merchandising plan based on self-service and reputation rather than on novelty. Even before the war, Ralphs seemed less an anomalous enterprise than an archetype, a standard for supermarkets of the future. By that time, the Los Angeles super was having a decisive impact on practices in other parts of the nation.

DIFFUSION

When Ralphs completed its first supermarket building campaign in 1931,
it is doubtful whether any other community outside southern California
could match the combination of operational structure, size, and elaborateness of its new stores. A decade later, Clements's recent buildings for the
company were likewise in the forefront, but they were no longer quite so
exceptional, either in their own region or in other parts of the United
States. By that time the supermarket had become a national phenomenon,
increasingly regarded as the most consequential thrust in food retailing of
the era. The precedents set in southern California arguably were the most
important to the type as it approached maturity by the early 1940s. However, the catalytic events that propelled the supermarket into the public
limelight across the country took place neither in Los Angeles nor in Houston, where the most significant prototypes existed, but in the New York
metropolitan area—western Long Island and northeastern New Jersey, the
land of the Muzaks—where nothing of this sort had been known prior to
the depression.

The first New York supermarket was in Flushing, opened in 1930
by Michael Cullen who, after unsuccessful attempts at persuading several
major retailers to adopt his ideas, developed an aggressive merchandising
plan on his own.[70] Cullen followed some practices of his former employer,
A&P, as well as those of other leading chains, in concentrating on major
brands. At the same time, the concept of an expansive store entailing a
number of concessions was probably shaped by his knowledge of the large
public markets in Los Angeles. Some of these emporia provided him with
the model for managing the operation as a fully integrated business. The
big southern California stores may also have inspired him to introduce
other common goods and services, which in his case included auto supplies, drugs, cosmetics, and dry goods as well as shoe repair, tailor, and barber shops.

Cullen departed from precedent, however, in featuring rock-
bottom prices throughout, buying from cash-starved jobbers who sold him
many items at a loss. To sustain his low prices, Cullen also minimized overhead. His first and subsequent King Kullen stores were housed in vacant
automobile garages and other utilitarian facilities, adapted without embellishment inside or out. The effect was of an industrial-age barn, with goods
displayed almost as if they lay in storage, an atmosphere Cullen called
"homey."[71] Apparently from the start, the huge selection of packaged groceries was self-service and most, if not all, food items were paid for at a single range of checkout stands—one of the first large-scale arrangements of
this kind other than at Ralphs stores. Self-service probably contributed to
the success Cullen enjoyed, along with the much-touted attributes of selection and value. The target audience was comprised for the most part of
modest-income households, many of whom were now experiencing hard
times. Up to this point, their choice among food stores had mostly been

limited to small neighborhood outlets run either by chains or by independent retailers. Perhaps with an understanding of what had already become commonplace in southern California, Cullen geared his business to the many thousands of such people who lived within driving distance of the store. Off-street parking was provided at a time when that feature was almost unknown for a single retail outlet in the region. Cullen knew his market well. In less than three years, he had a network of eight stores on Long Island and in the Bronx, ranging from 10,000 to 32,000 square feet.[72] Overnight, it seemed, he had gained a significant share of the trade.

Cullen laid much of the conceptual groundwork for a second and even more ambitious enterprise called Big Bear, which opened its first store in a vacant automobile assembly plant on the fringe of Elizabeth, New Jersey, during the 1932 Christmas season (figure 119).[73] The owners, Robert Otis and Roy Dawson, had years of experience working for Sears, Roebuck & Company as well as major variety and food store chains. They joined forces with a food wholesaler to present an array of merchandise in unprecedented volume. The store, which occupied 50,000 square feet of the 2,000,000 in the plant, included departments for drugs and cosmetics, radios, electrical supplies, sporting goods, and automobile accessories—which together occupied more than two-thirds of the selling area—in addition to those for food. Like Cullen, Big Bear's operators emphasized self-service and centralized checkout for food and retained tight control over concessions so that the entire store could sell popular brands at cutthroat prices. The trade area extended a radius of twenty miles, and many customers came from farther afield. A vast car lot, which probably had been created for the automobile workers, lay across the street and was now reserved for customer use. Patronage exceeded expectations. In the first year, the enterprise grossed over $3.8 million. The grocery department alone was responsible for more than half that amount, which represented almost four times the sales of a prosperous Los Angeles super.[74] Within short order, Big Bear began to expand to other locations; by the decade's end, stores could be found throughout the area.

In the eyes of retailers, especially those in the East and Midwest, the principal lesson of these New York–area emporia was that when people had little money to spend they were willing to forgo the conveniences of time, location, and service to reap substantial savings on food purchases. Low prices made a decisive difference in sales volume. At first, the convenience of self-service and centralized checkout was not viewed as a customer incentive, but it also became an important feature in the years that followed. Although numerous California merchants were already well aware of the dynamics of mass merchandising, for colleagues elsewhere the circumstances surrounding the King Kullen and Big Bear bonanzas seemed more dramatic and more applicable to their own situations. By 1934, the supermarket patterned on the King Kullen and Big Bear models was emerging as a conspicuous force in food retailing in many eastern and midwestern cities.[75] Three years later, the skepticism, fear, and loathing with which

119
Big Bear market, 963 Frelinghuysen
Avenue, Elizabeth, New Jersey, ca.
1910s/1920s, converted to market
1932; altered. Photo 1940. (Courtesy Progressive Grocer.)

the supermarket had been met in established circles of the trade there was
fast waning. The type could no longer be dismissed as a short-lived response to the depression. However, with widespread acceptance of the idea
came rejection of the bare-bones approach championed by King Kullen
and Big Bear. Price was no longer considered the sole criterion for sustained volume merchandising; the quality of goods and of the atmosphere
in which they were sold were now seen as equally significant.[76] In the rapid
diffusion of the supermarket nationwide after 1935, the New York experience provided the catalyst but did not offer an enduring paradigm.

      Until the mid-1930s, some retailers in New York and other met-
ropolitan areas began new operations modeled on King Kullen and Big
Bear; yet the general trend was more tentative in nature. Rather than dis-
carding their own established practices, merchants tended to adapt them
to meet the new demands of providing an increased variety of goods in
greater volume at lower prices in larger stores. The particulars of these operations varied considerably in organizational structure and scope of services
provided, but the physical plants almost always shared one attribute: makeshift appearance. Often the buildings were converted ones—sometimes
retail outlets, sometimes industrial or service plants, sometimes municipal
markets. The character of new buildings was not much different. Off-street
parking was an anomaly. For the most part, the supermarket had yet to

achieve a distinct physical presence.[77] Few resembled those in Los Angeles
and Houston, where well-established, innovative local companies erected
a network of sizable and sometimes elaborate owner-operated outlets.[78]

By the mid-1930s, as economic conditions began to improve in
many parts of the country and the supermarket idea no longer seemed
so experimental, some independent merchants commissioned stores that
looked more purpose-built.[79] Yet the major shift toward big and clearly distinctive buildings did not occur until the decade's end. Independents con-

tinued to set the pace in this regard; however, their work was now given an added impetus from the growing number of major chain companies that were entering the supermarket field.[80] Most chain supers were modest by the standards of southern California or even of some independents elsewhere, yet they contributed significantly to the development process, intensifying chain-independent rivalries. Improvements by one side fueled those by the other. As a result there was a swift rise in the value given to buildings that embodied popular notions of stylishness and modernity, places calculated to wow the Muzaks with a setting that matched the attributes of wide selection, low prices, and convenience. These internal trade dynamics were reinforced by the broad-based tendency in retail store design that gained its strongest following between the second half of the 1930s and the early 1940s. For merchants of all kinds, a modernization campaign that entailed major changes in store appearance emerged as a central concern in the drive to remain competitive and improve sales.[81]

The participation of chains also no doubt hastened the trend toward greater uniformity in the operational structure of big stores. Single ownership of departments became ever more the norm. Increasing chain involvement also no doubt helped shape the tendency to limit nonfood items. The variety and department store attributes that characterized the early New York stores fell from favor because they necessitated enormous facilities and reliance on concessionaires. Such changes represented a shift toward practices piloted by companies such as Ralphs, Weingarten, and Henke & Pillot at least a decade earlier.

While credit for the origin and spread of the supermarket idea cannot be ascribed directly or indirectly to any one company or place, southern California's contribution was central. In matters of appearance, the Los Angeles super was the standard-bearer. Work in no other region received more coverage in food and other retailing journals from the mid-1930s on. An editorial cartoon in *Super Market Merchandising* even depicted such a building as a symbol of "the new supermarket," "emerging from the chrysalis" of the makeshift store (figure 120).[82] Appearances among chain and independent outlets alike still varied. Local traditions in the trade, the personal taste of owners, and no doubt other factors contributed to an ongoing diversity in the particulars of supermarket design. Nevertheless, by the eve of World War II, a distinct industry trend emerged of building stores inspired by southern California examples, with buildings as sleek freestanding objects, their prominence enhanced by sizable parking lots, and with expansive, clear-span spaces, self-service, and a single range of check-out stands.[83] Standard Grocery Company, a fast-growing Midwest chain, borrowed rather overtly from Ralphs when it began to erect supermarkets of comparable scale in 1941 (figure 121). Even a pioneer such as Weingarten shifted to designs that emulated Los Angeles work in character if not in all details (figure 122).[84]

During the mid and late 1920s, the super service station had become southern California's first export in the realm of commercial architecture, emerging as a significant force in its field nationwide. A decade later much the same occurred with the supermarket. Its diffusion took longer and entailed a more complex process, affected by innovative practices elsewhere, but the type had a more profound and long-lasting impact on shopping routines as well as on the metropolitan landscape. Concurrently the drive-in market, by an even more circuitous path, began to exert an influence that would eventually alter shopping habits and the look of the land in a fundamental way.

IV

IS MAIN STREET DOOMED?

In 1931 *Popular Mechanics* featured an article on Frank Lloyd Wright's vision of future commercial development. For Wright, routine use of the automobile was a liberating force that demanded fundamental changes in the ordering of retail space. "Main Street" was doomed because it represented "a centralization made necessary in the past by the inefficiency of individual transportation." In its place would arise complexes expressly designed for the motorist—a new order already found in embryo with the gasoline station. Paraphrasing Wright, the journalist queried: "If this system of distribution works with the automobile, why not extend it to staple articles of food and clothing?" A few statistics were presented to indicate that the roadside stand, assumed to be an outgrowth of the filling station, was taking a significant amount of business away from merchants in the commercial core.[1] The drive-in market was cited as a more fully developed manifestation of the idea, although the reporter, and perhaps Wright himself, mistakenly believed that these facilities were additions to extant filling stations rather than adaptations of the auto service center concept (figure 123). Wright, of course, did not consider these buildings aesthetic models—he was probably aghast at the rendering prepared for the article, based upon the Mandarin Market in Hollywood—and he had no sympathy for the kinds of urban settings in which the drive-in was built and that it fostered. As were his younger colleagues Richard Neutra and Albert Frey, Wright was intrigued by the idea of a service center structured in direct response to the motorist. Furthermore, he was among the first individuals to

Is Main Street Doomed?

By CRAG DALE

LOOK at it!—the humble gasoline fill-ing station, ready to serve any auto-mobile with fuel.

If this filling system of distribution works with the automobile, why not ex-tend it to staple articles of food and cloth-ing? Already power is sold that way. Light sockets are electrical filling stations, maintained by a central-power unit.

In the opinion of Frank Lloyd Wright, an architectural pioneer of international fame, the gasoline-filling station rapidly is becoming a symbol of a trend away from Main Street—a centralization made necessary in the past by the inefficiency of individual transportation.

At every crossroads, and be-tween them, stand gasoline-fill-ing stations ready to serve any automo-bile with fuel. Since this system of dis-tribution works so well with the automo-bile, suggests Mr. Wright, why not ex-tend it to staple articles of food and clothing? And indeed in many places throughout the country Mr. Wright's idea already has been translated into action.

Government statistics show that there now are 110,000 roadside-stand owners, almost all of whom expanded from filling stations. Of that number, 45,000 are permanent year-around opera-tors, serving not only their own communities but tourists as well.

The 16,609 retail-store opera-tors who went into bankruptcy during the first eleven months of 1930 with liabilities of $244,578,-

Artist's Drawing of One of California's Marketing Centers, Where Even Theater Tickets Are Sold; It Has Grown Up around the Easily Accessible Filling Station

765

seize upon the notion that the drive-in market's layout could be expanded significantly to form a retail center that would replace commercial districts. Wright's concept soon was incorporated in his schematic plans for a new pattern of settlement, which he called Broadacre City, conceived to take full advantage of the opportunities afforded by mechanized transportation. Two years after the Main Street article, Wright himself began to publish on the subject, most extensively in his book *The Disappearing City* of 1932.[2] For Wright, the motorist's perspective was the principal means of experi-encing the decentralized landscape he envisioned:

It isn't difficult to see the great architectural highway with its roadside markets, super-service stations, fine schools and playgrounds, small, integrated, intensive farming units, great automobile objectives and fine homes winding up the beautiful natural features of the landscape into the Broadacre City of the future.[3]

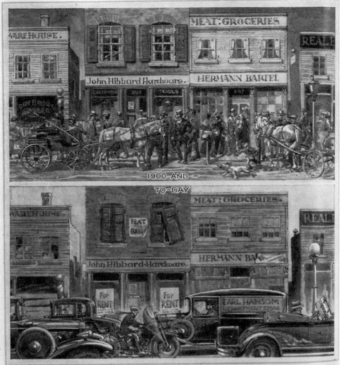

This Changing World and What Has Happened to Shop Keepers Since the Man on Foot Has Taken to the Crowded Roadway with Its Ever-Present "No Parking" Signs

000, face department of commerce figures showing that roadside marketing in 1930 took from the ordinary retail business of the country $500,000,000. In other words, it would seem that the business taken from retail stores last year by gasoline-filling stations and their accompanying roadside-marketing facilities more than doubled the total losses of the 16,609 retail bankruptcies.

A movement now is on foot, and has made great headway, to bring about a co-operative organization of filling stations engaged in selling commodities other than gas and oil. The latest census of gasoline-filling stations shows 317,000 in operation. That figure includes 6,000 owned and operated by the larger oil-producing companies, such as the Standard Oil company, which already is engaged in distributing tires through the service stations it owns or controls. An equal number is owned by the larger oil-producing companies but operated under lease. Independently organized companies operate 8,000, while individual oil producers and private operators maintain 105,000 filling stations. The remainder are run in connection with garages or are maintained as roadside pumps.

123
"Is Main Street Doomed?," lead pages of article. (*Popular Mechanics,* May 1931, 765–766.)

As Wright had suggested in 1931, the super service station, "neglected and despised" by proponents of traditional, centralized development, was the "embryo" for the "new store":

> The beginning of an important advance agent of decentralization by way of distribution and also the beginning of the establishment of the Broadacre City[,] . . . these now crude and seemingly insignificant units will grow and expand into various distributing centers of all sorts. . . . They would become, in the little, distributors of all that Marshall Field, Sears-Roebuck, or Wanamaker now find to distribute in the large . . . [providing] the most diversified modern unit to be found in all the features of the Broadacre City.[4]

Wright's "new store," which he later called the "great Roadside Market," was in fact a complete shopping facility where one could purchase "anything needed or desired at home." In 1934, when the first presentation models for Broadacre City were made, it became clear that the architect not only looked to the merchandising approach embodied in the super service station and drive-in market as a basis for this component of the scheme, he also drew directly from their form (figure 124).[5] As with many drive-in markets, the complex was bereft of obtrusive advertising and boasted handsome displays across its front. Yet Wright's proposal was enormous: its main portion occupied more than twelve acres with an adjacent U-shaped building, apparently containing additional stores, that consumed another nine. Two such markets, one somewhat smaller than the other, would house all retailing for a community of approximately 1,400 families. The size was too great for the population; nevertheless, the basic scale and configuration of Wright's plan came astonishingly close to those of community- and regional-sized shopping centers of the post–World War II era (figure 125).[6]

Wright's markets played an important role as places that helped define the landscape and as focal points of human activity in the new order he envisioned. The polemical designs for cities conceived by Neutra and other avant-garde architects of the period eroded the dense order of the traditional metropolis, but did not dissolve it. Wright's Broadacre City, on the other hand, was a settlement dominated by open space, with buildings of all sizes, freestanding and isolated, that appeared to have little obvious relationship to one another when viewed at ground level. In this matrix, the retail centers were among the few elements where the architecture conveyed a sense of spatial containment.

For Wright, the step from the modest, limited-purpose drive-in to the expansive complex that addressed all the shopping needs of a community was easy and expeditious. The process through which that change actually occurred, however, was complex and fragmented. Wright's manifesto had no impact on the pragmatic realm of business, and it is doubtful whether his hypothetical market plans became widely known until after World War II.[7] Traditional configurations—the legacy of "Main Street"—continued to exercise considerable influence on retail development through the 1940s.[8] For real estate developers and retailers, the major changes involved configuration, scale, and commitment to an integrated business structure. The last of these factors alone—building a complex that was singly owned and managed, its mix of tenants carefully selected so that each reinforced the presence of the others and the group chosen to appeal to an identified "target" audience—represented a pronounced break from conventional practices.[9]

Geographically, too, the course of change was irregular and unpredictable. Los Angeles was a logical place for the drive-in concept to be fused with that of the shopping center, but just as southern Californians quickly discarded the drive-in as a model for food stores, so they expressed little concern for its broader application, despite some precocious experiments in that realm. Instead, the most effective and ultimately influential fusion of the drive-in and shopping center ideas occurred far afield, in Washington, D.C. By the late 1930s, this development began to attract widespread attention and exert some influence nationally. After World War II, the idea began to be applied to much larger shopping centers and on a much more frequent basis. Within a decade, the shopping center configured as a drive-in facility was ubiquitous in urban areas coast to coast.

The supermarket also figured significantly in the transformation. Just as the drive-in lay the essential groundwork for the recasting of exterior space, so did the supermarket for the interior. Its use of large, open, nondirectional selling space, combined with self-service and volume sales of quality goods and reasonable prices—as pioneered by Ralphs in the late 1920s—became an important matrix for other kinds of emporia, starting with drug stores and variety stores. Those changes, moreover, both affected and were influenced by shopping center design after World War II.

EXPERIMENTS

The neighborhood shopping center provided the essential link between the drive-in market and a drive-in retail complex on the scale Wright envisioned. Consisting of about eight to twenty units, with a market as its anchor tenant and a drug store as a major support, the neighborhood center was an integrated facility planned to meet the everyday shopping needs of from three to fifteen thousand people who lived nearby or who frequently passed the premises. The origins of this type lay in the mid-nineteenth century, in store blocks designed as a basic component of comprehensively planned residential enclaves for the well-to-do. With the proliferation of such communities after World War I, the neighborhood shopping center became an increasingly popular phenomenon.[10] By the late 1920s at least one example could be found in many metropolitan areas, especially in the eastern half of the United States. It was quite exceptional, however, to construct a neighborhood center independent of planned residential tracts. The investment of time and money required to build the complex, secure a strong tenant mix, and manage the ensemble on an ongoing basis went beyond what many real estate speculators could or wished to undertake. For most parties involved in outlying retail development, taxpayer blocks and individual stores commissioned by chain companies were lucrative enough.[11] The neighborhood center appears to have been considered something of an indulgence, reserved for developers with large amounts of capital at their disposal and for discriminating customers who wanted conveniences close at hand but also wanted to have commerce physically contained so as not to encroach on their neighborhood.

In appearance, most neighborhood shopping centers of the 1920s did not differ significantly from some of the more embellished taxpayer blocks. Both sought visual compatibility with their residential environs. Similarly, too, the neighborhood center was laid out as a range of stores abutting the property line, its exterior entirely frontal in orientation. Curbside parking was deemed sufficient to meet customers' needs, but some-

124
Hypothetical design for a "roadside market" at Broadacre City, 1934, Frank Lloyd Wright, architect; project. Photo Roy Petersen, 1934. (Copyright © 1997 Frank Lloyd Wright Foundation, Scottsdale, Arizona.)

Miracle Mile Town and Country
Shopping Center, 3600–4000 E.
Broad Street, Columbus, Ohio,
1947–1948, C. Melvin Frank,
architect; altered. Photo ca. 1948.
(Courtesy Don M. Casto
Organization.)

times additional measures were taken to enhance motorist access. The work of J. C. Nichols, the Kansas City real estate developer who was nationally recognized as a leader in the building of planned communities and shopping centers, embodied the most advanced thinking of the period. The seven neighborhood centers Nichols constructed in his vast Country Club District between 1919 and 1931 were laid out with wider streets so that cars could park diagonally. After completing the first center, he also insisted that construction be limited to a single story so as to minimize the chances of vehicular congestion (figure 126).[12] Still, the primary difference between these planned nodes and a decorous taxpayer block lay in intangibles: integrated structure and enforced separation from other business development.

During the 1920s, Los Angeles saw the emergence of a more experimental type of facility that came close to the neighborhood shopping center in function.[13] The point of departure for this work came more from local precedent than from that exemplified by Nichols's buildings. Significantly, at an early stage of its own development, the drive-in market had been seen as the foundation from which more ambitious retail development could emerge. Like other drive-ins, these complexes were located some distance from retail nodes along thoroughfares that were zoned for and eventually supported many other businesses. While situated close to newly developing residential areas, they were not tied to a single tract. Food departments remained the basis of identity, but at least as much space was given to other, physically separated retail functions. The primary motive for such experiments was generating larger revenues. The line of reasoning was logical enough: If motorists came to a drive-in market because

126
Gregory and Oak Shops, 400–410 E. Gregory Boulevard and 7015–7019 Oak Street, Kansas City, Missouri, 1931, Edward W. Tanner, architect. Photo late 1930s/early 1940s. (Courtesy J. C. Nichols Company.)

Now we will drive the bus into the

LATCHSTRING

Glendale's Popular Drive-In Market

1300 to 1400 Blocks on
North San Fernando
Road

**LOTS OF ROOM
TO PARK**

A Regular Village with
many different kinds of
businesses under the
one roof.

We will leave the bus here in this convenient parkway while we make a tour of inspection of this interesting market.

It is hard to believe that only a few short years ago the site where this market stands was occupied by a very large ranch. Realizing that the way things were booming in this vicinity, that parking place would soon be at a premium, these people conceived and built this big village to which they gave the name of Latchstring Rancho, which means, "Ever Welcome—Always Open."

They gathered together a group of merchants who appreciated the value of service and particularly that of courtesy and quality in business, and started a drive-in market that today stands as one of the best in the country.

The foodstuffs departments are up-to-the minute in every detail, handling the very finest that the market affords. More than a million people patronized them in the last year because they had proven themselves in this regard.

You saw how convenient it was to just hop out and leave the bus here where we knew it would be safe while we looked around. That is the reason that Latchstring is so popular among the people who like to drive out to do their shopping.

DEPARTMENTS

Service Station	Chop Suey Parlor
Automobiles	Barber Shop
Hardware	Radio Store
Electric Store	Drug Store
Fruits and Vegetables	Builders Arcade
Bakery	All Night Lunch Room
Groceries and Delicatessen	Live Poultry Market
Meats	General Motors Trucks

it was convenient, more would come, and perhaps come more often, if the ensemble included an array of other frequently used outlets.

Probably the most ambitious scheme of this kind was the Latchstring Rancho Drive-In Market (1926–1927), the brainchild of Glendale entrepreneur George Clayton. Besides four large food concessions, the ensemble boasted drug, electrical, hardware, and radio stores; a lunch counter and "chop suey parlor"; a barber shop; and an outlet for live poultry (figure 127).[14] Clayton's real estate office and automobile showroom provided the visual centerpiece, supplemented by a super service station, automobile paint shop, and truck sales agency. The scope of the development suggests it was intended to serve as a business center for the many new residential tracts in nearby Burbank as well as others in northwest Glendale, where Clayton had been active in fostering growth. Strategically placed near the boundary between the two towns, along the heavily traveled San Fernando Road, the Latchstring was more than a place to stop in transit; it was a destination conceived to attract consumers from an extended area who could easily drive to the premises.

The size of the Latchstring probably determined its linear form, allowing the array of businesses to be seen easily from the street. There was no forecourt as such, but rather an access road, wide enough to permit cars to parallel park on the outer side. This zone was not so much private space as it was an extension of the public domain of the street. The arrangement prevented patrons from pulling their cars directly up to the stores; instead, they had to cross the path of moving vehicles. More importantly, space was

127
Latchstring Rancho Drive-In Market, 6311–6329 N. San Fernando Road, Glendale, 1926–1927; Genevieve Lund, designer/builder; no longer standing. (*Glendale News Press,* 26 April 1928, II-9.)

not adequate for cars to park near the most heavily used stores during peak shopping periods. In physical terms, the complex was much like a series of taxpayer blocks set back from the property line. The awkward aspects of the plan coupled with its added costs did not offer compelling evidence that it was preferable to the norm.

Configuration was not the only problem in devising such ventures. Securing a strong mix of desirable tenants likewise presented a challenge, particularly for those not experienced in retail development. Several months before construction began on the Latchstring, plans were unveiled for a project almost as large (21,000 square feet) located on Colorado Boulevard, well to the east of downtown Pasadena.[15] In its basic configuration and appearance, the scheme was indebted to the prototypical drive-in market, Ye Market Place, and was even to bear that name, minus the pseudo-archaic prefix. At the same time, other aspects of the scheme represented a significant departure. The plan was bifurcated by a side street, with mirror-image, L-shaped buildings and forecourts on either side (figure 128). As a result, the extent of the complex was clearly evident to passing motorists, and the off-street accommodations for cars were made to seem spacious as well as accessible.

The strengths of the Market Place's layout were not matched by its business plan. The enterprise was conceived by Frank Dishbrow, who for over two decades had run a citrus nursery on the site. Like many other southern Californians, he now sought to capitalize on the rapidly escalating value of land induced by residential growth. Dishbrow's initial idea was to create a public market with multiple concessions, but he had failed to sign tenants by the time construction was completed seven months later. Close to another year elapsed before the facility opened, now under the name of Mother Goose Market and modified in scope to include an array of other stores. Besides four major food concessions, there was a restaurant, filling station, and outlet for automobile accessories. Negotiations were under way for a barber shop, beauty salon, radio store, music store, and hardware store. Dishbrow seems never to have consummated his new tenant plan, however, and sold the property within nine months.[16]

The drive-in market was not the sole basis for new approaches to shopping center configuration. Perhaps the earliest such scheme arranged around an area devoted exclusively to off-street parking to be realized in

128
Mother Goose Market, 1949–1989 Colorado Boulevard, Pasadena, 1926, Walter Folland, architect; altered. (*Los Angeles Times,* 7 February 1926, V-11.)

E. R. MAUZY ENGLISH VILLAGE SHOPS
9988 Sunset Blvd., at Larrabee Street

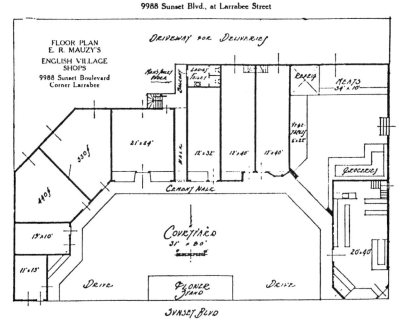

129
English Village Shops, 8830–8840 Sunset Boulevard, West Hollywood, preliminary design, 1924, Richard Bates, architect, V. D. Van Akin, associate; no longer standing. (*Hollywood Daily Citizen,* 22 September 1924, 6.)

Los Angeles or anywhere else was developer E. R. Mauzy's English Village Shops, which opened in December 1924, just a few months after Ye Market Place (figure 129).[17] Located on Sunset Boulevard outside the city limits in a then thinly settled area of West Hollywood, the complex was intended to complement Mauzy's modest grouping of "English cottages" nearby and serve an area that seemed more rural than urban. The design of the retail center appears to have been inspired by the shopping court—another type still considered new in the commercial field—comprised of small specialty stores picturesquely grouped around a patio.[18] Here the arrangement was modified to address the street, with the patio becoming a "courtyard" for automobiles, a change probably inspired by the super service station. There was also a difference in tenant structure. Whereas the shopping court was for the most part a collection of outlets purveying unusual goods and services, Mauzy planned his facility to serve basic needs. The ensemble was to include a bank, food stores, dry cleaner, barber shop, doctor's office, and florist, as well as drug, dry goods, hardware, plumbing supply, paint, and shoe repair stores—a mix Nichols would have endorsed.

As realized, the English Village Shops had a more limited array of tenants. The size of the units was inadequate to meet the increasing space requirements of a competitive market or drug store. Mauzy's building appears to have attracted little or no attention outside the immediate area when it was built, nor did it have any impact on subsequent work in the region. But whatever the shortcomings, they probably were not the central reasons why this or analogous experimental ventures failed to influence retail development patterns in southern California. Modifications to size, configuration, or business structure stood a good chance of occurring as long as some entrepreneurs believed the underlying concept to be a strong one. That the concept of the drive-in shopping center itself failed this test is further suggested by the very different approaches taken toward the end of the decade in a second round of experiments to enlarge the scale and scope of the drive-in market.

A decisive break in what had become by the late 1920s the conventions of design for drive-ins was manifested in the Chapman Park Market (1928–1929).[19] The complex lay on two acres amid an eighty-five-acre tract in the mid–Wilshire district owned by Charles Chapman, whose vast real estate holdings ranged from oil wells to downtown office buildings. Most of the Wilshire property was sold for the construction of houses and apartment buildings, but Chapman's own commercial development, one block off Wilshire Boulevard on Sixth Street, clearly reflected an effort to foster the precinct as the region's most stylish for shopping. Both market and adjacent store buildings were designed by Morgan, Walls & Clements in an opulent variation on the Hispanic mode rendered for Ralphs (figure 130).[20] As with many of the specialty shops in the area, the market was conceived as an areawide attraction. Chapman used billboards to advertise the facility along thoroughfares in many parts of the metropolitan area—a costly method almost never employed for a single food outlet. But the most unusual aspect of the development was its retail complexion. Three sizable food stores occupied the building, each with a somewhat different composition of goods and services (figure 131). One offered self-service on a cash-and-carry basis; the second provided clerk service, charge accounts, and delivery; the third combined cash-and-carry with a delivery option.[21] Complementing, but also competing against, one another, these stores were intended to provide an unusually wide range of choices. Eight store units, with loft space above for offices and studios, also were part of the package, yet neither their arrangement nor tenancy suggests they were developed as an integral part of the merchandising plan.[22] With lavishly decorated exteriors, these end parts of the building were the most ornate, while their interior spaces enhanced the respectability of the ensemble. Here the mass appeal of a large food outlet was balanced by the more elite draw of the specialty shop purveying fine goods.

The pursuit of a stylish aura also may have led to a complete rejection of the forecourt. The complex was commonly referred to as a drive-in, and its parking area, with space for about sixty cars, was perhaps the largest of any Los Angeles market when the facility opened.[23] This important feature was little apparent from the street, however (figure 132). Much like the public face, the car lot was cast in a historicizing tone, with a courtyard or patio, complete with decorative fountain, that adapted a centuries-old Spanish tradition to the motor age (figure 133). The arrangement retained the drive-in's direct relationship between selling space and cars,

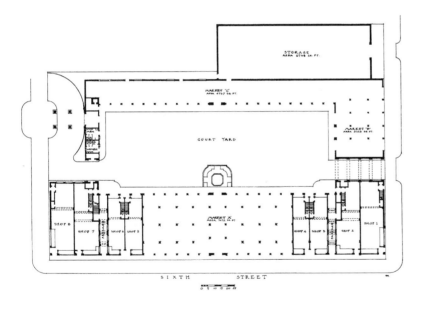

130
Chapman Park Market, 3451–3479
W. Sixth Street, Los Angeles, 1928–
1929, Morgan, Walls & Clements,
architects. Photo ca. 1929. (Special
Collection, University of California,
Los Angeles.)

131
Chapman Park Market, ground floor
plan. (Drawn by Brenden Meyer
after original in Huntington Library.)

while reestablishing the primacy of the street for its orientation and
identity.

    The Chapman Park's layout was probably influenced by pragmatic
as well as aesthetic concerns. The basic configuration bears affinity to those
of wholesale food distribution centers where the inner open space, or yard,
served a vital purpose in both the movement and display of goods. Morgan, Walls & Clements designed the first large facility of this kind in Los

132
Chapman Park Market, parking
court. Photo ca. 1929. (Special Collections, University of California,
Los Angeles.)

133
Chapman Park Market, parking
court. Photo ca. 1929. (Courtesy
Progressive Grocer.)

134
Union Wholesale Terminal, 1302–
1396 E. Seventh Street, Los Angeles,
1917–1918, et seq., John Parkinson,
architect. View of yard. Photo Gra-
ham, 1923. (Huntington Library.)

Angeles, the City Market, in 1909.[24] Soon thereafter work was begun on a
far more extensive plant for the Union Wholesale Terminal, which became
one of the earliest local demonstrations of how important motor vehicle
movements were in the arrangement of space. Encompassing ten acres, the
complex included a yard over 1,500 feet long surrounded by two-story
buildings that housed a retail market, bank, shops, restaurant, offices, and
a rooming house in addition to wholesale and warehousing spaces (figure
134).[25] Adjacent lay several ranges of six-story buildings designed for bulk
storage and the manufacture of food products. The yard itself was organized to facilitate the circulation of hundreds of trucks and cars that passed
through its gates every day. A filling station, repair facility, and accessories
store were included on the premises along with a portable tank to replenish
trucks with gas and oil while they were transferring goods in the yard.

 When it opened for business in 1918, the terminal had few peers.
It became a much-heralded landmark—a symbol of the city's rapid growth
and of the skill with which produce from one of the nation's richest agri-
cultural areas could be processed, sold, and distributed to the growing
population. As much as any other building then realized in the region, the
terminal stood as a popular emblem of progress in the upstart metropolis,
while revealing how important motor vehicles were to that progress. Chapman probably had some firsthand knowledge of the terminal, for among

MAMMOTH MARKET WILL BE ERECTED

Highland-Avenue Site Chosen for Spanish Building

Investment of $1,500,000 to Be Made on 600-Foot Frontage

135
Market, Highland Avenue, Los
Angeles, 1928, Walker & Eisen, architects; project. (*Los Angeles Times*,
23 December 1928, V-2.)

his extensive holdings were three large ranches on which he raised oranges
and other fruits. His experience as a producer, in turn, may have led him to
hire Arthur Goodwin, a nationally prominent authority on the design and
operation of wholesale and retail markets, to lay out his building.[26]

Regardless of who initiated the concept, the wholesale plant appears to have been considered a model for developing a retail facility with
extensive spaces both for food sales and motor vehicles. While the Chapman Park Market was still under construction, plans were unveiled for an
even grander enterprise of much the same type on the edge of downtown
Hollywood (figure 135). Costing $1.5 million, the complex entailed a mar-
ket, numerous shops, offices on the second floor, and a four-story refrigera-
tion unit at the rear, all set around a large "patio" for parking, from which
motorists presumably could gain direct access to the selling areas.[27] The
size of the building—its frontage extended 600 feet—made the scheme
a singular one. On the other hand, the emphasis given to its food-selling
role suggests that, like the Chapman Park Market, this ensemble was not
planned as an integrated business development. Indeed, the tendency
toward a substantial increase in the scale of outlying retail facilities that
occurred in the years just prior to the depression often was not founded
on serious study of what functions would be the most mutually reinforcing
or even compatible. For some entrepreneurs, even those with considerable
experience in real estate development, size itself appears to have been the
major objective.

Finding a solution in which form and business structure worked
together must have seemed a formidable challenge even to those few who
recognized the need for such an integrated scheme. A good illustration of
the problems faced in meeting this challenge is afforded by an unrealized
project designed in 1929 by Richard Neutra for the Dixie Drive-In Market in Lexington, Kentucky (figures 136, 137).[28] Food concessions occupied the entire ground level, consuming more space than generally found
in Los Angeles counterparts. Upper stories formed a major component of

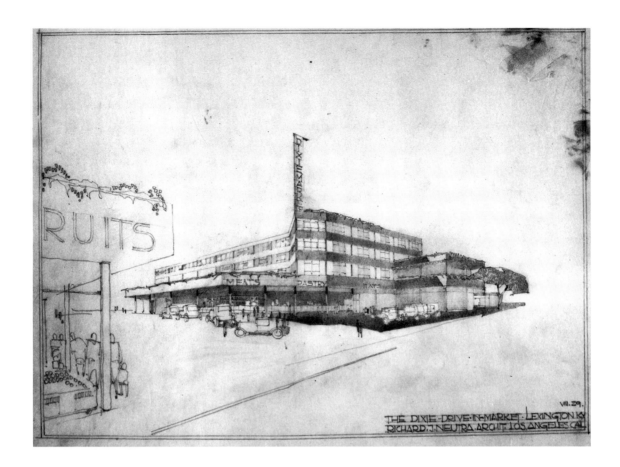

the ensemble; a restaurant, shopping arcade, and roof terraces lay at the second level, offices at the third and fourth. Equally unusual was the configuration, which was oriented around a car lot that connected two nearly parallel thoroughfares. This use of a linear, open-ended space, bracketed by a multistory building on one side and a canopied vending area on the other, may well have been inspired by the California Produce Terminal, an important wholesale facility in Los Angeles's Central Manufacturing District completed two years earlier, for which Neutra professed admiration (figure 138). From his perspective, this updated version of the Union Terminal possessed an almost lyrical simplicity in both form and character—an elegance predicated on utilitarian needs, which he sought to express with greater élan at the Lexington complex.[29]

The constricted site, however, posed problems that the architect seems not to have recognized. In contrast to the expansive layout and more or less single purpose of the produce terminal, here there was a compressed mixing of multiple activities that was more suggestive of a European hill town: market stalls lining a center square and shops, cafes, and apartments terraced up the slope on one side. The automobiles around which the solution was conceived would have caused problems, however. The court was not conducive to the free movement of more than a few cars at a time, especially if circulation was two-directional. Furthermore, that movement would have discouraged shoppers from crossing the space to patronize mer-

136
Dixie Drive-In Market, Vine and High streets, Lexington, Kentucky, 1929, Richard Neutra, architect; project. (Special Collections, University of California, Los Angeles.)

137
Dixie Drive-In Market. Site and
floor plans. (Special Collections,
University of California, Los
Angeles.)

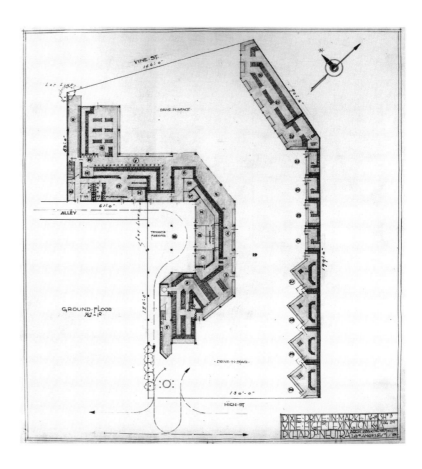

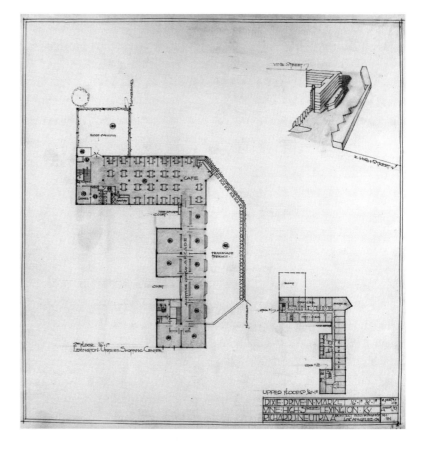

138
California Produce Terminal, E. Ninth and Camulos streets, Los Angeles, 1927; no longer standing. (Richard Neutra, *Amerika,* pl. 99.)

chants on the other side. Pedestrians on the street might have felt even less welcome in an area without sidewalks. Parking was woefully inadequate, assuming that patrons of the shops, restaurant, and offices were as inclined to drive as were those of the market, especially because the former group would be likely to leave their cars for longer periods. In 1929 the provision for *any* large off-street parking area to serve a retail complex remained far more the exception than the rule, and in using this space as the primary organizing component for the overall plan, Neutra revealed his thinking to be well ahead of many colleagues'. If vision outdistanced practicality, it did so out of lack of experience rather than out of lack of concern.

No doubt the expansiveness of the modern wholesale food terminal, with low-slung buildings stretching across vast yards to facilitate the movement of hundreds of motor vehicles, made the type seem exemplary for adaptation to the modern shopping center. Yet basic differences in function made that relationship impractical. Patterns of movement and parking common to trucks in a staging area and to cars on a shopping expedition were not at all similar. With the escalation of scale from the conventional drive-in found at both Chapman's and Neutra's complexes, the market function remained predominant; there was little apparent study of how other business activities might relate to it. The idea that the facility's retail structure, size, and configuration should go hand in hand was not as easy to recognize as hindsight might suggest.

Functional considerations notwithstanding, southern Californians in the real estate and retail fields proved reluctant to accord much visual emphasis to the parking lot. The fact that this element was treated as residual space in the development of most supermarkets and other shopping facilities through the 1940s suggests a prejudice rooted in basic ideas about the form and the character of the city. Despite Angelenos' partiality to the automobile, parking was seen as a necessary evil. The allocation of off-street space for cars was proving an important factor in a competitive business climate, but emphasizing that space in concrete terms through the site plan or architectural expression, as had occurred with some of the drive-in markets, was generally shunned.[30] This largely unspoken cultural outlook, combined with the practical ones of food merchandising, stymied the drive-in's further development. Though it might seem the most obvious course in retrospect, the drive-in never went far as a model in southern California.

139
Park and Shop, 3507–3523 Connect-icut Avenue, N.W., Washington, D.C., 1930, Arthur Heaton, archi-tect. Photo Horydczak, early 1930s. (Prints & Photographs Division, Li-brary of Congress.)

140
Park and Shop, plan. (Prints & Pho-tographs Division, Library of Congress.)

PARK AND SHOP

Amid the sporadic experiments of the late 1920s and early 1930s, one even-tually validated the use of the drive-in concept not just for food stores but for neighborhood shopping centers as well. In 1928, an official of Shan-non & Luchs, a leading Washington, D.C., real estate firm with consider-able experience in selecting locations for chain stores, took notice of the drive-in markets while on a business trip to Los Angeles. These complexes apparently impressed him enough to convince associates back home to ex-plore utilizing the idea. West coast examples were studied, as were Wash-ington retail market and traffic conditions. The findings were sufficiently positive, despite the stock market crash, that Shannon & Luchs was able to entice investors into forming a subsidiary corporation, Parking Stores, for the purpose of erecting a 50,000-square-foot complex, considerably larger than most drive-in markets. This center, in turn, was to serve as a proto-type for a dozen more in the metropolitan area and perhaps additional ones in other cities. Worsening economic conditions precluded creating such a network, but not the construction of the first center, called the Park and Shop, which began in April 1930 and was completed less than nine months later.[31]

The Park and Shop's L-shaped form, with stores facing two sides of a large forecourt, was adopted directly from the drive-in market (figures 139, 140). Similarly, too, the building's simple mass and composition were related to the forecourt and aimed at attracting the eye of the motorist. On the other hand, the complex included a number of stores housed in dis-crete units, catering to a range of everyday shopping needs, a mix character-istic of neighborhood shopping centers. Two chain-owned food outlets served as the anchor tenants, yet neither their physical presence nor their hi-erarchical stature approached the dominance enjoyed by the food-selling area of the drive-in market. The Park and Shop had eight additional units—a bakery, chocolate shop, delicatessen/restaurant, hardware store, laundry call station, beauty salon, and barber shop—which constituted a major share of the program. A third of the property was set aside for a super service station and auto laundry, which were constructed two years later. A major selling point of the setback of the drive-in market was the direct spatial tie between indoors and out across the long front, permitting

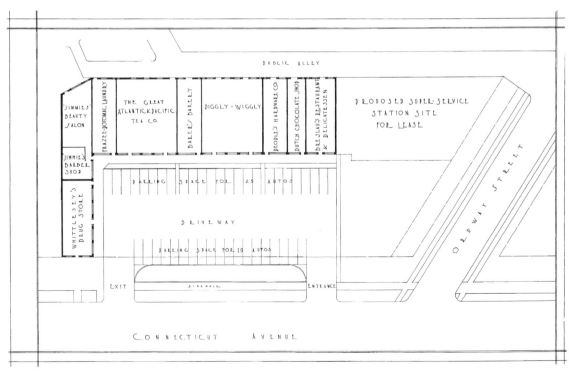

extensive open-air displays. The fully enclosed stores at the Park and Shop proved that this feature was unnecessary; the attributes of off-street parking and planned tenancy were sufficient to secure a highly profitable trade. Although preliminary drawings labeled the complex a drive-in market, Shannon & Luchs clearly had the shopping center just as much in mind.

Several factors probably contributed to the real estate firm's embarking on such an unconventional scheme during adverse market conditions and in a place where tastes were more conservative than in Los Angeles. Washington had experienced less business decentralization by 1930 than many cities because the great majority of its workplaces remained in or close to the urban core and the fabric of residential districts was compact. Furthermore, curtailment of retail facilities in outlying areas began to receive official sanction in 1920 when the city's first zoning ordinance was adopted. In that document, commercial functions were banned from several arteries and limited to a few small nodes along Connecticut Avenue, a major thoroughfare to emerging middle- and upper-middle-class enclaves. Within a few years similar restrictions were adopted for other key routes. As the city started to experience a significant lateral spread in its residential development during the 1920s, the opportunities for creating large commercial service districts were limited. Although the situation was quite the opposite of that in Los Angeles, Shannon & Luchs's leadership seems to have realized that these circumstances could work to their benefit. Gathering compatible functions in a carefully planned ensemble, they could acquire a strategic advantage in relatively underutilized territory. At the same time, space limitations mandated by the zoning ordinance along Connecticut Avenue, where the Park and Shop was built, contributed to the potential for congestion unless off-street parking was an integral feature. The forecourt was a conspicuous attraction that was virtually unique in the nation's capital and other east coast cities.

The degree to which the Park and Shop represented a departure from conventional practices is underscored by comparing it to a complex in Shreveport, Louisiana, which, when it opened in 1929, represented one of the most advanced designs for a store group oriented to motorists to be found outside southern California. Well removed from downtown, on an artery leading to the premier residential sections of the city, the ensemble was undertaken by the locally based food retailer Big Chain Stores as its flagship facility.[32] Flanking the lavishly adorned market, purportedly the biggest in the region, were a drug store, laundry call station, beauty salon, and service station (figure 141). Storefronts were set back from the property line to allow a row of cars to park in front, and a side lot provided space for perhaps two dozen additional vehicles. Billed as a commercial center, the group was more ambitious and carefully planned than most taxpayer blocks. The scale and embellishment of the food emporium made it a major attraction in its own right, and the other outlets were chosen to enhance its draw. But the scope of outlets was far more limited than at the Park and Shop or other fully developed neighborhood shopping centers. Furthermore, the configuration was basically a traditional one, modified by

the slight setback and open side yard to accommodate automobiles; it was one of the numerous schemes developed over the next dozen years that moved toward, but fell short of embracing, the drive-in concept.

More than most experiments of the period, the Park and Shop drew widespread national attention and eventually exerted considerable influence. Within six months of its opening, the complex was illustrated in the *Architectural Record* as the only U.S. example in an article on new tendencies in store design. The following year, 1932, the Park and Shop was even more prominently featured in the *Record* as the logical alternative to the disparaged "Main Street." Equally important was the series of diagrammatic plans that appeared on the following pages, showing possible layouts for such centers (figure 142). Drawn by Albert Frey, these sketches followed the repertoire of configurations employed for drive-in markets modified, much like the Park and Shop, to accommodate a range of stores. While the accompanying text, coauthored by Frey and *Record* editor A. Lawrence Kocher, primarily consisted of notes on programmatic considerations, the pictorial assemblage implied that the drive-in neighborhood shopping center was the best answer to the needs of retail development for a motorized populace. Since the *Record* then enjoyed the largest readership among architects and these illustrations remained a rare compendium of the type for some years, the piece likely had a significant impact on the shape of neighborhood centers once the drive-in concept gained favor for retail facilities toward the decade's end.[33]

Frey's graphic lexicon was given added importance by a 1934 essay, again in the *Record,* that focused on the need for planned shopping centers. Written by Clarence Stein and Catherine Bauer, two of the nation's leading exponents of reform in housing and community design, the essay was one of the most detailed presentations on building shopping centers to be published during the interwar decades. The authors marshaled an array of statistics to make their case: in 1929 50 percent of the nation's stores grossed less than 9 percent of the total dollar volume; 25 percent of independent food stores netted their proprietors no more than 32 cents per day; 45 percent of all groceries that began operation in Louisville, Kentucky, between 1921 and 1928 closed within a year. Such performances

141
Big Chain Commercial Center, 1500–1518 Fairfield Avenue, Shreveport, Louisiana, 1928–1929, Jones, Rossle, Olschner & Wiener, architects; altered. (*Chain Store Review,* February 1930, 49.)

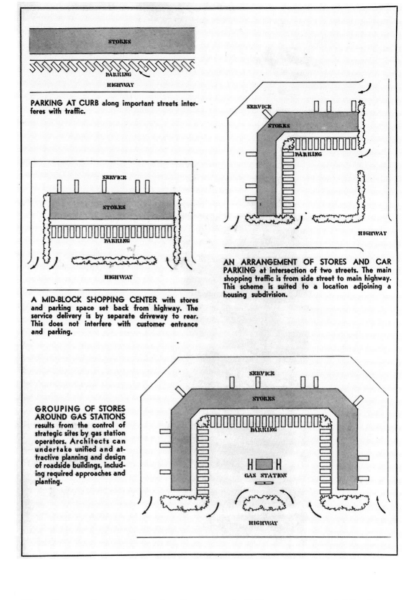

Diagrammatic plans for shopping
center layout. Drawings by Albert
Frey, ca. 1932. (*Architectural Record,*
May 1932, 326–327.)

affected not only merchants but investors, building owners, neighboring
residents, and the community tax base. The depression may have intensified these problems, the authors asserted, but laissez-faire development practices had caused them. Numerous poorly run stores and an oversupply of
stores in general contributed to the high casualty rate. They argued that retail outlets could secure a more stable existence in outlying areas only by
grouping complementary services as an ensemble, carefully planned in its
size, location, appearance, and ability to accommodate motorists with off-
street parking. Stein and Bauer concluded that "the California drive-in market has come closest to a recognition of the functional requirements of
a modern shopping center," and chose the Palm Market in Beverly Hills
along with the Park and Shop, which they mistakenly identified as a drive-
in market, to illustrate their thesis.[34]

The financial picture that Stein and Bauer drew was all too famil-
iar in retail and real estate as well as planning circles by the mid-1930s.

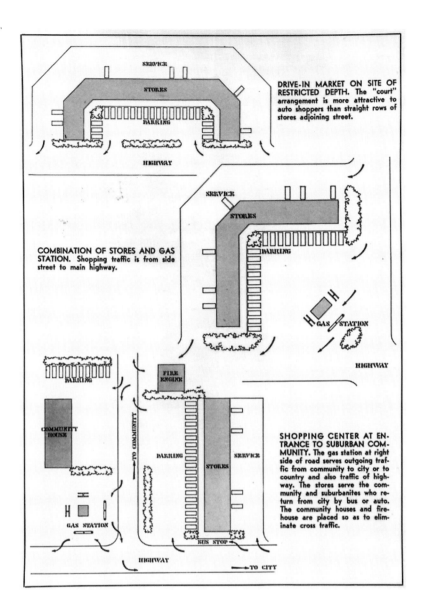

DRIVE-IN MARKET ON SITE OF RESTRICTED DEPTH. The "court" arrangement is more attractive to auto shoppers than straight rows of stores adjoining street.

COMBINATION OF STORES AND GAS STATION. Shopping traffic is from side street to main highway.

SHOPPING CENTER AT EN-TRANCE TO SUBURBAN COM-MUNITY. The gas station at right side of road serves outgoing traf-fic from community to city or to country and also traffic of high-way. The stores serve the com-munity and suburbanites who re-turn from city by bus or auto. The community houses and fire-house are placed so as to elim-inate cross traffic.

Weak business practices were acknowledged to be a major problem, but by no means the only one. Long before the depression, some real estate inter-ests expressed nervousness over the amount of land identified for commer-cial development in outlying areas relative to that being profitably used. Some Angelenos were among the first to understand the problem. A promi-nent local spokesman for the industry stressed in 1928 that from "a stand-point of economics it is far better to zone or restrict too few lots for business use, than too many." The current excess, omnipresent in Los Angeles, he explained, was a financial time bomb. Vacant lots encumbered large amounts of capital that otherwise could be channeled into more pro-ductive improvements. Furthermore, these long stretches of unused arterial frontage ultimately affected the value of property in the whole precinct.[35]

One of the main problems in Los Angeles and many other cities was that the areas zoned for commercial use in ordinances of the previous decade far exceeded the demand in either the immediate or the foreseeable future. Harland Bartholomew, who had prepared many of these ordinances, explained in 1931:

[During the 1920s] the automobile was upon us and there was a great desire to limit the rapidly increasing number of stores, filling stations, "hot-dog" stands, and what not which were springing up overnight in many desirable residential areas.

Since it was observed that many of these uses came along established main thoroughfares, it was but logical to assume, in the absence of comprehensive surveys and city plans, that all main thoroughfares were logical business locations and that any property on any main thoroughfare was consequently a potential business site. It was a very considerable advance step to be able suddenly to protect large areas of residential property from this potential menace, and there was no means of gauging whether all of the frontage along main thoroughfares was too much or too little for actual business needs. In fact, there was very little thought given to this phase of the subject.

He added, with regret:

In recent years it has become increasingly evident that not all frontage on all main thoroughfares, even those zoned as business, could fully develop as good business property. On the contrary, there appeared to be a very painfully evident surplus of unused property.[36]

Well before Bartholomew's lament, the financial implications of overzoning spurred a few planning agencies to study the problem. Ordinances generally were not amended as a result of such probes; instead, the studies presented ways of controlling retail growth, in the hope that landholders might heed them.[37] A scheme devised in 1927 by the Los Angeles city planning office was among the first, calling for nodal concentration where major arteries intersected (figure 143).[38] Stores were set back to be aligned with neighboring houses, but more importantly to provide space for parking. Two years later the Los Angeles County planning office expanded the model's scope to encompass a matrix for the development of new residential areas (figure 144). Apartments now faced the thoroughfares, offering a buffer for the single-family houses behind. Lying in the center, the commercial node was less conventional than its forebear. Each group of stores was related to an off-street parking area in ways probably inspired by the drive-in market, which planners now saw as a useful means to foster their objectives. That tie was made explicit in 1932 when drive-in shopping facilities serving a similar precinct were featured on the cover of the city planning office's annual report (figure 145).[39]

In their pursuit of a blueprint for community development, planners in Los Angeles and many other cities drew heavily from the neighborhood unit concept created by Clarence Arthur Perry during the 1920s, which was perhaps most widely known as a component of the Regional Plan of New York. Perry employed land-use and other zoning tools to organize the structure of growth in response to demands imposed by the automobile; his work had a wide-ranging impact on the planning profession nationally well into the post–World War II era.[40] At the same time, Los Angeles practitioners adapted a local type that suited the driving public's needs far better than did the standard streetfront store grouping delineated by Perry.[41] Like Shannon & Luchs's officers, the Los Angeles planners also sensed that the drive-in market held the key for localized retail develop-

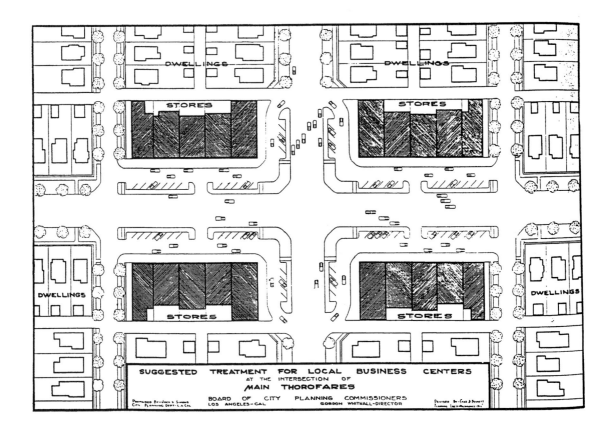

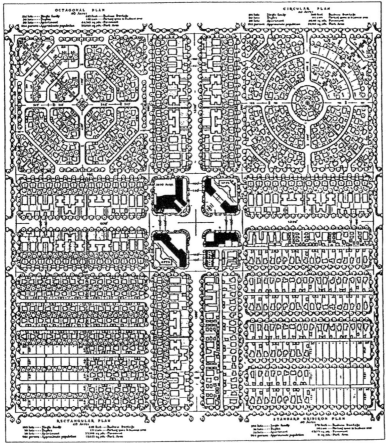

143

"Suggested Treatment for Local Business Centers at the Intersection of Main Thoroughfares," Board of City Planning Commissioners, City of Los Angeles, 1927. (*American City,* February 1928, 144.)

144

"Zoning by Design," schematic plan, Regional Planning Commission, County of Los Angeles, 1929. (*Annals of the American Academy of Political and Social Science,* May 1931, 84.)

145
Sketch of hypothetical neighborhood plan, showing drive-in markets
in foreground. (Los Angeles, Board
of City Planning Commissioners,
Annual Report, 1931–1932, cover.)

ment in the future. Even though the drive-in was a central factor in the
spread of scattered-site, linear commercial development, it was seized upon
to demonstrate the merits of containing that activity in tightly defined
clusters. Through this instrument, municipal regulation might advance
the cause of neighborhood stability, not just for the well-to-do but for the
citizenry at large.

Stein and Bauer had much the same notion. The appeal of the
Park and Shop no less than the drive-in market lay in its compactness.
Here stores and automobiles could be concentrated in an efficient way that
was at once physically integrated with, yet not intrusive upon, the places
they served. However, these complexes were not seen as true community
centers in themselves. Bauer criticized Frank Lloyd Wright for implying
that his huge markets could fulfill that function. She maintained that his
"ideal society seems to live in a sort of endless Road Town; its entire social
structure and its ideal of freedom are based on intensive use of the automobile. . . . A minimum of communal facilities—shopping centers, clubs—
is clustered around the gas station."[42] Instead, Stein and Bauer argued, the
shopping center should be part of a larger whole, which included schools,
recreation facilities, meeting halls, and other places conducive to social interaction. If commercial development was limited to these planned centers,
which in turn were designed as part of a greater public arena, then, Stein

146
Brentwood Shopping Center, Washington, D.C., preliminary design, 1937, Raymond Snow, architect; altered. (*Insured Mortgage Portfolio,* September 1937, 9.)

and Bauer believed, their full potential would be realized. From this perspective, the Park and Shop and its Los Angeles progenitors were not seen foremost as business facilities, but rather as means to far more significant aesthetic and social ends. The excesses of laissez-faire, now intensified by the depression, necessitated a reorientation of values.

The reformers' advocacy of the drive-in neighborhood shopping center as an element of community design had an immediate impact on planning done under the auspices of New Deal programs. The most widespread application was at projects insured by the Federal Housing Administration, which incorporated the concept into its guidelines in 1936. Over the next two decades, perhaps hundreds of shopping centers were built as part of FHA-insured residential developments (figure 146).[43] The private sector, however, mostly ignored the suggestions for contained commercial development made by national leaders and by planning officials in Los Angeles and other cities. Even though overzoning for commercial use became a widely acknowledged problem, property owners tended to hold out for a time when their land would achieve its imagined value. Only when federal oversight required it, or when a large-scale developer such as J. C. Nichols elected to take such a course, was retail building so neatly confined.

Even under a program of comprehensive planning, it is unlikely that the drive-in shopping center would have been adopted had not the attributes of the Park and Shop been appealing from a retail perspective. From the mid-1930s until U.S. entry into the Second World War, market forces provided the major impetus for advancing the type. The economic pitfalls of uncoordinated retail growth enunciated by Stein and Bauer were of broad concern. But at least equally important was the need for facilities in new locations once the economy began to improve and residential construction in outlying areas was again occurring at a substantial pace. Renewed demand, coupled with the leaner, more competitive approach to retailing that was an outgrowth of the depression, enabled the drive-in shopping center to establish a foothold as a sound business investment.

Interest was predictably slow at first. Building a shopping center required not only more money than most forms of retail development beyond the city center, but more time and effort to assemble the land in a suitable place and to secure a strong tenant mix. Moreover, the success of such planning was still little proven outside affluent residential enclaves. Many developers lacked the capital required to embark on such undertakings or were reluctant to assume the risks. Individual stores designed for the needs of a tenant or taxpayer blocks of a more generic sort usually remained an easier, quicker, and cheaper endeavor. Unplanned arterial development might be financially unsound, just as Stein and Bauer had described; on the other hand, it could be very profitable. Acceptance of the more difficult path of shopping center development stemmed from the realization that off-street parking was a valuable asset, even in new, small commercial districts on the urban periphery. Equally important was the understanding that if this amenity was combined with the strengths of an integrated business structure, the complex could be a formidable contender against conventional strip development along thoroughfares, and not just in the protected setting of an exclusive residential enclave. The economic concerns Stein and Bauer raised to argue for the drive-in center as a component of planned communities proved just as germane in less controlled settings, as the Park and Shop demonstrated. Once this conceptual shift was made, the type began to gain popularity among retail and real estate interests alike. By 1941 the drive-in shopping center was being characterized as a significant new trend in the field.[44]

Washington, D.C., was the major proving ground for the drive-in neighborhood shopping center during these crucial years. Thirteen such complexes were operating in the metropolitan area by 1938, when examples were just beginning to appear in other parts of the country.[45] Several factors contributed to the local proliferation of the type. Washington was unlike most other cities in that its principal employer, the federal government, not only attracted a large middle-class population but spared the local economy from the worst ravages of the depression. Increases in the federal workforce under Franklin Roosevelt's administration precipitated a marked rise in residential construction beginning in 1935. Thereafter, the metropolitan area enjoyed one of the highest residential growth rates anywhere in the nation. After the Park and Shop, Washington's drive-in centers were built almost entirely to serve those new residential districts, both within the city limits and in the adjacent counties. From 1935 to 1939, twelve out of fifteen centers were constructed, like the Park and Shop, independent of any single housing tract. That ratio was reversed over the next three years as the area became a primary location for FHA-insured housing projects targeted to moderate-income households.[46] The great majority of Washington centers lay apart from concentrated retail activity, but most of them were situated along projected business corridors and some were extensions of established outlying business precincts. Collectively, this work presented ample evidence that the drive-in shopping center was an economically strong facility for a broad audience irrespective of whether it stood in isolation or amid competitors.

By the time the United States entered World War II, drive-in neighborhood centers could be found in many cities, from Philadelphia to Tacoma, Buffalo to Birmingham, although no other place came close to matching the volume of work done in Washington. A few of these complexes were being planned in 1937; most were constructed between 1939 and 1941. In most cases, they deviated little in siting, size, tenancy, or character from what could be found in the nation's capital. These circumstances suggest that Washington played a decisive role in the diffusion of the type and in its rise to national prominence.[47] The details of this process are difficult to ascertain, however, owing to the dearth of firsthand accounts. Material published in the *Architectural Record* during the early 1930s no doubt contributed, but was hardly a sufficient impetus in itself. The lessons drawn from concrete experience were likely of much greater importance in persuading developers of the type's worth. The neighborhood centers of J. C. Nichols were known to many colleagues elsewhere, but their integral relation to the surrounding residential tracts of the Country Club District may have cast them as a special case. Moreover, none of Nichols's centers made use of the drive-in concept prior to the war. Washington was the only other place where more than a few examples could be found. Whether by word of mouth, discussions at trade meetings, on-site visits, or journal coverage, developers became increasingly aware of them.[48]

Outside of Washington, a likely agent in reinforcing the acceptance of the drive-in neighborhood shopping center in the late 1930s was the drive-in market itself. Even though the drive-in market had fallen from favor in the food industry and had generated no more than fleeting interest in other circles early in the decade, it now came to be seen as a useful springboard, just as Wright, Frey, Stein, Bauer, and Shannon & Luchs had believed early on. The drive-in market remained a ubiquitous feature of the urban landscape in southern California and was seen often by the numerous visitors to the region. The type continued to be cited as an important contributor to the shopping center idea in literature directed toward other retail interests, developers, and architects. Indeed, the distinction between the two does not appear to have been great in many observers' minds. Carl Feiss, an architect and planner then teaching at Columbia University, was probably not alone when he characterized the drive-in market along with Washington complexes as "types" of shopping centers.[49] Under the circumstances, the fact that the drive-in market had proliferated in a region recognized as a pioneer in meeting the needs of motorists may have helped convince developers elsewhere that the shopping center idea was worth exploring.

The interplay of sources that affected the diffusion process is well illustrated by the River Oaks Shopping Center in Houston (1937), which was the most publicized and praised example of its kind until the post–World War II era. The complex was realized as part of River Oaks, a large, comprehensively planned residential area on the city's west side begun in 1924 by two rich, civic-minded entrepreneurs, Will and Mike Hogg, and a prominent attorney, Hugh Potter. Numerous planned developments were visited in the course of preparation; among them, Nichols's Country Club District probably exerted the greatest influence. Land was set aside for a shopping center at an early date.[50] The River Oaks center was conceived in phases. Initially the complex was to provide everyday goods and services, but also some specialty items. Buildings would be added to the complex as demand grew. Preliminary studies began around 1932, but the scheme was not finalized until five years later, when Potter believed the economic climate had improved decisively.[51] Two young Houston architects, Oliver C. Winston and Edward Arrantz, were commissioned to prepare plans and spent several months developing studies. Arrantz died soon thereafter, and his place in the firm was taken by Slayton Nunn. Then, in 1934, Winston became project planner for the Public Works Administration's housing division in Washington, D.C. The new job exposed him to the concerns for reform in commercial development espoused by Stein and Bauer and, no doubt, to the example that they used as a paradigm, the Park and Shop. Winston's "unusual interest" in the River Oaks project, along with what must have been a good working relationship with his client, led Potter to invite him to complete the process once an investor committed to financing the enterprise in the early fall of 1936. Winston was able to take only a month's leave of absence from his federal post, so while he concentrated on the design, responsibility for the working drawings and supervision went to Nunn and his associate, Milton McGinty.[52]

The four-year delay proved crucial to the design. As built, the River Oaks center consisted of two nearly identical units on either side of a cross street that was a direct route to downtown, along which subsequent commercial expansion was to occur (figure 147). Winston organized each of the units around a forecourt, much as if two of the Washington centers were paired face to face. At the same time, the crescent form, created to permit a clear view of all storefronts by motorists entering the forecourt, together with the abstract, minimalist vocabulary, stood in contrast to Washington work and to most retail design at that time. Both features correspond closely to Neutra's unrealized drive-in schemes of the late 1920s (see figures 66, 67). Like Neutra, too, Winston treated the front as a transparent surface, with signs and roof canopy above used to particularly dramatic effect at night through indirect lighting.[53] The corner filling station—an element seldom incorporated in shopping centers in Washington or elsewhere but common to drive-in markets, including Neutra's designs—further suggests that these southern California buildings provided inspiration. Through the combined efforts of an enlightened developer and a talented architect, the examples of the Washington centers and the drive-in market were fused in an arresting design that was at once heralded as a showpiece of its city.

The River Oaks complex also was touted as a model nationally for nearly a decade. Even after the shopping center began to experience

147
River Oaks Shopping Center, 2020–2048 W. Gray Avenue, Houston, 1937, Oliver C. Winston, Slayton Nunn, and Milton McGinty, associated architects; altered. Photo Paul Peters, ca. 1939. (*Architectural Record,* June 1940, 114.)

dramatic, fast-paced change after World War II, River Oaks was lauded as a pioneer in the field.[54] Potter played a central role in fostering this legacy. In 1940, he joined J. C. Nichols and other colleagues in forming the Urban Land Institute, a Washington-based organization devoted to improving the standards for new development. He served as the group's third president (1943–1944) and in 1950 succeeded Nichols as chairman of its Community Builders' Council, which had become the principal proponent of and source of information about shopping centers. In the late 1930s, when the type was still considered an unusual venture of perhaps limited application, and when the drive-in concept was likewise seen as experimental for most purposes other than automobile service, River Oaks offered convincing evidence that such ventures had a sound practical basis. No other example so successfully presented the shopping center concept, crafted in a vocabulary that exuded promise, as a solution that appeared not only realistic but inevitable. Main Street, it seemed, did not stand a chance.

RECONCILIATION

In one respect, however, River Oaks was much like Main Street. Its design, and that of contemporary work in Washington, allotted multiple tenants modest amounts of space each—at most about 2,500 to 4,000 square feet—as was still characteristic of the majority of outlying stores. The supermarket was not part of River Oaks's program, even though a number of examples could be found in Houston by 1937, perhaps because Potter believed it would overwhelm the complex and run counter to the intimate atmosphere his well-heeled clientele preferred. On the other hand, a company such as Henke & Pillot saw no advantage in sharing a car lot and other facilities with a group of small shops. The supermarket, after all, was large enough to be a destination without a supporting cast. In this respect, River Oaks was more a reflection of the past than a harbinger.

The supermarket and drive-in shopping center generally remained separate concepts through the prewar years. This tendency was quite evident in southern California, where the Park and Shop idea elicited no interest. The profusion of supermarkets planned as discrete buildings, sometimes near but still independent of the increasingly ambitious store groups in new outlying areas, reflected the strength of the local industry. In the very few cases where supermarkets were built as part of integrated retail complexes in those years, off-street parking was relegated to the rear so that the huge supermarket could maintain a commanding presence from the street and could exhibit produce across its open front with minimum encumbrance. Not until the 1950s, when the shopping center became fully accepted and the demand for such complexes intensified, was the forecourt arrangement again accepted in the region.[55] That shift was part of a national phenomenon in which the supermarket played a significant role.

The shopping center's rise in the decade following the war was shaped by several related factors. Large new areas around population centers were being occupied by middle-class and prosperous working-class residential developments. These tracts were generally far removed from existing retail outlets. By the late 1940s, it also became widely apparent that building retail centers on a large scale was the most effective way to avoid being outflanked by the many competitors eager to increase their share of the lucrative new market. Modest projects quickly became outmoded. Often zoning restrictions were minimal and readily modified to suit specific proposals. All these conditions argued against the traditional form of linear, street-oriented, unplanned retail centers that had been the norm in outlying areas since the rise of horsecar lines in the nineteenth century. As an integrated business development, the shopping center afforded greater leverage and security for all involved. River Oaks and others of its kind provided a basic precedent, but one that required modification because the mass-merchandising techniques of the supermarket were now considered optimal to attract the new middle market under these equally new circumstances.[56]

The growth rate of this second-generation shopping center was extraordinary. In 1954, the editorial staff of *Chain Store Age,* one of the retail field's primary organs, estimated that, of the roughly 1,000 such complexes in operation, the great majority had been built since 1945, and that nearly 2,000 more were being erected or were in the planning stage. Once the momentum was established, retailers who targeted this clientele had little choice but to participate. *Chain Store Age* editor S. O. Kaylin noted: "The question no longer is: 'Should we consider going into centers?' Today, chain-store operators are asking: 'Which centers should we go into. . . ?'"[57] By 1950 the shopping center was transforming the supermarket from a lone-wolf operation into an anchor unit of a considerably larger enterprise. But the supermarket also was key to transforming the shopping center into a complex that was substantially larger than examples of the previous decade. Not only were major stores several times the size of their precursors, but there was often a more extensive supporting cast.

Neighborhood centers now commonly had twenty units, and many examples were classified as community shopping centers, with twenty to forty units. Furthermore, it was now seen as essential to allocate two or three times as much ground area to parking as to buildings, to accommodate a clientele that had become almost entirely reliant on cars for transportation. The supermarket further affected shopping centers by the influence it was exerting on some of the other retail outlets that were important parts of these new complexes.

SELLING SPACE

By the 1950s, characteristics pioneered by Ralphs and other Los Angeles supers were widely emulated across the country.[58] A vast, unbroken space, neutral in character, with all the emphasis given to display; wide aisles, without any visual divisions between departments; unencumbered movement, with most if not every section self-service, all became hallmarks of new food stores coast to coast (figure 148). The labor shortages caused by World War II accelerated the shift to self-service. While usually limited to grocery departments until that time, self-service was adopted by many supermarket operators for meat, dairy, baked goods, and other departments between 1942 and 1945. Public approval was strong; customers did not feel rushed by others in line, nor did they feel they might be getting less than

148
Von's market, probably at 6651 Van Nuys Boulevard, Los Angeles, 1948–1949. Interior. Photo "Dick" Whittington, 1949. (Whittington Collection, Department of Special Collections, University of Southern California.)

optimal advice from the sales force—indeed many enjoyed the opportunity to choose for themselves. As a result, purchases were greater while staffing costs were reduced. Within a few years of the war's end, supermarkets that largely relied on self-service were becoming the norm. Having a single checkout point, with the row of checkout stands that Ralphs pioneered more than a decade earlier, emerged as a common feature. The average size of stores continued to increase, responding to the incessant need to maintain profit margins and stave off competition.[59]

At the same time, the supermarket was exerting a significant influence on the design of other retail facilities, in particular the drug store and the limited-price variety (or five-and-ten-cent) store. In contrast to the supermarket's own history, major chain companies assumed the leading role in this change, which thus was not locally based but national, channeled through prominent trade networks.[60] On the other hand, the underlying motive was much the same, namely that volume sales, induced by low prices, good value, and convenience, significantly boosted profits. Like the supermarket's development, too, the transformation was an incremental one that took years to consummate, beginning in the 1930s.

The drug store of 1930 seemed an unlikely candidate for sweeping change. A few large units existed in the city center, but the great majority were modest affairs of perhaps 1,000 to 2,500 square feet, were situated in outlying areas, were independently owned, and served a local clientele (figure 149). But even when unassuming in size, these emporia were becoming more diversified in merchandise. Besides the traditional pharmaceuticals and toiletries, drug stores were carrying such items as luggage and leather accessories, china and glassware, sporting goods, watches and jewelry, toys and novelties, electrical appliances, and stationery. Soda fountains

149
Commercial block, including Munro Drug Company store, Santa Monica Boulevard and Roxbury Drive, Beverly Hills, ca. 1920s; no longer standing. Photo Rode, 1932. (Hearst Collection, Department of Special Collections, University of Southern California.)

often functioned as full-fledged lunch rooms, much to the dismay of restaurateurs. Some drug stores even had beauty parlors.[61] Chain companies were especially aggressive in broadening their retail base, but many independent operations also did so, paralleling the trend toward expansion among food stores.[62] As a result, space tended to be compartmentalized. The bigger the sales area, the greater was the number of stations for making purchases, loosely following the arrangement common to the open floors of a department store.

The shrinking market caused by the depression bolstered the tendency to sell goods in greater quantity and variety. Chain companies with substantial amounts of capital reserve seized the initiative to expand, building large new units and adding to existing ones. Much of this activity occurred apart from the city center. One of the most ambitious schemes of this kind was announced in August 1934 by Michael Katz, president of the Kansas City-based Katz Drug Company. Located in a major outlying commercial district catering to the middle and upper markets, the new store contained 21,000 square feet, making it probably the largest example beyond downtown anywhere in the country (figure 150). Almost as much land was allocated to parking, with space for 300 cars. The venture was costly; several buildings, all constructed in the previous decade, were demolished to secure the site. The new store sold a spectrum of merchandise developed for the five existing downtown units and unmatched by other drug chains in the region, including hardware, household goods, men's and women's apparel, electric appliances, toys, automobile accessories, and many other items, emulating, perhaps, the diversity found at King Kullen

150
Katz Drug Company store, 3944–3954 Main Street, Kansas City, Missouri, 1934, Clarence Kivett, in association with Robert Bloomgarten and Kent Frohwerk, architects; altered. Photo author, 1972.

and Big Bear stores. Katz kept the drug store designation so that units could operate in the evening and on Sundays; however, he proudly stated that this was the first "supermarket" in the field and seems to have hoped it would set a national precedent.[63]

In sharp contrast to the barnlike markets of the East, Katz's "super-service store," designed by his nephew, Clarence Kivett, drew from the sleek fronts of the latest Los Angeles supers, which were then almost the only other stores of comparable size, configuration, and appearance.[64] Like the supermarket, and in contrast to the vast majority of drug stores anywhere, the business occupied an entire building specifically created for the purpose and with an image strongly tied to the chain. Katz continued to expand in outlying areas of Kansas City over the next half-dozen years, although not at quite so grand a scale. The supermarket analogy, in merchandising and image, remained strong nevertheless. Those ties were strengthened with the introduction of self-service in many departments in 1940.[65]

The Katz store may have been an anomaly when it opened, but other chains soon began to assume some of its characteristics. This trend was conspicuous in Los Angeles, where the Sontag Drug Company opened a 16,000-square-foot "super" store in April 1936 in the Miracle Mile on Wilshire Boulevard.[66] Somewhat more typical was the 6,000-square-foot Thrifty drug store begun three months later several miles to the west on Wilshire, with a simple, sculpted front reminiscent of a supermarket's (figure 151). Both companies undertook ambitious expansion plans. In 1930, Sontag and Thrifty had had only downtown stores; ten years later, each had twenty units in outlying areas of the city. From mid-decade on, their designs were carefully planned to foster mass-merchandising methods adapted from the supermarket.[67] Downtown ceased to be the sole province of large-scale drug retailing.

Expansion continued at a fast pace after the war. In outlying areas of Los Angeles, for example, Thrifty increased its units to over thirty by 1950, and other chains aggressively following suit. Stores of 8,000 square

feet or more were not uncommon.[68] Increasingly, too, the drug store's exterior appearance approximated that of the supermarket, sometimes to the point that only corporate signs distinguished one from the other (figure 152). The siting of drug stores still tended to be different, however. Most were centrally located in shopping districts, built either as part of a larger group of stores or alongside existing ones. But sometimes the drug store, like the supermarket, was constructed as a catalyst for other business development. The Owl store that opened in 1952 in Norwalk, then a fast-growing residential community in Orange County, was the second unit in what was envisioned as a large shopping center, initiated the previous year with the All American Market. Encompassing more than 10,000 square feet of sales area, set back from the street with a parking lot, and announced by a large pylon on one side, the complex could easily have been mistaken for many supermarkets of the era (figure 153).[69]

Among the most overt moves taken in the drug store's adoption of supermarket characteristics was to combine the two facilities under one roof. In southern California, the Owl Drug Company undertook several such ventures with supermarket chains. The initial project, completed in 1949, was for a mammoth, 30,000-square-foot building in Pasadena, planned with Alpha Beta Food Markets (figure 154).[70] Situated less than

151
Thrifty Drug Stores, 332 Wilshire Boulevard, Santa Monica, California, 1936, Norstrom & Anderson, architects; no longer standing. (*Architectural Concrete* 6 [1940], 350.)

152
Thrifty Drug Stores, #98, 4901 Whittier Boulevard, East Los Angeles, 1950; altered. Photo 1950. (Hearst Collection, Department of Special Collections, University of Southern California.)

153
Owl Drug Company store, 11726 E.
Firestone Boulevard, Norwalk, Cali-
fornia, 1951–1952; altered. Photo
Marcia & Ramsey, 1952. (Hearst
Collection, Department of Special
Collections, University of Southern
California.)

154
Alpha Beta Market–Owl Drug
Company store, 237–273 N. Los
Robles Avenue, Pasadena, 1949,
John Kewell, architect; no longer
standing. (Hearst Collection, Depart-
ment of Special Collections,
University of Southern California.)

two blocks from the main shopping district and with an off-street parking
capacity of nearly 300 cars, the facility was intended to attract patrons
throughout Pasadena and nearby communities. Each company emphasized
that having the other in a continuous space greatly enhanced customer convenience and selection. While separately operated, drug store and food
store were nearly one and the same. Such an integration was only possible,
of course, with the drug store's full acceptance of what had become a key
feature of supermarket merchandising, self-service.

Self-service was the decisive, but also generally the last, step taken in the transformation of the drug store, just as it had been for many supermarkets. The shift to mass merchandising, begun in the 1930s, first focused on ways to improve circulation, overall visibility, and product display. These objectives were widespread among retailers of the period; what set many drug stores apart was a reliance on the straightforward, open, and visually unified lateral space of the supermarket.[71] Still, the prevailing tendency was to retain discrete departments, each with its own staff. While an increasing number of goods were displayed on the open shelves of gondolas adapted from those devised for supermarkets, many other items were still in cases. Irrespective of the presentation mode, purchases were made department by department. Retailers harbored fears that shoplifting would skyrocket with self-service and that patrons would bemoan the lack of personal attention that had long been the drug store's hallmark. Thus, well after World War II, many large new drug stores—such as Owl's 16,500-square-foot unit at the Broadway-Crenshaw Center, the company's "largest and finest" when it opened in 1948—resembled supermarkets in overall appearance but remained organized in this more traditional way (figure 155).[72]

Experiments with self-service were initiated before the war. Along with Katz, Dallas-based Skillern's Drug Stores embraced the concept at an early date, modeling its stores closely on the supermarket in every re-

155
Owl Drug Company store, Broadway-Crenshaw Shopping Center, 4145 Crenshaw Boulevard, Los Angeles, 1945–1947, Albert B. Gardner, architect; demolished 1987. Interior view. Photo Leon Miller, ca. 1947. (Hearst Collection, Department of Special Collections, University of Southern California.)

spect. Many of these enterprises proved unsuccessful, however, and their owners returned to more conventional merchandising methods.[73] Other pioneers kept up the practice while remaining circumspect about its broad application. On the west coast, for example, Thrifty opened an immense, 30,000-square-foot self-service store in downtown Los Angeles in 1942; but only twelve of its ninety-two units were using self-service seven years later. On the other hand, a new, locally based rival, Sav-On, utilized self-service in all six of its stores by 1949. California and other western states were considered among the nation's leaders at the close of the decade, although the shift was still tentative.[74]

Then, over the next three years, chain companies embraced self-service with a swiftness that surprised industry observers and insiders alike. By January 1953 over a third of chain units nationwide were estimated to have adopted the practice.[75] Self-service was now the rule for new units, and many established ones were converting as well. The sudden shift was precipitated in part by threats. Supermarkets were increasingly carrying important staples of the drug store, such as health and beauty aids and housewares, or were establishing their own departments that functioned as complete drug stores.[76] The threat was intensified by the proliferation of supermarkets themselves in many parts of the country where they had been scarce, combined with the dominance they could enjoy in new outlying areas. Equally important, large new drug stores, like supermarkets, were being planned primarily as part of shopping centers by the early 1950s. To address the competition head on, drug chain executives often chose to locate next to the big food emporia and have their stores look and operate like them. The drug store, they believed, could only meet the supermarket's challenge by emulation. Enough industry leaders were convinced of this strategy and they controlled enough stores to induce a swift change in the course of the field as a whole.

That shift still might never have occurred had self-service not been found to possess distinct advantages. The cost of installation for a new self-service store was about half that of a conventional plant. Although personnel costs remained about the same, the staff could now devote more time to restocking and displays, while customers could devote more time to perusing merchandise. Self-service functioned better at peak sales periods and during promotions when large numbers of people came to a store. Predictions of extensive shoplifting proved unfounded, as did those that consumers would resent the lack of attention from salesclerks. Instead, patronage, unit sales, and overall volume tended to increase markedly once a store switched to self-service. Having acclimated to the practice at supermarkets, the public now welcomed the freedom and flexibility of the new supermarketlike drug store (figure 156). Some debate continued over details of layout, especially for those few functions, such as the pharmacy, that did not lend themselves to self-service. But once the desirability of self-service became clear to the industry, the trend became widespread.

The relationship between the supermarket and the variety store was more complex. Unlike most food and drug stores around 1930, major

variety outlets were already in sizable quarters and carried a diverse array of goods. Furthermore, self-selection, the ability to examine goods without the aid of clerks, had been a defining characteristic of these emporia from an early date. The primary changes to occur in the depression decade were a further increase in the scope of the goods carried and a rise in their price ceiling. National chain companies led this move in order to become more competitive with other retailers.[77] In the process, many stores were enlarged as well as modernized. Downtown and major outlying commercial districts were the focus of this expansion before and after World War II. Through the mid-1950s, variety chains continued to make substantial investments in adding to or constructing new multistory buildings in central locations.[78] In no other retail sphere was the commitment to bolstering the urban core more conspicuous during the postwar years.

But variety chains also expanded in less concentrated outlying areas, continuing a course that had gained considerable momentum in large cities such as Philadelphia, Chicago, and St. Louis during the 1920s. Los Angeles, for example, had eighteen units among its three major chains (Kress, Newberry, Woolworth) situated beyond the city center in 1930, and forty-one in 1940.[79] Many of these new stores served low-density residential neighborhoods, the same places where the supermarket flourished.

156

Thrifty Drug Stores, unidentified unit, perhaps in Riverside, California. Interior view. Photo William B. Andrews, 1956. (Hearst Collection, Department of Special Collections, University of Southern California.)

Often they were single-story and occupied 7,000 to 10,000 square feet, which was markedly more floor area than had been found in counterparts of the previous decade. Like the drug store, variety stores were almost always built amid existing retail facilities or as part of a new group of stores. In setting and appearance, they suggested an updated version of conventional Main Street emporia more than they resembled the supermarket (figure 157).

The supermarket did, however, seem to have an impact on the design of a few variety stores prior to the war. Among those showing the most obvious signs of influence was the Akron, Ohio, unit erected in 1940 by Scott-Burr Stores of Chicago. Located in the heart of downtown, across the street from the city's two major department stores, the building occupied a sprawling, 18,500-square-foot area on a single floor (figure 158).[80] Such a configuration may have been spurred by deflated land values; nevertheless, most variety stores built in the urban core still had two or three stories. The low-slung mass had a strong horizontal emphasis, counterpointed by a corner pylon, an arrangement for which the supermarket was the obvious source. The selling area, 108 feet wide, was unencumbered by structural supports, forming a continuous space clearly inspired by the supermarket as well as by the grandeur associated with department stores

(figure 159).[81] The unusual nature of what Scott proclaimed its "most outstanding store" suggests careful study of the supermarket as a new point of
departure for the physical plant if not for merchandising strategy. Such ties
grew more common after World War II, when many new units in outlying
areas were built as "super" stores, with expansive, clear-span spaces on a
single floor and exteriors that were configured more like contemporary
supermarkets than like most retail outlets. The sprawling Newberry store
in Los Angeles's Westchester Business Center—that company's largest self-
service unit to date—represented an advanced state for the type when it
opened in 1953, but it soon became the norm for new work (figure 160).[82]

  The move to self-service was the variety chains' most decisive adaptation of supermarket techniques. Much like the drug store, the variety
store experimented in this vein before the war. The best-known example
within the industry was the west coast–based Sprouse-Reitz Company,

which opened a trial unit in 1940. The resulting 25 percent increase in
sales led to converting 40 units out of 170 over the next year and a half.
But most other early ventures were by independent merchants and had
little impact on national practices. Another decade would elapse before variety store executives believed self-service had any value save, perhaps, for
small stores where no competition existed.[83]

   In both timing and nature, the shift to self-service in variety stores
paralleled that in drug stores. Within a few years—1952 to 1955—a number of variety chain executives adopted self-service as a key component of
store operation. The move was led by the F. W. Woolworth Company,
which had 435 such units, over a fifth of its total, by January 1956.[84] Fears
of shoplifting and of customer disorientation were offset by the need to re-
coup a share of the market that had been declining steadily since 1945.
Trial ventures showed that shoppers greatly preferred self-service and purchased more goods when allowed complete freedom. Sales volume expanded an average of 28 percent, it was found, without increases in
operating costs. Just as with drug stores, self-service improved efficiency
during peak shopping periods and increased the opportunities for display
and the restocking of merchandise. Shoplifting rose only marginally or not
at all. Large stores of 20,000 to 30,000 square feet proved just as conducive
to this form of merchandising as ones of 5,000 to 6,000 square feet, theretofore considered the optimal size for it. Not everyone embraced the practice; S. H. Kress & Company was among the most prominent chains to
remain skeptical. Within a few years, however, self-service was virtually a
universal practice.[85]

   The transition was not easy, in part because variety store executives had long viewed their plants as being more prestigious than those of
food markets. Kress had begun to set that industry standard in the 1910s,
constructing emporia with ornate facades and handsomely appointed main
selling floors, their ceilings as high as 30 feet, that helped make the variety
outlet a destination of respectability as well as of thrift (figure 161).[86] While
competing chains seldom commissioned facilities that were as elaborate,
they pursued the same general course during the 1920s and, especially, the

161
S. H. Kress & Company store, 11 E.
Main Street, Alhambra, California,
ca. 1923, remodeled 1937, Edward
F. Sibbert, architect; altered. Interior.
Photo, 1937. (Kress Collection, National Building Museum, gift of
Genesco, Inc.)

1930s. Downtown stores in major cities were built or remodeled as show-cases, more suggestive of a department store than of a bargain center. As late as 1954, the editor of *Variety Store Merchandiser* touted buildings of the trade as "the largest, best-appearing . . . [ones] in the shopping section of the average American city—barring only a relatively few department stores of the highest caliber."[87] Under the circumstances, chains were reluctant to forfeit the association for one of ostensibly lower stature. Despite advice that conversion to self-service should result in a complete change of appearance, many units experienced only minor modifications. A Woolworth's store on Crenshaw Boulevard in Los Angeles was probably typical: existing counters were moved to eliminate the salesclerk's aisle, and additional shelving for display, new lights, and checkout stands near the entry were added, but the store's overall image was still more reminiscent of times past than of the impending transformation (figure 162).[88]

The underlying impetus for more fundamental change in variety stores seems to have come from the shopping center, although the correlation was not acknowledged in trade literature of the period. Until the early 1950s, most variety chains viewed their downtown stores as flagships; units in outlying areas were of secondary rank, carrying fewer goods in less competitive settings. If these peripheral locations grew to be important retail centers in their own right, the store was expanded or rebuilt as a smaller version of those downtown.

The shopping center changed that perspective. Here, ample space existed for a large store on a single level; most developers discouraged basements or second floors due to the construction costs they incurred. Developers also sought to create a generally uniform appearance for shopping center exteriors, minimizing differences between one storefront and another. Finally, by the mid-1950s, there was a growing realization among retailers that the market to which these centers catered was different from traditional ones. Their consumers shunned the upscale pretensions of many downtown stores and the bargain-basement atmosphere of many others. Instead, the demand was for what Perry Myers, research director of Allied Stores, one of the nation's largest retail chains, called "middle styling"—lines that were neither too expensive nor seemed too cheap.[89]

Real estate developers seem already to have sensed this basic shift in outlook. The new shopping centers that were attracting consumers in such numbers were simple and straightforward in appearance not just for economic reasons, but also to provide a setting that was conspicuously unlike older business districts. However disparaged by some, the postwar shopping center seemed modern, clean, and convenient to much of its target audience. It had abundant space and light, looked "better" than the old neighborhood strip, and offered a much greater range of shopping choices, but it was also a place that invited casual activity and possessed no hint of elite stylishness (figure 163). For similar reasons, this clientele embraced self-service and thus ensured that it would become a basic staple of retailing generally.

162
F. W. Woolworth Company store,
5436 Crenshaw Boulevard, Los
Angeles, 1930–1931; altered. Inte-
rior as remodeled for self-service.
Photo "Dick" Whittington, 1953.
(Whittington Collection, Depart-
ment of Special Collections,
University of Southern California.)

163
Northwood Shopping Center, Loch
Raven Boulevard and Havenswood
Road, Baltimore, Maryland, 1949–
1950, Ring Engineering Co.,
designer; altered. Foor Fair market at
left, Acme market at center, S. S.
Kresge store at right. Photo ca.
1950. (Author's collection.)

These conditions were particularly favorable for the supermarket,
which had embodied such a merchandising atmosphere for over a decade.
By expanding into new lines, the supermarket was also challenging the variety store's role in retailing, although less so than it challenged the drug
store. From the developer's perspective, both supermarket and variety store
were essential—complementing and competing against each other—to
draw the vast middle market that was resettling on the urban periphery.[90]
Combined, the two types provided the anchor for the increasing number
of community shopping centers and were key components for regional centers as well. Supermarkets and variety stores had to be large—around
20,000 to 30,000 square feet—if these centers were to attract the critical
mass of shoppers needed to be profitable in an intensely competitive arena.
At first, variety store executives were lukewarm to the potential advantages
of shopping center locations; by the mid-1950s, however, as these retail
complexes became the primary form of concentrated retail development
and the most advantageous arena in which to hold the supermarket in
check, variety chains adjusted their building programs.[91]

Under the circumstances, maintaining a traditional identity made
little sense. As two of the largest—and often *the* largest—components of
the shopping center and as equals in its hierarchy, the supermarket and variety store assumed a generally similar appearance (figure 164). Inside, the variety store also became much like the supermarket, with a broad and open
selling floor, wide aisles separating tiered counters and gondolas, and a
single checkout point. The character of space was as neutral as its organization, relying entirely on displays for visual stimulus. Once its strengths were
revealed, self-service was a logical extension of this arrangement, and shopping center units became the front line for the industry's shift. By the close
of the decade, even the conservative Kress Company was fully engaged in
this new mode (figure 165).

164
Miracle Mile Town and Country Shopping Center, Columbus, Ohio. Albers supermarket at left, F. W. Woolworth Co. at center. Photo ca. 1950. (Courtesy Don M. Casto Organization.)

165
S. H. Kress & Company store, Metcalf Plaza, N. Main Street, Santa Ana, California, 1959; altered. Interior. Photo 1959. (Kress Collection, National Building Museum, gift of Genesco, Inc.)

By the mid-1950s the shopping center and mass merchandising became closely interwoven phenomena, in large part due to the supermarket's rapid ascent as a model for retailing practices. By this circuitous route, the two spatial orders pioneered by the drive-in and the Los Angeles super during the interwar decades were finally integrated. The shopping center helped diffuse the transformation of retail space initiated by the supermarket. At the same time, these complexes underscored the efficacy of having large stores operate as part of an integrated development arranged according to the drive-in concept. This mix eventually helped ensure that the supermarket did not become a dominant, all-purpose store, but rather that its identity remained with food while the drug and variety stores continued to fulfill their own basic functions. Meanwhile, the increased size of sales areas—especially in supermarkets, variety stores, and drug stores—and of the clientele to which they catered, helped transform the drive-in shopping center from the modest neighborhood complexes of the 1930s into sprawling affairs, often with twenty to forty stores and car lots occupying at least twice as much space as the building. Frank Lloyd Wright had envisioned this new scale of lateral space, indoors and out, when the shopping center and the supermarket were in their infancies, but the actual steps needed to achieve it were too numerous and varied for anyone to predict. Ultimately, of course, pragmatism guided the development, just as it had led to the invention of the prototypes. Yet the collective results were revolutionary. The location of retail facilities, the scale and arrangement of their spaces, the underlying merchandising strategies, and the shopping routines that were induced all had fundamentally changed. From metropolis to small town, Main Street would never be the same.

NOTES

Introduction

1
Richard Longstreth, "The Lost Shopping Center," *The Forum,* Bulletin of the Committee on Preservation, Society of Architectural Historians, 20 (Oct. 1992), whole issue; idem, "I Can't See It; I Don't Understand It; and It Doesn't Look Old to Me,"

Historic Preservation Forum 10 (Fall 1995), 8–9. For an example, see Amy Arget-
singer, "End of the Road for 1st Enclosed Mall in the East," *Washington Post,* 30
Nov. 1997, B1, B8.

2

The years used in the title of this book are, like most such dates, somewhat arbi-
trary. The first super service station, discussed in chapter I, was erected ca. 1914;
1941, after which most retail developments of the interwar decades came to a
temporary halt due to U.S. entry into the world war, affords a convenient endpoint.
Analyzing the influence of the supermarket on commercial space, however, necessi-
tates some coverage of the postwar decade.

3

For background, see Richard Longstreth, *City Center to Regional Mall: Architecture,
the Automobile, and Retailing in Los Angeles, 1920–1950* (Cambridge: MIT Press,
1997), esp. chap. I; Scott L. Bottles, *Los Angeles and the Automobile: The Making of the
Modern City* (Berkeley: University of California Press, 1987); and Robert M. Fogel-
son, *The Fragmented Metropolis: Los Angeles 1850–1930* (1967; rpt. Berkeley: University of California Press, 1993).

4

Postwar shopping centers have become the subject of considerable study in recent
years; see Longstreth, *City Center to Regional Mall,* chaps. IX and XI, and references
cited on p. 357, n. 7; and "AHR Forum: Shopping Malls in America," *American
Historical Review* 101 (Oct. 1996), 1049–1121. The rise of interest among graduate
students is suggested by a session I chaired but did not assemble, entitled "A New
Retail Environment," at the Seventh National Conference on American Planning
History held in Seattle in October 1997.

I Monkey-Wrench Merchandising

1

James H. Collins, "Monkey-Wrench Merchandising," *Printer's Ink Monthly* 16 (Apr.
1928), 49.

2

Ibid.

3

See n. 46 below.

4

Exceptions did not begin to appear until the late 1920s. The most significant one
was Bullock's Wilshire department store (1928–1929); see Richard Longstreth,
*City Center to Regional Mall: Architecture, the Automobile, and Retailing in Los Angeles,
1920–1950* (Cambridge: MIT Press, 1997), 112–123. Other examples are discussed in idem, "Don't Get Out: The Automobile's Impact on Five Building Types
in Los Angeles, 1921–1941," *Arris,* Journal of the Southeast Chapter of the Society
of Architectural Historians, 7 (1996), 32–56.

5

Longstreth, *City Center to Regional Mall,* 43–55.

6

For general discussion, see Richard Longstreth, *The Buildings of Main Street: A Guide to American Commercial Architecture* (Washington: Preservation Press, 1987); and idem, "Compositional Types in American Commercial Architecture," in Camille Wells, ed., *Perspectives in Vernacular Architecture, II* (Columbia: University of Missouri Press, 1986), 12–13.

7

Tom Wilder, "Planning Filling Stations for Efficiency," *MA* 40 (6 Oct. 1921), 16. See also Alexander G. Guth, "The Automobile Service Station," *Architectural Forum* 45 (July 1926), 33–56. Historical studies include John A. Jakle and Keith A. Sculle, *The Gasoline Station in America* (Baltimore: Johns Hopkins University Press, 1994), chap. 5; Chester H. Liebs, *Main Street to Miracle Mile: American Roadside Architecture* (Boston: New York Graphic Society, 1985), 96–98; and Daniel I. Vierya, *"Fill'er Up": An Architectural History of America's Gas Stations* (New York: Collier, 1979), 4, 7.

8

"Finest Fuel . . . ," *LAT,* 16 Nov. 1913, VIII-8. The six initial stations were located at sites then considered relatively far from the city center in an arc extending from the southwest to the northwest of that core: Grand and Washington, Vermont and Washington, Wilshire and Mariposa, Pico and Alvarado, Seventh and Wilshire, and Vermont and Hollywood. It is unclear whether the company continued to build units, but its purpose was soon assumed by major oil companies, which began to distribute their own products in the area on a large scale by the decade's end. Similarly basic facilities continued to be built by local chains into the next decade. See, for example, *LAT,* 24 May 1924, I-9.

9

Fear of poor-quality products lingered for some time among local motorists, if advertisements are an accurate gauge. See, for example, *LAT,* 30 Oct. 1920, VI-6.

10

"California Man Claims Credit for Planning First Filling Station," *FS* 1 (Jan. 1922), 51; "Now Comes the Service Town, Going the Service Station One Better," *FS* 1 (Dec. 1921), 51; Jakle and Sculle, *Gasoline Station,* 131–142; Vierya, *"Fill'er Up,"* 4, 6–7, 10; Liebs, *Main Street,* 97. One account suggested Los Angeles's first filling station was built ca. 1902 by the Union Oil Company, but I have yet to find verification of this claim; see "Old Service Station . . . ," *LAT,* 25 Apr. 1926, VI-18.

11

Accounts of the period leave little doubt that the type originated in southern California and that the region influenced work done elsewhere. For Los Angeles examples, see "Now Comes Service Town," 51, 53; B. V. Ellzey, "Something Growing Helps Appearance around the Station," *FS* 2 (Mar. 1923), 21, 23, 25, 27; idem, "Experimenting with 'Super-Service' on the West Coast," *FS* 2 (Mar. 1923), 83, 85, 87; William V. Gross, " 'Super Service' in California Means Everything for the Automobile," *FS* 6 (10 Sep. 1925), 31, 33; James V. Murray, "This Super-Service Station Idea—Will It Spread East?" *FS* 7 (10 Jan. 1926), 26–28; William E. Green, "Super Service Stations Thrive Best Operated by Individual Owner," *NPN* 20 (14 Mar. 1928), 97, 101. To date, I have found only one source that offers a conflicting account: H. A. Haring, "Merchandising for Filling Stations," *Printer's Ink Monthly* 15 (Aug. 1927), 48. For general discussion of the type, see William H.

McGrew, "Sound Fundamentals Support the Super-Service Station," *FS* 12 (Aug. 1928), 41–43, 71, 74, 76; (Sep. 1928), 73–74, 78, 82, 86, 88, 90.

12

"Now Comes Service Town," 51, 53. The only image I have been able to find of the complex is contained in this account but is of such poor quality as to preclude reproduction here. Concerning Western Avenue, see Longstreth, *City Center to Regional Mall,* 67–71.

13

"Now Comes Service Town," 51, 53; Gross, "'Super-Service' in California," 31–33; "Something New in Line," *LAT,* 21 Aug. 1921, VI-2.

14

"Now Comes Service Town," 53; W. Harold Hawkins, "From Soup to Nuts," *FS* 7 (10 Jan. 1926), 32; Green, "Super Service Stations Thrive," 101; McGrew, "Sound Fundamentals," 73, 82, 86; Brad Mills, "Mullers' Complete Service," *FS* 13 (June 1929), 22; Frank H. Williams, "Appealing to Women Buyers," *FS* 9 (25 May 1927), 19–20; R. M. Ward, "Bigger Profits for Better Merchandising," *FS* 16 (Aug. 1930), 30–32, 62, 64, 66.

15

Gross, "'Super-Service' in California," 31.

16

See, for example, "Is Service a Business?" *MA* 39 (10 Mar. 1921), 13; B. M. Ikert, "Average Service Station Lacks Tone," *MA* 40 (22 Sep. 1921), 7–9, 13; B. M. Ikert, "Making Maintenance Pay," *MA* 41 (30 Mar. 1922), 7–9, (6 Apr. 1922), 17–21; Sam Shelton, "Sources of Profit," *MA* 51 (5 May 1927), 10–11; L. Z. McKee, "Looking Over an Overlooked Field," *MA* 53 (28 June 1928), 32–33, 38. For an early Los Angeles example, see "Applying the Department Store Idea to the Dealer's Business," *MA* 41 (23 Feb. 1921), 10–13. Some businesses that started in automobile repair also expanded in this manner, such as Los Angeles's Master Service Company; see Roy Alden, "Specialization in Maintenance Develops Quarter-Million Annual Business," *MA* 49 (21 Jan. 1926), 10–12. In the region, both types seem to have developed an unusually high standard of service early on; see Fred M. Loomis, "What Good Roads Have Done for California," *MA* 37 (13 May 1920), 7–9, 37.

17

Ellzey, "Experimenting with 'Super-Service'", 82.

18

Arthur E. Goodwin, *Markets: Public and Private* (Seattle: Montgomery Printing Co., 1929), 29–31. See also Helen Tangires, "Feeding the Cities: Public Markets & Municipal Reform in the Progressive Era," *Prologue,* Quarterly of the National Archives and Records Administration, 29 (Spring 1997), 16–26.

19

"Unique Arcade Structure . . . ," *LAT,* 15 Mar. 1914, VI-2. For other early examples, see "Up-to-Date Market," *LAT,* 30 Mar. 1913, VI-4; and "New Market Place for West Seventh," *LAT,* 27 Jan. 1918, V-1. A large downtown market occupied the former quarters of a major department store; see "Great Market for North End," *LAT,* 14 Nov. 1915, V-1.

20

Public markets continued to be built in the city center during the immediate post-war years as well; see: "Will Establish . . . ," *LAT,* 1 Aug. 1920, V-1; "Public Market Building . . . ," *LAT,* 17 Oct. 1920, V-3; *LAT,* 20 May 1921, II-10; *Western Architect* 31 (July 1922), pl. 15; and "Public Market for Olive . . . ," *LAT,* 4 Feb. 1923, V-1.

21

These firms included Sam Seeling, E. A. Morrison, and Young's Market Company.

22

"Public Market Opening . . . ," *HDC,* 16 Jan. 1920, 1.

23

"Western Avenue Site . . . ," *LAT,* 18 Sep. 1921, V-2, 5; "New Beverly-Western . . . ," *HDC,* 3 Feb. 1922, 3, 8; *Southern California Business* 1 (Sep. 1922), 12. Others in the area included the Gardner Junction Market, 7503–7507 Sunset Boulevard (*HDC,* 14 Nov. 1919, 13); East Hollywood Public Market, 1724–1726 N. Vermont Avenue (*HDC,* 14 Nov. 1919, 16); Cahuenga Public Market, Cahuenga and Selma avenues (*HDC,* 12 Aug. 1921, I-11; "New Cahuenga Public Market . . . ," *HDC,* 19 Aug. 1921, I-11); Hollywood and Western Avenue Public Market, 5504–5506 Hollywood Boulevard (*HDC,* 3 Nov. 1921, 8); Sunset-Bronson Public Market, 1645 Highland Avenue (*HDC,* 3 Feb. 1922, 16); the Shopping Center, 5950 Hollywood Boulevard ("New Shopping Center Opens," *HDC,* 10 Feb. 1922, 7, 9); Holly-Serrano Public Market, 5403 Hollywood Boulevard (*HDC,* 17 Feb. 1922, 2); Holly-Sunset Market, 6507 Sunset Boulevard ("Sunset to Get . . . ," *HDC,* 20 Mar. 1922, 1; "New Market . . . ," *HDC,* 9 June 1922, 5); and Hollywood Quality Market, 6658 Hollywood Boulevard (*HDC,* 14 July 1922, II-2).

24

"Work Started . . . ," *LAT,* 18 Feb. 1923, V-10. For other examples, see *LAT,* 15 Feb. 1920, V-4; *LAT,* 10 June 1920, I-5; "Market . . . Completed," *LAT,* 3 Dec. 1922, V-2; "Glendale's Gateway Markets . . . ," *GNP,* 19 Jan. 1922, 1; "Gateway Building . . . ," *GNP,* 27 Apr. 1923, Southern Glendale Sect., 2; and "A California Grocery Store," *PG* 4 (Apr. 1925), 12.

25

See, for example, "Growth of San Francisco Filling Station Shows Trend . . . ," *FS* 9 (10 Jan. 1927), 20–21; J. M. Lind, "Professional Touch of Modern Equipment," *FS* 9 (10 Apr. 1927), 50; Aldon Andley, "Greenfield Makes It a Personal Matter . . . ," *FS* 9 (10 May 1927), 14.

26

"Muller Brothers' New Service Station," *HDC,* 22 July 1922, 5; "Muller Brothers Success . . . ," *HDC,* 3 Sep. 1922, 5; James V. Malone, "A Particular Service for Particular People," *MA* 43 (3 May 1923), 24–25; James V. Murray, "Super-Service Station . . . ," *FS* 9 (10 Jan. 1927), 24–25; "Station Is Open . . . ," *HDC,* 27 May 1925, 15; "Muller's 'Oil'em Up' Shop," *HDC,* 22 July 1925, 16; "Frank and Walt Muller . . . ," *HDC,* 28 July 1926, 16; "Everything for the Car on One Lot," *NPN* 20 (25 July 1928), 83, 86; Mills, "Mullers' Complete Service," 22–23; "Muller Brothers Patrons . . . ," *HDC,* 8 Aug. 1928, 11, 12.

27

"'Chain' System to Serve Autoists," *LAT,* 9 Nov. 1919, V-2; "Standard Motor Service . . . ," *LATMN,* 1 Jan. 1920, VII-4. As with many other proposals for chain operations of the period, it is doubtful whether more than the initial unit was erected.

28

Williams, "Appealing to Women Buyers." Contemporary accounts sometimes mention features specifically tailored to a female clientele; see, for example, "Super Station Designed as Mosque," *NPN* 20 (18 Apr. 1928), 94. More often, the subject is addressed through inference, by emphasizing decorative embellishments and even landscaping (Ellzey, "Something Growing"; Murray, "This Super-Service Station Idea").

29

"Muller Brothers' New Service Station."

30

Liebs, *Main Street,* 39–73, offers a provocative discussion of the general subject.

31

The assembly-line-like arrangement of the service building suggests that the company may have sought to induce customers to have several maintenance or repair jobs performed during a single visit; but, given the diverse nature of those jobs, such a system would have been impractical. Cars may have been able to enter and exit at other points.

32

"New Features Found . . . ," *LAT,* 6 Nov. 1927, VI-2.

33

For examples, see W. Lee Sloan, "Two Thousand Customers Visited This Station's Formal Opening," *FS* 5 (10 Feb. 1925), 25–27; "Filling Station Is Central Unit of 'Auto Department Store,'" *FS* 6 (25 Dec. 1925), 42; Mandus E. Bridston, "Four Times the Outlet Equals Twelve Times the Gross," *FS* 9 (10 May 1927), 11–12; idem, "Can the Super Station Manager Really Merchandise?" *FS* 10 (25 July 1927), 15–16; "A $100,000 Idea and Worth Every Cent of It," *MA* 52 (11 Aug. 1927), 29, 32; William H. McGrew, "Chicago Adopts the Super Service Station," *FS* 11 (11 Dec. 1927), 13–15; A. W. Roe, "Location—Equipment—Service," *MA* 54 (4 Oct. 1928), 28–30; William H. McGrew, "Modern Oil Company Has Three Types of Station Management," *FS* 12 (Dec. 1928), 34–36; Wallace Davis, "Get Business with Guns," *FS* 13 (Apr. 1929), 38–39; Leonard Muddimer, "Ohio Super Station Embodies Latest Development of Construction," *FS* 14 (July 1929), 24–26; N. M. Mainpa, "Even Colors Picked to Help Sales at Ohio Standard's New Stations," *NPN* 21 (5 June 1929), 94–96, 98; and Roger B. Stafford, "90 Day Battery Guarantees Gain Friends for One-Stop Station Operator," *NPN* 21 (18 Sep. 1929), 83–84, 87–88, 90–92.

The south-central states, especially Texas, appear to have been another important area for the super service station's development. Work may have occurred there as a result of local influences as much as, if not more than, in emulation of that in southern California. Super service stations frequently differed in their physical characteristics, the most obvious being a roof structure that covered the entire facility. The desirability of shade during much of the year was no doubt a key factor in such designs. For examples, see "This Station Seems to Prove That the Building Is Important," *FS* 7 (25 Jan. 1926), 43, 45, 47; and A. W. Roe, "Does This Use of Station Windows Have Double Value?" *FS* 8 (10 June 1926), 35, 37, 43. Similar configurations also became popular in regions where winters were severe; see Ward K. Halbert, "Super Service Stations under One Roof," *NPN* 19 (22 June 1927), 81–82, 84, 86; and "'Master' Station in Omaha Offers Wide Services," *NPN* 20 (26 Sep. 1928), 64. The Midwest may have provided other models as well; see A. H. Packer, "Community Service Stations," *MA* 44 (6 Sep. 1923), 23–24; "A Service Station of Tomorrow," *MA* 47 (26 Mar. 1925), 14–15; and Ward K. Halbert and William H. McGrew, "Chicago Adopts the Super Service Station," *FS* 11 (11 Dec. 1927), 13–15.

34
E. L. Barringer, "One-Stop Manager Needs Sales Ability, Technical Knowledge of Work," *NPN* 22 (28 May 1930), 34, 36–37.

35
C. Edward Packer, "There's Money in the Automobile Laundry Business," *MA* 50 (16 Sep. 1926), 12; "Here's Our History—Capsule Form," *ALN* 7 (Oct. 1959), 19; "Cleaning Cars by Air and Water," *MA* 38 (12 Aug. 1920), 11, 28; "Washing Eight Hundred Cars a Day," *Popular Science Monthly* 96 (Apr. 1920), 35; "Auto Laundries for Gasoline Stations," *NPN* 19 (28 Dec. 1927), 25–27, 45. For illustrations of small auto laundries, see "If You Service Cars—," *MA* 38 (7 Oct. 1920), 15; "Cars Washed and Polished in Modern Auto Laundry," *PM* 26 (Oct. 1921), 558; and *FS* 14 (July 1929), 89.

36
"A Wash Bowl for Automobiles," *MA* 41 (8 June 1922), 30; "Cleaning Auto Running Gear in a Wash Bowl," *PM* 38 (Aug. 1922), 178–179; "Big Wash Bowl Shakes Mud from Cars," *Popular Science Monthly* 101 (Oct. 1922), 67; "Washing Cars in a 'Wash Bowl'," *MA* 48 (3 Sep. 1925), 14. Chicago was also the location of an enclosed facility, erected in 1921, which had an elaborate facade but unsophisticated equipment; see "Automobile Laundry for Washing and Polishing Cars While You Wait," *MA* 41 (23 Mar. 1922), 13.

37
HDC, 21 July 1923, 8; W. E. Green, "This Car Washing Establishment Turns Them Out Quickly," *FS* 2 (10 Sep. 1923), 21, 23.

38
"New Auto Wash Bowl," *HDC,* 14 Nov. 1924, 2; "Hundreds Will Attend . . . ," *HDC,* 27 Feb. 1925, 11; "Pacific Auto Laundries . . . ," *HDC,* 1 Sep. 1927, Pacific Auto Laundry Sect.; "Ultimate Service Found . . . ," *LAT,* 6 Nov. 1927, VI-1; Brad Mills, "The Super Auto Laundry Has Hit the West Coast," *FS* 10 (10 Nov. 1927), 17–18; "Auto Laundries for Gasoline Stations," 25; "New Holly Auto Laundry . . . ," *HDC,* 29 July 1928, 16; "Plant Will Care . . . ," *LAT,* 28 Sep. 1930, VI–3; *LAT,* 24 Oct. 1930, I-11; "Who Remembers the 1925 Bean-Elder System for Laundering Automobiles?" *ALN* 6 (Dec. 1978), 6–7, 10, 30. By 1925 Chicago had a facility rivaling the most ambitious ones in southern California; see "Auto Laundry Cleans Car Every Minute," *PM* 43 (Jan. 1925), 7–9; "Cars Are Washed in 12 Minutes," *MA* 47 (11 June 1925), 12–13; and "Here's Speed in Car Washing," *MA* 50 (17 Feb. 1927), 15.

39

"New Automobile Cleaning Firm," *HDC,* 15 June 1927, 17; "El Patio Laundry Success," *HDC,* 17 Aug. 1927, 11; Ward K. Halbert, "Department Stores for Auto Servicing Planned for 200 Cities," *NPN* 20 (3 Oct. 1928), 17.

40

"Tell It to Sweeney," *MA* 52 (8 Sep. 1927), 42; "Car Wash Plant Opens in Pasadena," *LAT,* 2 Oct. 1927, VI-3; Halbert, "Department Stores," 17–19; Gerald F. Champ, "The Latest in Auto Laundries," *San Diego Magazine* 4 (Apr. 1928), 19; "New Type of Auto Plant . . . ," *Long Beach Press-Telegraph,* 17 June 1928, C-4, C-5; Joseph C. Coyle, "Automobile Laundry as a Retail Outlet for Petroleum," *FS* 12 (Dec. 1928), 68, 70; Ward K. Halbert, "Sinclair Goes In for Car Washing with Two Gillespie Units," *NPN* 21 (20 Feb. 1929), 31–32; "Speed without Sacrificing Thoroughness . . . ," *NPN* 21 (20 Mar. 1929), 118–119, 122, 124–125; "Sinclair Takes Another Step in One-Stop Service," *FS* 13 (May 1929), 15–16, 38.

41

See, for example, "Auto Laundry Cleans Car Every Minute," 7–9; "Car Laundering Brings Service to This Plant," *MA* 50 (23 Sep. 1926), 12–13, 31; "Tell It to Sweeney," 32–33, 42; Mandus E. Bridston, "The Profits Come Out in the Wash," *MA* 53 (2 Aug. 1928), 20–21, 36; R. W. Davis, "Latest Car Washing Methods Adopted in the Southwest," *FS* 14 (Aug. 1929), 30–35; Roger B. Stafford, "Straight Line Moving Platform for Car Laundering," *NPN* 21 (7 Aug. 1929), 92–94.

42

"New Features Found in Car Wash Plant," *LAT,* 6 Nov. 1927, VI-2; Richard Longstreth, "The Forgotten Arterial Landscape: Photographic Documentation of Commercial Development along Los Angeles Boulevards during the Interwar Years," *Journal of Urban History* 23 (May 1997), 445–449.

43

Champ, "Latest in Auto Laundries," 19.

44

"Muller Bros. . . . ," *HDC,* 28 Mar. 1928, 11; "Muller Brothers, Oldest Car Wash . . . ," *ALN* 7 (Apr. 1959), 6–7, 26–27, 29–30.

45

See, for example, "New Service Station Opens," *HDC,* 24 Feb. 1923, 13; "Colonial Auto Service . . . ," *HDC,* 29 Aug. 1923, 10; "Lubrication Expert . . . ," *HDC,* 5 Sep. 1923, 10; "Becker-Duemer Co. . . . ," *HDC,* 8 Aug. 1924, 5; "Rival Towns . . . ," *HDC,* 12 May 1926, 16; "They Hustle . . . ," *HDC,* 19 May 1926, 16; "They Thought . . . ," *HDC,* 26 May 1926, 16; "Another Hustler . . . ," *HDC,* 2 June 1926, 14; "Keith Lloyd's Speed . . . ," *HDC,* 9 June 1926, 12; "Guasti-Giulli, Inc. . . . ," *HDC,* 23 Feb. 1927, 18; "Paul W. Cowan . . . ," *HDC,* 1 Mar. 1928, 11; and "'Hight's Tower' . . . ," *HDC,* 17 Oct. 1928, 13.

46

For examples, see "Novel Building Attracts Considerable Attention on West Coast," *ALN* 5 (Jan. 1957), 8–9, 27; "Happy Employees Are Good Employees!" *ALN* 5 (Feb. 1957), 6–7, 19, 27; "An Ultra Modern California Style Auto Laundry in the $150,000 Class . . . ," *ALN* 5 (June 1957), 6–9; "You Can't Stand

Still—You Have to Keep Going Forward," *ALN* 6 (Jan. 1958), 6–7, 12, 14;
"'Sopp's Little Acre,'" *ALN* 6 (1 July 1958), 6–7, 11–14, 20, 27; and "Pasadena
Auto Wash . . . ," *LAT,* 12 July 1959, VI-20.

47

HDC, 10 June 1921, I-2; "El Camino Station . . . ," *HDC,* 10 June 1921, I-7;
"New El Camino Station," *HDC,* 1 July 1921, I-1, 12; "Something New in Line."
Early examples could be found elsewhere as well; see L. P. Bott, Jr., "Playing the
Telephone Number in Advertising," *FS* 2 (Apr. 1923), 23, 25, 27; and "Complete
Service under One Roof," *MA* 47 (25 June 1925), 11.

48

William H. McGrew, "The Tire Men Look Over the Super-Service Station," *FS*
13 (Feb. 1929), 322–34; C. H. Williams, "Successful One-Stop Management
Analyzed," *FS* 18 (Oct. 1931), 19–23.

49

For early examples, see "Super Station Embodies Unique Architectural Design," *FS*
14 (July 1929), 44; B. V. Ellzey, "Where Do We Go from Here?" *FS* 14 (Nov.
1929), 26–27; "Oil Companies May Aid Tire Dealers in Building Super Stations,"
NPN 21 (1 May 1929), 40a–40b; Roger B. Stafford, "Linking Beauty with Quick
Service," *NPN* 21 (14 Aug. 1929), 96, 98–99; M. S. Sullivan, "How Firestone
Sells 600,000 Gallons a Year at Two Stations," *NPN* 22 (4 June 1930), 107–108;
"Multiple Service Auto Station in Detroit," *AR* 70 (Dec. 1931), 455–457.

50

Jakle and Sculle, *Gasoline Station,* 38–43, 50–60.

51

Gary Triplett, "Two Ways to Super Station," *FS* 12 (Mar. 1929), 43–44; Green,
"Super Service Stations Thrive," 97, 101. During the early 1920s, the organ of automobile dealers editorialized that the filling station was not conducive to selling accessories or service; see "The Gas Station as a Business Booster," *MA* 39 (21 Apr.
1921), 17.

52

Liebs, *Main Street,* 102–105; Gary Triplett, "Tires Are Here," *FS* 16 (Sep. 1930),
27–28; E. L. Barringer, "One-Stop Service," *NPN* 22 (17 Dec. 1930), 35–36, (24
Dec. 1930), 59–60, 62, (31 Dec. 1930), 62, 64, 67, 23 (7 Jan. 1931), 91, 93–94.

53

For early examples, see "Union Employs Super-Service Type for Key Stations," *FS*
22 (Aug. 1933), 14–22; "Display Holds First Place in New Outlets of Associated
Oil Company," *FS* 23 (May 1934), 18–21; C. Henri Rush, "In the Shell Design
the Modern Holds Hands with the Useful," *FS* 24 (Aug. 1934), 10–14; E. L. Bar-
ringer, "Better Materials and Fittings Available at Moderate Cost . . . ," *NPN* 24 (4
May 1932), 47, 49–52; "Mid-Continent Builds Ultra-Modern Station," *NPN* (12
Aug. 1931), 65; and "Planning Techniques for . . . Service Stations," *Architectural
Forum* 66 (Feb. 1937), 86–92.

54

Precisely the opposite trend was occurring in many other parts of the retail field, as
discussed in later chapters.

1

Corine Orff, "'Ye Market Place' Is Unique . . . ," *GNP,* 20 June 1923, 2. Subsequent accounts include "'Ye Market' to Solve . . . ," *GNP,* 20 June 1924, 4; "'Ye Market Place' . . . ," *GNP,* 2 Aug. 1924; "Ye Market Place . . . ," *GNP,* 23 Oct. 1924; "First Shopping Unit . . . ," *GNP,* 24 Oct. 1924, 1; and "'Ye Market' to Have . . . ," *GNP,* 24 Oct. 1924, 13. I am grateful to Barbara Boyd of the Glendale Public Library for tracking down the market's opening date and finding several of the above references for me.

2

"Business Center Develops . . . ," *GNP,* 1 Jan. 1923, II-1; H. Thomas Rich, "Realty Values Increase . . . ," *GNP,* 27 Apr. 1923, South Glendale Sect., 1, 4; "1923 Banner Year . . . ," *GNP,* 31 Dec. 1923, 13. Traffic flow along Los Feliz Boulevard increased very substantially between counts taken in 1922 and 1924; see Frederick Law Olmsted, Harland Bartholomew, and Charles Henry Cheney, *A Major Traffic Street Plan for Los Angeles* (Los Angeles: Committee on Los Angeles Plan of Major Highways of the Traffic Commission of the City and County of Los Angeles, 1924), 22–23.

　　The area failed to develop as a major business center, perhaps in part because it was too close to downtown Glendale to avoid redundancy of function, and also because tracts just to the west, lying along the principal north-south line of the Union Pacific Railroad, were primarily attractive for industrial and related functions. Long-distance traffic on the San Fernando Road soon diminished with the widening of the Cahuenga Pass in 1926.

3

"'Ye Market' Now Open to Public," *GNP,* 27 Oct. 1924.

4

Morgan wrote the most extensively on the drive-in market at that time: "California Drive-In Markets Serve Motorists on the Go," *CSR* 1 (Sep. 1928), 29–31; "'Drive Ins' Drive On while Stores Sleep," *CSR* 2 (May 1929), 15–16, 30–32; "At Last—A Place to Park!" *American Builder* 47 (July 1929), 58–61; "Stores the Road Passes Through," *Nation's Business* 17 (July 1929), 45–46; and "The Super Drive-In Emerges from Competitive Whirl," *CSR* 3 (Oct. 1930), 10–12, 40. See also "Drive-In Markets Popular in West," *PG* 7 (June 1928), 22–23; Walter Van de Kamp, "An Innovation in Retail Selling," *Magazine of Business* 56 (July 1929), 42–43; Arthur E. Goodwin, *Markets: Public and Private* (Seattle: Montgomery Publishing Co., 1929), 70–74; Marc N. Goodnow, "Drive In and Shop," *Forbes* 25 (1 Feb. 1930), 15–17; S. Lewis Brevit, "Drive-In 'Department Stores' Gaining Popularity in West," *Sales Management* 25 (17 Jan. 1931), 118; Crag Dale, "Is Main Street Doomed?" *PM* 55 (May 1931), 765–768; Albert Frey, "Amerikanische Notizen," *Werk* 20 (Oct. 1933), 314; and Clarence S. Stein and Catherine Bauer, "Store Buildings and Neighborhood Shopping Centers," *AR* 75 (Feb. 1934), 185–186. Recent accounts include Richard Longstreth, "The Perils of a Parkless Town," in Martin Wachs and Margaret Crawford, eds., *The Car and the City: The Automobile, the Built Environment, and Daily Urban Life* (Ann Arbor: University of Michigan Press, 1992), 141–153, 310–313; and idem, "Innovation without Paradigm: The Many Creators of the Drive-In Market," in Thomas Carter, ed., *Images of an American Land: Vernacular Architecture Studies in the Western United States* (Albuquerque: University of New Mexico Press, 1997), 231–264.

Morgan believed that a market built in 1925 by Alexander Haddad was the first drive-in, and no other accounts of the period suggest otherwise. My own examination of directories, Sanborn fire insurance maps, newspapers, contract notices, and trade literature has uncovered nothing remotely akin to Ye Market Place to have been conceived, designed, or erected at an earlier date; indeed, it is the only example I have documented to predate Haddad's. Nevertheless, the evidence that Ye Market Place was the first remains circumstantial and almost impossible to verify completely.

5

For discussion, see chapter I.

6

Besides Haddad's Beverl'y Open Air Market (1925) (illustrated in Longstreth, "Innovation", 249), early examples include Los Feliz Drive-In Market (1925–1926) at 3070–3074 Los Feliz Boulevard; Citizens' Community Market (1925) at S. Vermont Avenue and 30th Place (*HDC,* 6 Sep. 1925, II-3); Los Angeles Motor-In Market (1926) at 2301–2315 Beverly Boulevard (*LAT,* 3 Oct. 1926, V-6); Mother Goose Market (1926) at 1949–1989 Colorado Boulevard, Pasadena (see chapter IV); Mission Market (1927–1927) at 1425–1437 Sunset Boulevard (*LAT,* 26 Oct. 1926, V-5; Longstreth, "Innovation," 254); Latchstring Rancho Drive-In Market (1926–1927) at 6311–6329 San Fernando Road, Glendale (see chapter IV); and Hattem's Market (1927) at 4267–4277 S. Western Avenue ("Great Crowds Greet Market . . . ," *SWW,* 23 Dec. 1927; "Market to Open . . . ," *SWW,* 9 Dec. 1927; "Hattem's Market Holds Opening . . . ," *SWW,* 16 Dec. 1927; Maurice I. Hattem, "I. M. Hattem and His Los Angeles Supermarket," *Western States Jewish Historical Quarterly* 11 [Apr. 1979], 243–246). All of these have been destroyed or altered almost beyond recognition save the Mission Market, whose fabric remains remarkably intact.

7

Basic data on the drive-in market presented in this chapter was compiled from contracts and other notices in *SWBC,* telephone directories, Sanborn fire insurance maps, site visits and coverage in area newspapers, including *Alhambra Post Advocate, BHC, GNP, HDC, Huntington Park Signal, Inglewood Daily News, LAT, Long Beach Press-Telegraph, PSN, Santa Ana Register, SMEO, South Gate Tribune, SWW, Van Nuys News,* and *Venice Evening Vanguard.*

8

For detailed discussion, see Longstreth, "Innovation," 239–243. For a sampling of accounts profiling owners, see "E. F. Bogardus Opens . . . ," *HDC,* 28 Sep. 1928, 17; "Structure Is Dream . . . ," *BHC,* 10 Jan. 1929; "Sponsor Is Man of Achievement . . . ," *HDC,* 23 Mar. 1929, 16; "Clock Market to Open . . . ," *BHC,* 9 May 1929, 8; "Tower Market to Open . . . ," *BHC,* 30 May 1929, 5; "Modern Market Building . . . ," *Van Nuys News,* 1 June 1929, 1, 3; "Friday and Saturday . . . ," *HDC,* 4 Oct. 1929, 13; "Drive-In Market . . . ," *PSN,* 28 Mar. 1930, 25; and "Woestman's Drive-In . . . ," *PSN,* 11 July 1930, 25.

9

Morgan, "California Drive-In Markets," 29; Stanley L. McMichael, "The Influence of the Automobile on Real Estate," *Annals of Real Estate Practice* (Chicago: National Association of Real Estate Boards, 1928), 212; Van de Kamp, "Innovation," 42; Brevit, "Drive-In," 118; interview with Ben Schwartz, Commerce, California, 13

Nov. 1989. Schwartz began his career in food retailing at a drive-in department operated by his father in the early 1930s.

10

Quoted in Morgan, "California Drive-In Markets," 30, 31.

11

J. Gordon Wright, "Passing of the California Drive-In Market," *SMM* 3 (Aug. 1938), 14.

12

Van de Kamp, "Innovation," 42; Brevit, "Drive-In," 118; McMichael, "Influence of Automobile," 212; Morgan, "'Drive-Ins' Drive On," 16.

13

Morgan, "California Drive-In Markets," 29–30; idem, "'Drive-Ins' Drive On," 31; idem, "Super Drive-In," 40; Schwartz interview. Schwartz recalled that developing a full spirit of cooperation among concessionaires was one of the most difficult tasks at a drive-in market and was not fully achieved in a number of instances.

14

Theodore W. Braun, "The Independent Retailer Adopts Chain Methods," *Southern California Business* 9 (Feb. 1930), 16–17, 32. For discussion of chain store expansion during the period, see Richard Longstreth, *City Center to Regional Mall: Architecture, the Automobile, and Retailing in Los Angeles, 1920–1950* (Cambridge: MIT Press, 1997), 71–74.

The extent to which independent grocers were concerned with reform is reflected in the contents of *PG,* one of the major journals of their trade. Store appearance, including layout and displays, was the subject of interest to the point that the magazine undertook the design of a model store, discussed in a series of articles by the editor, Carl W. Dipman: "Better Grocery Stores . . . ," 6 (Nov. 1927), 10–15, 59, 62, 66, 68; ". . . What Is a Good Store?" 6 (Dec. 1927), 20–23, 76, 81–82, 86, 88; "Building a Grocery Store Step by Step," 7 (Jan. 1928), 10–17, 70, 72; "The Finishing Touches of a Modern Grocery Store," 7 (Feb. 1928), 10–19, 68, 72, 74; "Hundreds of Grocers Have Increased Sales by Rearranging Their Stores," 7 (June 1928), 10–16, 108; and "You May Think You Have a Good Store . . . ," 8 (Jan. 1929), 20–23, 78, 80, 84. See also "And Now Grocery Stores Go Modern," *Printer's Ink Monthly* 20 (Apr. 1930), 36–37; and W. P. Hamilton, "Good Looks Made Good Stores," *CSA* 6 (June 1930), 65–66. This extensive campaign may well have influenced details of the internal arrangements of drive-in markets.

15

Godfrey M. Lebhar, *Chain Stores in America* (New York: Chain Store Publishing Corp., 1952), 76–77. The personal relationship that often existed between neighborhood merchants and their clientele was a constantly reoccurring theme in publications oriented toward the independent food trades during the second half of the 1920s, including the Los Angeles–based *Grocer's Journal;* see, for example, Ralph Borsodi, "Independent Merchant's Place Not Filled by Mass Distribution," 1 July 1927, 7, 17; Ralph L. K. Martin, "My Neighborhood Store," 21 Oct. 1927, 11; and Harry W. Walker, "The Neighborhood Grocer," 6 Jan. 1928, 8.

16

Morgan, "At Last," 60; idem, "Stores the Road," 45; Van de Kamp, "Innovation," 42. The ninety-three out of one hundred failure rate claimed by Van de Kamp for independent food store operators has not been verified and may be an exaggeration.

17

For a sampling of accounts of concessionaires, see "The Vineyard . . . ," *HDC/ HES,* 17 June 1927, 1; "New Drive-In Market . . . ," *SMEO,* 30 Aug. 1927, 3; "New Drive-In Market . . . ," *SMEO,* 29 Jan. 1928, II-1; "Yale Drive-In Market . . . ," *GNP,* 13 Apr. 1928, 12–13; "Gala Opening Planned . . . ," *BHC,* 14 June 1928, 17; "New Mission Drive-In Market . . . ," *SMEO,* 3 Oct. 1928, II-1; "Elaborate Radio Programs . . . ," *GNP,* 12 Oct. 1928, 12–13; "Tower Drive-In Market . . . ," *GNP,* 26 Oct. 1928, 10–11; "Grand Opening . . . ," *GNP,* 2 Nov. 1928, 12–13; "New Market to Open . . . ," *South Gate Tribune,* 1 Jan. 1929, 1; "Sunset Hills Market . . . ," *BHC,* 19 Jan. 1929, 22–24; "Yale Drive-In Market . . . ," *SMEO,* 11 Jan. 1929, 2; "Mandarin Market . . . ," *HDC,* 23 Mar. 1929, 20; "Palm Market Is Largest . . . ," *BHC,* 18 Apr. 1929, 20A; "Clock Market to Open," *BHC,* 9 May 1929, 8; "Tower Market to Open . . . ," *BHC,* 30 May 1929, 5, 12; "Formal Opening . . . ," *Van Nuys News,* 27 Aug. 1929, 8; "New Drive-In Market . . . ," *Santa Ana Register,* 6 Dec. 1929, 22; "Drive-In Market . . . ," *PSN,* 28 Mar. 1930, 10; "Latest Type of Market . . . ," *Santa Ana Register,* 18 July 1930, 11; "Aurora Drive-In Market . . . ," *GNP,* 18 July 1930, 5; "City's Latest Drive-In . . . ," *Inglewood Daily News,* 15 Aug. 1930, 2; "Modern Marketplace . . . ," *HDC,* 19 Dec. 19230, 8; and "Thousands Acclaim . . . ," *Alhambra Post-Advocate,* 15 Sep. 1911, 2.

18

Morgan, "California Drive-In Markets," 30; idem, " 'Drive-Ins' Drive On," 15; idem, "At Last," 61; Brevit, "Drive-In," 118.

19

Chester H. Liebs, *Main Street to Miracle Mile: American Roadside Architecture* (Boston: New York Graphic Society, 1985), 39–44; Longstreth, *City Center to Regional Mall,* 58–71; idem, "The Forgotten Arterial Landscape: Photographic Documentation of Commercial Development along Los Angeles Boulevards during the Interwar Years," *Journal of Urban History* 23 (May 1997), 442–445.

20

After business hours, the front of grocery stores or markets was secured generally with folding metal doors. Accordion gates were used instead in some cases, predominantly in towns, where security needs were less. The same hardware was used for drive-in markets.

21

R. E. Skillern, "Front Door Parking Space Stimulates Trade of Neighborhood Stores," *CHM* 11 (June 1927), 141; E. A. Wood, "Space for Head-In Parking Relieves Congestion and Facilitates Suburban Street Widening," *AC* 40 (Feb. 1929), 127. Extensive fieldwork in these regions indicates the practice was widespread, sometimes into the post–World War II years.

22

Morgan, " 'Drive-Ins' Drive On," 16.

23

Morgan, "At Last," 60.

24

Morgan, "'Drive-Ins' Drive On," 30.

25

Richard Longstreth, *The Buildings of Main Street: A Guide to American Commercial Architecture* (Washington: Preservation Press, 1987), 54–63.

26

Morgan, "'Drive-Ins' Drive On," 16.

27

These averages were derived from Sanborn fire insurance maps, which, even in updated form, document a large majority of the drive-in markets realized. Averages were somewhat lower for drive-ins in towns on the periphery of or outside the metropolitan area.

28

For discussion of the latter, see the articles by Carl W. Dipman cited in n. 14 above.

29

Morgan, "'Drive-Ins' Drive On," 30–31. Concerning Moderncraft, see Richard Longstreth, "Don't Get Out: The Automobile's Impact on Five Building Types in Los Angeles, 1921–1941," *Arris,* Journal of the Southeast Chapter of the Society of Architectural Historians, 6 (1997), 42, 48.

30

"Arcadia Drive-In Market," *San Gabriel Valley Digest,* Apr. 1930, 16; interview with Edward Schmidt, Whittier, California, 9 July 1987.

31

I have found only two other examples: in the Clearwater district (*Long Beach Press-Telegram,* 25 Aug. 1929, C-2) and in Santa Ana ("New Drive-In Market . . . ," *Santa Ana Register,* 21 Feb. 1930, 9).

32

For discussion, see Longstreth, "Innovation," 248–255.

33

Donald E. Marquis, "The Spanish Stores of Morgan, Walls & Clements," *Architectural Forum* 50 (June 1929), 902.

34

For information on how these facilities were secured after hours, see n. 20 above.

35

Morgan, "'Drive-Ins' Drive On," 30.

36

Concerning the Mandarin Market, see "Mandarin Market to Open . . . ," *HDC,* 4 Feb. 1929, 11; "Mandarin Market Opens . . . ," *HDC,* 19 Mar. 1929, 15; *HDC,* 23 Mar. 1929, Mandarin Market Sect.; and "Picturesque Charms of the Mandarin Market," *Saturday Night* 10 (8 Mar. 1930), 17. Concerning the Persian Market, see *LAT,* 16 June 1929, V-2. For good illustrations of Venice, see Jeffrey Stanton, *Venice of America: 'Coney Island of the Pacific'* (Los Angeles: Donohue Publishing, 1987).

37

For discussion, see Longstreth, "Innovation," 246.

38

The demand for such formed ornament seems to have made the cost of the form-work relatively low; see *Forms for Architectural Concrete* (Chicago: Portland Cement Association, 1936).

39

For illustration, see M. Roux-Spitz, *Exposition des Arts Décoratifs, Paris, 1925: Batiments et Jardins* (Paris: Albert Levy, [1928]), pls. 2–4, 7.

40

Morgan, "Super Drive-In," 12. For background on the complex, see "Tower Market to Open . . . ," *BHC,* 30 May 1929, 5, 12; *BHC,* 6 June 1929, 8–9; and "Announcement Made . . . ," *BHC,* 20 Oct. 1932, 13.

41

"Plaza and Business Center . . . ," *LAT,* 18 Nov. 1928, V-2. See also refs. cited in nns. 50, 61, and 62 below.

42

"Palm Market Is Largest . . . ," *BHC,* 18 Apr. 1929, 20-A; *BHC,* 25 Apr. 1929, 8–9. See also refs. cited in n. 52 below.

43

The designs predate September 1928 and July 1929, respectively, when they first appeared in print, but a precise chronology is lacking. Another Neutra drive-in project is discussed in chapter IV.

Morgan quoted Neutra and discussed his projects in "California Drive-In Markets," 29, 31; "At Last," 59–61; "Stores the Road," 45–46; and "Super Drive-In," 11–12. Neutra's interest in an automobile-related architecture is the subject of Thomas S. Hines, "Designing for the Motor Age: Richard Neutra and the Automobile," *Oppositions* 21 (Summer 1980), 35–51. See also idem, *Richard Neutra and the Search for Modern Architecture* (New York: Oxford University Press, 1982), 60–64.

Neutra and Morgan knew each other well, for the architect hired Morgan to photograph his early California work and used other Morgan images to illustrate his books of the period. The late Dione (Mrs. Richard) Neutra and her sister, the late Regula Fybel, confirmed the architect's close working relationship with Morgan during the period (interviews, Los Angeles, 25 June 1987, 28 June 1987). When Morgan left California for the East Coast, Neutra searched for another young architectural photographer and chose Julius Shulman, on whom he relied for the rest of his career.

44

"Modern Market Place . . . ," *HDC,* 19 Dec. 1930, 8; "Corrugated Galvanized Iron, Yucca-Vine Market, Hollywood, California," *American Architect* 90 (Mar. 1932), 22–23; David Gebhard and Harriette von Breton, *Lloyd Wright, Architect* (Santa Barbara: Art Galleries, University of California, Santa Barbara, 1971), 49–50, 53.

45

See, for example, the Nakoma Country Club, Madison, Wisconsin (1942); San-Marcos-in-the-Desert, near Chandler, Arizona (1927); San Marcos Water Gardens tourist cabins, Chandler (1927); and design for a village service station (1928), all illustrated in Henry-Russell Hitchcock, *In the Nature of Materials: The Buildings of Frank Lloyd Wright 1887–1941* (New York: Duell, Sloan and Pierce, 1942), pls. 267–268, 281–284, 287–288, 291–292. See also Anthony Alofsin, *Frank Lloyd Wright: The Lost Years, 1910–1922* (Chicago: University of Chicago Press, 1993), chap. 9; and David G. De Long et al., *Frank Lloyd Wright: Designs for an American Landscape 1922–1932* (New York: Henry N. Abrams, 1996), 100–120.

Significantly, however, the Yucca-Vine Market's geometry appears to have been developed in direct response to the irregular, constricted site.

46

"Train-Shed Type Market Developed," *LAT,* 15 Feb. 1931, V-2; Gebhard and von Breton, *Lloyd Wright,* 54–57. In the latter account, the project is incorrectly identified as possibly having been for a site in Arcadia.

47

See, for example, *L'Architecture Vivante,* Autumn 1925, 6, 24, and Autumn 1929, 12; *Moderne Bauformen* 27 (May 1928), 169–171, and 29 (Mar. 1930), 144; K. Weidle, "Lichtreklame," *Baumeister* 26 (Dec. 1928), B252–B258; Dr. Fier, "Über Architektur und Schrift zu den Berliner Geschäftshausfassaden der Brüder Luckhardt und Alfons Anker," *Baumeister* 27 (Nov. 1929), 349–358; *Moderne Ladenbauten Aussen- und Innenarchitektur* (Berlin: Ernst Pollak, [1929]); René Clarence, *Nouvelles boutiques . . .* (Paris: Albert Levy, [ca. 1929]); Adolf Schumacher, *Ladenbau . . .* (Stuttgart: Julius Hoffmann, 1934); Louis Parnes, *Bauten des Einzelhandels. . . .* (Zurich and Leipzig: Orell Fussli, [ca. 1935]); René Herbst, *Boutiques et Magazins* (Paris: Charles Moreau, n.d.); and Arthur Korn, *Glas im Bau und als Gebrauchsgegenstand* (Berlin: Ernst Pollak, n.d.), 135–159.

48

See, for example, Herbst, *Boutiques,* pl. 46; *Baumeister* 24 (Oct. 1926), 220; "La Loi Loucheur," *L'Architecte* n.s. 6 (Feb. 1929), 9–14; *L'Architecture Vivante* Summer 1929, 28–29; "Die Neugestaltung des Paradeplatzes und anderer Verkehrsplätze in Zürich," *Baumeister* 27 (June 1929), 181–201; and "Ein Bauten in den Strassenraum," *Baumeister* 29 (May 1931), 181–187.

49

Although Neutra did not see any projects for tall buildings realized until well after World War II and is most remembered as an architect of houses, the skyscraper was of great interest to him from the outset of his career in the United States, as is made clear in his own writings, such as *Wie Baut Amerika?* (Stuttgart: Julius Hoddmann, 1927) and *Amerika: Die Stilbildung des Neuen Bauens in den Vereinigten Staaten* (Vienna: Anton Schroll, 1930), and in Hines, *Neutra.*

50

For a general discussion of the subject, see Reyner Banham, *A Concrete Atlantis: U.S. Industrial Building and European Modern Architecture 1900–1925* (Cambridge: MIT Press, 1986); however, for unexplained reasons the text fails to mention Neutra.

51

Frey, "Amerikanische Notizen," 312–316; interview with Albert Frey, Palm Springs, California, 27 June 1987.

52

Coverage in trade magazines with national circulation included V. Cahalin, "Spanish Type Houses Pay," *Building Age* 51 (May 1929), 37; Morgan, "'Drive-Ins' Drive On," 15, 16, 30, 31; "Store Buildings," *AR* 65 (June 1929), 603; Morgan, "At Last," 60–61; idem, "Super Drive-In," 11; Frey, "Amerikanische Notizen," 314; and Stein and Bauer, "Store Buildings," 186.

53

The first of the two Neutra schemes discussed may well have been a source for the River Oaks Shopping Center in Houston; see chapter IV.

54

Alan Hess, *Googie: Fifties Coffee Shop Architecture* (San Francisco: Chronicle Books, 1985), 8, 21–22.

55

For discussion, see Longstreth, "Innovation," 246.

56

See, for example, "Roadside Markets the Modern Solution of the Marketing Problem," *CHM* 6 (Aug. 1922), 180–181.

57

See Longstreth, *City Center to Regional Mall,* 73. For a detailed discussion of the locational methods of Safeway Stores, one of the largest grocery chains in the metropolitan area by the late 1920s, see H. S. Wright, "Locating Grocery Stores," *CSA* 1 (Aug. 1925), 10–11.

58

Olmsted, Bartholomew, and Cheney, *Major Traffic Street Plan.* See also *Report and Recommendations on a Comprehensive Rapid Transit Plan for the City and County of Los Angeles* (Chicago: Kelker, De Leuw & Co., 1925); *A Comprehensive Report on the Regional Plan of Highways, Section 2-E, San Gabriel Valley* (Los Angeles: Los Angeles County Regional Planning Commission, 1929); *A Comprehensive Report on the Regional Plan of Highways, Section 4, Long Beach—Redondo Area* (Los Angeles: Los Angeles County Regional Planning Commission, 1931); and *Report of a Highway Traffic Survey in the County of Los Angeles* (Los Angeles: Regional Planning Commission, County of Los Angeles, 1934).

59

The detailed survey of new residential building construction, conducted by the Los Angeles Railway Company, was printed in February or March issues of *Los Angeles Realtor* during the 1920s. Three of the remarkable maps made for these surveys are reproduced in Scott L. Bottles, *Los Angeles and the Automobile: The Making of the Modern City* (Berkeley: University of California Press, 1987), 188–190.

60

A very rare exception was a block-long complex of buildings proposed in 1929 at Western and Florence avenues in the Southwest district. Little, if any, of the plan was realized, however. See *LAT,* 21 Apr. 1929, V-5.

61

Walter H. Leimert, "Leimert Park Subdivision . . . ," *CHM* 12 (Feb. 1928), 46–47; Cahalin, "Spanish Type," 37–40; "Residence Area . . . ," *LAT,* 16 Aug. 1931, V-2;

interview with Walter H. Leimert, Jr., Los Angeles, 14 July 1987. The significance of the endeavor is emphasized in Greg Hise, *Magnetic Los Angeles: Planning the Twentieth-Century City* (Baltimore: Johns Hopkins University Press, 1997), 14–22.

62

According to Walter H. Leimert, Jr. (interview), property in the business center was sold to a number of retail and investment interests that met with his father's approval. Precisely what criteria the latter used is unknown. Leimert established some design restrictions, but otherwise exercised no control over the development of the center once the initial agreement was made. Concerning individual projects there, see "Plans for Store . . . ," *LAT,* 23 Aug. 1931, V-3; "Erection of Playhouse . . . ," *LAT,* 3 Jan. 1932, V-2; "Beautiful Leimert Theater . . . ," *SWW,* 19 Apr. 1932, 1; "Two New Stores . . . ," *LAT,* 1 May 1932, V-3; *SWW,* 22 Nov. 1935, 17; *SWW,* 2 Nov. 1937, 5; *SWW,* 5 Nov. 1937, 24; *SWW,* 14 Jan. 1938, 10; "Store-Unit Building . . . ," *LAT,* 20 Nov. 1938, V-2; *SWW,* 25 Nov. 1938, 2; *SWW,* 6 Dec. 1938, 1; "Drug Store Unit . . . ," *LAT,* 27 Aug. 1939, V-4; and "Parking Planned . . . ," *LAT,* 15 Dec. 1940, V-3.

   The other major examples developed in the region before World War II were at Westwood and Palos Verdes Estates; see Longstreth, *City Center to Regional Mall,* chap. VI. Concerning the phenomenon generally, see idem, "The Diffusion of the Community Shopping Center Idea during the Interwar Decades," *JSAH* 56 (Sep. 1997), 268–293.

63

The Los Angeles Investment Company prominently featured the Mesa-Vernon Market to promote sales in its Viewpark Tract across Chenshaw Boulevard; see *LAT,* 17 Nov. 1928, I-3. For further discussion of the subject, see chapter IV.

III The Los Angeles Super

1

Craig Davidson, "What about Supermarkets?" *Saturday Evening Post* 211 (17 Sep. 1928), 23.

2

M. M. Zimmerman, *The Super Market Grows Up* (New York: Super Market Publishing Co., 1939), 3.

3

J. C. Furnas, "The Super Market Basket," *Forbes* 48 (15 Dec. 1941), 24. Besides the articles cited above, useful accounts of the supermarket written before World War II include M. M. Zimmerman, "Super-Markets," *Printer's Ink* 176 (9 July 1936), 7, 10, 90–92; (16 July 1936), 53, 56, 58–59, 62; (23 July 1936), 53, 57, 60, 62; (30 July 1936), 71–72, 74–76, 78; (6 Aug. 1936), 51–52, 56–57, 60; (13 Aug. 1936), 73, 76–77, 80–81; (20 Aug. 1936), 81–82, 84, 86–87; (27 Aug. 1936), 85–86, 88; (3 Sep. 1936), 69, 72–73, 76–78; (10 Sep. 1936), 73–74, 76–77, 80 (the early installments of which were reprinted in *SMM* 1 [Nov. 1936], 7, 27, 29, 30; [Dec. 1936], 8, 20–21; 2 [Jan. 1937], 9–10, 21; and [Feb. 1937], 7, 20–21); M. M. Zimmerman and F. R. Grant, "Warning: Here Comes the Super-Market!," *Nation's Business* 25 (Mar. 1937), 20–22, 96–99; and Emmanuel Rapaport, "The Economic Significance of the Super Market," *SMM* 3 (Feb. 1938), 84–85, 92. Zimmerman was the most knowledgeable and prolific writer on the subject; he also was among its most ardent champions, as the pages of *SMM,* which he edited, suggest.

Not all observers were so enthusiastic. Carl Dipman, editor of *PG,* an organ with primary allegiance to small-scale independent retailers, downplayed the phenomenon. See, for example, his "What Is the Super-Market's Real Place in the Grocery Business?," *PG* 16 (Aug. 1937), 24–26, 101–102, 104, 108, 110; and "Merchandising Trends in the Food Trade . . . ," *Journal of Marketing* 3 (Jan. 1939), 269–273.

Zimmerman further provided the most detailed retrospective account of the subject from a business perspective: *The Super Market: A Revolution in Distribution* (New York: McGraw Hill, 1955). See also Frank J. Charvat, *Supermarketing* (New York: Macmillan, 1961); and Rom J. Markin, *The Supermarket: An Analysis of Growth, Development, and Change,* rev. ed., Washington State University, Bureau of Economic and Business Research, Bulletin No. 43, Feb. 1968.

Two recent historical studies of the supermarket's physical development are Chester H. Liebs, *Main Street to Miracle Mile: American Roadside Architecture* (Boston: New York Graphic Society, 1985), 124–135; and James M. Mayo, *The American Grocery Store: The Business Evolution of an Architectural Space* (Westport, Conn.: Greenwood Press, 1993), chaps. 4 and 5.

4

Definitions of the period vary to a considerable degree, as do many offered in later years. For a sampling, see Zimmerman, "Super-Markets" (9 July 1936), 90; Zimmerman, *Super Market Grows Up,* 5; Dipman, "Merchandising Trends," 270; Zimmerman, *Super Market,* 18; and Markin, *Supermarket,* 4–5. The earliest use of the term "supermarket" I have found in print is in a notice published in *SWBC* 75 (18 Apr. 1930), 48. The term may have been employed on occasion some years earlier, as was suggested by Zimmerman, *Super Market,* 17–18. The pioneering Ralphs stores discussed below were called "store Building" or "mercantile Building" in contract notices published in *SWBC.* By the mid-1930s, "super-market" was part of common parlance, and most people in the trade were under the impression that the term was coined in southern California.

5

Period sources leave no doubt that work in southern California provided the key prototype, both in terms of design and operational structure and that this contribution was widely recognized within the trade. See, for example, A. E. Holden, "Is Price-Wrecking Wrecking the Supermarkets?," *CSA/GME* 9 (June 1933), 82; Donna Collister, "Inside Story, of a Supermarket," *PG* 13 (Aug. 1934), 40; Zimmerman and Grant, "Warning," 90–98; M. J. Rowoldt, "How Supers Operate in California," *PG* 16 (Oct. 1937), 30; Rapaport, "Economic Significance," 84–85; "Today's Super-Markets," *PG* 17 (July 1938), 23–25; "How Margins Vary in Different Food Markets," *PG* 17 (Nov. 1938), 34; and M. M. Zimmerman, "A Cross Country Impression," *SMM* 5 (Apr. 1940), 37, 40.

6

"Review of Business Conditions in 1931," *Eberle Economic Service* 9 (1 Jan. 1932), 5–6; "Building Activity in Los Angeles in 1933," *Eberle Economic Service* 11 (11 Jan. 1934), 115–116. Data on the drive-in markets is based on sources cited in chapter II, n. 7.

7

Figures published in *SWBC* suggest this to have been the case; however, they provide only a rough picture. Construction costs cited are estimates, and not all contracts appear to have been included.

8

Rapaport, "Economic Significance," 84–85; Charvat, *Supermarketing*, 37–40; Ruth Schwartz Cowan, *More Work for Mother: The Ironies of Household Technology from the Open Hearth to the Microwave* (New York: Basic Books, 1983), 128–139; Sigfried Giedion, *Mechanization Takes Command* (New York: Oxford University Press, 1948), 602–603.

9

Holden, "Price-Wrecking," 83; Zimmerman, "Super-Markets," 9 July 1936, 10. It is uncertain whether the figures cited in the latter article refer to units in the city or county of Los Angeles, or perhaps to even a larger geographic area. Furthermore, Zimmerman may well have included some of the larger drive-in markets in his estimates. Nevertheless, ample evidence from other sources can be found to indicate that numerous stores of the kind described in the text below existed in the region by that time.

10

A. E. Holden, "Super-Markets on Coast Set Modernization Pace," *CSA/GE* 11 (May 1935), 20.

11

Holden, "Super-Markets," 20, 58; Holden, "Price-Wrecking," 83; J. Gordon Wright, "Passing of the California Drive-In Market," *SMM* 3 (Aug. 1938), 14, 36–37; J. Gordon Wright, "Food and Functionalism," *California Arts and Architecture* 54 (Oct. 1938), 28; Ben O'Connor, "Super Markets: The Office of Stiles Clements, Architect," *AR* 90 (Oct. 1941), 72–73; Ben O'Connor, "Planning the Super-Market," *Architect & Engineer* 146 (Dec. 1941), 18.

12

Useful sources for background on the company include "Story of Ralphs Store Growth Is Like Fiction," *SMEO,* 20 Nov. 1929, 18; J. Gordon Wright, "Sharing Economies with Public, Ralphs' Policy," *SMM* 2 (Sep. 1937), 6, 8; "Early Years of Firm Recalled," *LAT,* 28 Apr. 1939, IV-3; Lucius S. Flint, "The Los Angeles Super," *CSA/GE* 26 (June 1950), J34; and an untitled, undated manuscript prepared by the company.

13

For examples of downtown food palaces elsewhere, see Claire Giles, "F. J. Kanper —and What He Is Doing for the Grocery Business," *PG* 2 (May 1923), 7–11, 64; John A. Donohue, "When the Bell-Weather Deserts the Flock," *CSA* 2 (Feb. 1926), 7–9, 38–40; Fred B. Barton, "Davidson's Idea of a Real Food Store," *CSA/GE* 5 (June 1929), 5–6, 31–32; and Ralph F. Linder, "Butter Built America's Greatest Grocery Store," *PG* 10 (Jan. 1931), 12–17, 64, 66, 70, 72.

14

Concerning Safeway, see Richard Longstreth, *City Center to Regional Mall: Architecture, the Automobile, and Retailing in Los Angeles, 1920–1950* (Cambridge: MIT Press, 1997), 73–74. The additional Ralphs stores were at 2604 Pasadena Avenue

(1910); 100 N. Western Avenue (1920); 201 W. Broadway, Glendale (1922); 926 W. Seventh Street (1923); 7257 Sunset Boulevard (1925); 5470 Crenshaw Boulevard (1925); and 3617 W. Washington Boulevard (1926).

15

I have found little published information on these stores. For exceptions, see "Ralphs Glendale Market . . . ," *GNP,* 6 Feb. 1922, 1; and "Pioneer Grocers Enter Hollywood," *HDC,* 19 May 1925, 3. Since all these buildings were later modified by the company to serve as modest-sized supermarkets, information on updated Sanborn fire insurance maps does not record the original selling area. Estimates cited in the text are rough approximations. The selling area shown in figure 81 below is probably typical.

16

These attributes were frequently stressed by the company in its publicity; see, for example, Dorothea Howard, "Ralphs Serve 51 Years . . . ," *HDC/HES,* 30 Apr. 1926, 1; and "Story of Ralphs Store."

17

"Grocery Firm to Build . . . ," *LAT,* 16 May 1926, V-11; "Ralphs to Open New Structure," *HDC,* 15 Nov. 1926, 6. See also Howard, "Ralphs Serve 51 Years."

18

Harriet Burdsal, "Ralphs Buildings and Methods Reflect Age," *HDC/HES,* 8 June 1928, 11; "Both Hollywood Stores . . . ," *HDC,* 5 June 1929, 9; "Ralphs Firm . . . ," *Alhambra Post-Advocate,* 11 Sep. 1929, Ralphs Grocery Sect., 1, 5; "Ralphs Adjusts Marketing System . . . ," *HDC/HES,* 2 Jan. 1930, 9.

19

The company did not disclose its annual earnings during the period. I am basing this rough estimate on the fact that while Ralphs nearly doubled the number of its stores (ten in 1927, nineteen in 1932), the size of the new units was considerably larger than that of the biggest ones of previous years.

Stores constructed in Ralphs's first supermarket campaign included: 2651 Florence Avenue, Huntington Park; 5615 Wilshire Boulevard (1928); 5711 Hollywood Boulevard; 510 W. Main Street, Alhambra; 171 N. Lake Street, Pasadena; 1142 Westwood Boulevard (1929); 2024 E. Tenth Street, Long Beach; 6121 W. Pico Boulevard (1931); and 7813 S. Vermont Avenue (1932). All but the Westwood unit have been demolished.

20

LAT, 29 Apr. 1928, V-1; and Harriet Burdsal, "Thousands Enjoy Opening . . . ," *HDC,* 21 Sep. 1928, 9. Concerning the Miracle Mile, see Longstreth, *City Center to Regional Mall,* 127–141.

21

Two exceptions were stores at Huntington Park (1928), a predominantly blue-collar community where ornateness may not have seemed necessary, and at Westwood Village (1929), where unity of the ensemble was the overriding concern. See "Ralphs Celebrate Opening . . . ," *HDC,* 13 Apr. 1928, 13; *LAT,* 14 July 1929, V-5; and "Ralphs Opening 16th Store . . . ," *SMEO,* 20 Nov. 1929, 14–18. Concerning the mode, now known as Spanish Colonial Revival, see David Gebhard, *George Washington Smith, 1876–1930: The Spanish Colonial Revival in California* (Santa Barbara: Art Galleries, University of California, Santa Barbara, 1964); idem,

"The Spanish Colonial Revival in Southern California (1895–1930)," *JSAH* 26 (May 1967), 131–147; idem, *Santa Barbara— The Creation of a New Spain in America* (Santa Barbara: University Art Museum, University of California, Santa Barbara, 1982); and Longstreth, *City Center to Regional Mall*, 108–109.

22

Why Collins was retained as architect of Ralphs stores after the Wilshire unit was built is unknown, but it may have stemmed from previous ties with the company. Collins was probably following client orders in basing many aspects of his later work for Ralphs on Clements's design.

23

Concerning the Pasadena store, see *LAT,* 28 Apr. 1928, V-8; and *PSN,* 2 Oct. 1929, 21–24.

24

Concerning the Hollywood store, see *LAT,* 20 Jan. 1928, V-8; "Ralphs Will Build . . . ," *HDC,* 18 Jan. 1928, 16; *LAT,* 20 Jan. 1928, V-8; and *HDC,* 5 June 1929, Ralphs Sect. Concerning the Alhambra store, see *LAT,* 28 Apr. 1928, V-8; and *Alhambra Post-Advocate,* 11 Sep. 1929, Ralphs Grocery Sect.

25

Concerning the W. Pico Boulevard store, see "Store and Warehouse . . . ," *LAT,* 17 May 1931, V-3; "Market Opening Celebrated . . . ," *HDC,* 17 Sep. 1931, 12; and *LAT,* 4 Oct. 1931, V-3. Concerning the S. Vermont Avenue store, see *SWW,* 13 Apr. 1932, Ralphs Special Ed.; and "Ralphs Celebrates Opening . . . ," *HDC,* 14 Apr. 1932, 17.

26

A brief description of the lamella system is provided in Carl W. Condit, *American Building Art: The Twentieth Century* (New York: Oxford University Press, 1961), 39–41. For a contemporary account, see "Lamella Roof Affords Floor Clear of Posts," *HDC,* 5 June 1929, 11. Locally, advertisements for the lamella system began to appear in *SWBC* in 1925 (see, for example, 66 [30 Oct.], 32), the year it was introduced to the United States. Building types for which the manufacturer, Trussless Arch Roof Company, identified its application included garages, warehouses, theaters, hangars, industrial buildings, churches, and armories. The system also was used for a number of drive-in markets.

27

Burdsal, "Thousands Enjoy Opening"; and idem, "Ralphs Buildings and Methods. . . ."

28

Burdsal, "Thousands Enjoy Opening"; "Ralphs Chain Is Just Starting Up," *SMEO,* 20 Nov. 1929, 17; "Story of Ralphs Store."

29

"Beautiful New Ralphs Store," *SWW,* 13 Apr. 1932, Ralphs Special Ed., 1.

I have found no indication of when Ralphs introduced wheeled grocery carts to its stores, but they were likely available by the early 1940s. The first commercially used cart was purportedly developed by an Oklahoma City retailer in 1937 and was first advertised in June of that year; see Terry P. Wilson, *The Cart That Changed the World: The Career of Sylvan N. Goldman* (Norman: University of Oklahoma Press, 1978), chap. 4. However, advertisements for a cart manufactured by the American Wire Form Company of Jersey City appear in early issues of *SMM,* beginning with 2 (Feb. 1937), 5.

30

Burdsal, "Ralphs Buildings"; Burdsal, "Thousands Enjoy Opening"; "Both Hollywood Stores . . . ,"; interview with Ben Schwartz, Commerce, California, 13 Nov. 1989.

31

The decentralization trend in movie palace building is discussed in Douglas Gomery, "The Picture Palace: Economic Sense or Hollywood Nonsense?," *Quarterly Review of Film Studies* 3 (Winter 1978), 23–36. That the film industry was influenced by retailers, especially chain store companies, in developing this strategy is argued by Gomery in "The Movies Become Big Business: Public Theatres and the Chain Store Strategy," *Cinema Journal* 18 (Spring 1979), 26–40.

32

Ruel McDaniel, "Fancy Grocery Appeal Speeds Texas Chain's Turnover," *CSR,* 2 (March 1929), 39–41; "Weingarten's Grocery . . . ," *HP,* 27 Sep. 1930, 4; Abe Weingarten, "Designing Stores for Maximum Display," *CSA/AE* 9 (June 1933), 41–43.

33

HP 30 Nov. 1923, 6–7; 7 Dec. 1926, 7–9; 12 Dec. 1931, Henke & Pillot Sect.; 1 Apr. 1938, Henke & Pillot Sect.; 1 Nov. 1940, Henke & Pillot Sect.; Charles N. Tunnell, "Henke & Pillot Supermarket Grew from Houston Public's Demand," *SMM* 2 (Feb. 1937), 3–5; "Employees Buy Henke & Pillot Supers for $1,500,000," *SMM* 5 (Aug. 1940), 10, 27; "Big Volume in 1922," *CSA/GE* 26 (June 1950), J50–J51.

34

"Watkin Plans New A-B-C Store . . . ," *HP,* 22 May 1927, Real Estate Sect., 2. I am grateful to Stephen Fox for bringing this and several other references to my attention.

35

In the absence of concrete documentation, this analogy must remain hypothetical. However, such courthouse squares were the principal sources of inspiration for the large parking area conceived by Dallas real estate developer Hugh Prather for his Highland Park Village shopping center begun in 1929; see Richard Longstreth, "The Diffusion of the Community Shopping Center Concept during the Interwar Decades," *JSAH* 56 (Sep. 1997), 276–279.

36

For illustration, see Weingarten, "Designing Stores," 43.

37

For an illustration of Young's downtown facility, see *LAT,* 17 May 1908, V-20. Concerning the Seventh Street buildings see "New Year Gets Send-Off," *LAT,* 6 Jan. 1924, II-1, 16; "Young's Food Emporium," *LATMN,* 1 Jan. 1925, I-36; *LAT,* 3 March 1924, II-6; "Market Building Is Notable Structure," *SWBC* 65 (6 Mar. 1925), 44; "De Luxing the Hotel Supply," *Pacific Coast Record* 16 (Apr. 1925),

25–26; Emil Held, "They Call It the World's Finest Grocery Store," *PG* 4 (Sep. 1925), 9–12, 44. Concerning other aspects of the operation, see "Fourteen Young's Markets . . . ," *HDC/HES,* 6 Nov. 1925, 1, 5; "Young's Standard of Service . . . ," *GNP,* 3 Oct. 1929, 4; and "Readers Taken on Trip . . . ," *HDC/HES,* 4 Apr. 1935, 14.

38

Just when the downtown store ceased to function as the parent facility is uncertain, but it may well have been as early as 1923, when the business office moved to the new store on West Seventh Street.

39

For discussion, see chapter I.

40

Concerning Westra, see "Expert Heads Food Project," *GNP,* 3 Oct. 1929, 4; and "Competitive System . . . ," *HDC/HES,* 9 Apr. 1931, 13. Concerning the Home-croft, see "Home Croft Market Opens . . . ," *SWW,* 18 Apr. 1930, 1, 3; and "Homecroft Mkt. Section," *SWW,* 6 Nov. 1931, 7. On Hattem, see "New Open Mart . . . ," *LAT,* 16 Mar. 1930, V-3; Maurice I. Hattem, "I. M. Hattem and His Los Angeles Supermarket," *Western States Jewish Historical Quarterly* 11 (Apr. 1979), 246–248.

41

Concerning the Great Southwest Market, see "Celebrates Fourth Anniversary," *SWW,* 24 June 1932, 1, 14. See also n. 60 below. Concerning the Metropolitan Market, see *SWBC* 74 (29 Sep. 1929), 77; and "Big Metropolitan Market . . ." *SWW,* 12 July 1935, 1. For other examples, see "Everything Is in Readiness . . . ," *PSN,* 23 Mar. 1928, 15; "Ocean Park's New Public Market . . . ," *SMEO,* 26 Apr. 1929, II-1; "Jess Willard's Food Dept. Store . . . ," *HDC,* 3 Oct. 1930, 9, 12; *LAT,* 3 May 1931, V-3; *LAT,* 28 June 1931, V-3; "Grand Central Market . . . ," *SWW,* 10 July 1931, 3; "New Southwest Market . . . ," *SWW,* 24 July 1931, 2; "Market Fiesta . . . ," *SWW,* 14 Aug. 1931, 2; "The Marketplace to Open Saturday," *BHC,* 12 Nov. 1931, 1, 4A; "Many Cars Pass . . . ," *LAT,* 6 Dec. 1931, V-2; "New Smith's Public Market . . . ," *SWW,* 11 Dec. 1931, 2; and "El Dorado Market . . . ," *BHC,* 19 May 1932, 16.

42

"Grand Central Market . . . ," *GNP,* 4 Oct. 1929, II-2.

43

Andrew Westra's Union Public markets in Glendale and Hollywood were an exception in this respect. Upon completion of the latter, he announced plans for two more, on Western Avenue and in Alhambra, neither of which seems to have been realized; see "Competitive System."

44

For examples from the late 1920s, see "New Highland Avenue Market Opens," *HDC/HES,* 4 Mar. 1927, 1; "Public Invited . . . ," *SMEO,* 1 July 1927, II-1; "Imagination Used . . . ," *HDC/HES,* 12 Aug. 1927, 1; "E. A. Morrison to Open . . . ," *HDC,* 22 Feb. 1929, 13; "Roberts Market Opens . . . ," *SMEO,* 7 Feb. 1930, 12; and "Pioneer Market Re-Opening . . . ," *SMEO,* 4 May 1930, II-2.

45

Contract notices in *SWBC* provide the key information about the number, size, and materials of these buildings.

46

Interview with Ben Schwartz. For a later example of the type, see R. G. Agee, "Van's Watch Local Needs in Policy Changes," *SMM* 6 (Apr. 1941), 24, 26–27.

47

For a sampling of accounts, see *HDC*, 23 Oct. 1930, 16; "Safeway Opens . . . ," *SWW*, 30 Oct. 1936, 5; "Safeway Stores Open . . . ," *SWW*, 22 Jan. 1937, 10; "New Safeway Store . . . , *SWW*, 13 Aug. 1937, 2; "New Safeway Store . . . ," *BHC*, 19 Nov. 1937, 14; "Safeway Store Opens . . . ," *SWW*, 22 Apr. 1938, 2; "New Safeway Store . . . ," *BHC*, 20 May 1938, 7; "New Safeway Store . . . ," *SWW*, 10 June 1938, 25; "Modern Safeway Store . . . ," *SWW*, 23 Dec. 1938, 2; "New Safeway Store . . . ," *SWW*, 31 Mar. 1939, 11; *SWW*, 7 Apr. 1939, 2; "Modern Safeway Store . . . ," *BHC*, 4 Aug. 1939, 28; "New Safeway Store . . . ," *BHC*, 4 Aug. 1939, 8; *Montebello Messenger*, 16 Nov. 1939, 5; "Leimert Park Will Welcome . . . ," *SWW*, 2 Feb. 1940, 17; "New Safeway Opens . . . ," *SWW*, 16 Feb. 1940, 16; "Safeway Opens . . . ," *SWW*, 26 Apr. 1940, 4; "What Public Relations Did," *Retail Executive* 31 (July 1940), 8; "New Safeway Unit . . . ," *Belvedere Citizen*, 31 Jan. 1941, 1; and "Robertson Blvd. Safeway . . . ," *BHC*, 27 Mar. 1942, 8. Additional information on square footage and parking facilities was gleaned from Sanborn fire insurance maps.

48

Schwartz interview; Zimmerman, "Cross Country," 37, 40. Zimmerman noted that A&P was the one major national chain food store to have entered the supermarket field in southern California (Safeway was still considered regional at that time), but that its impact there was relatively minor. A good sense of the company's shift to larger stores can be gleaned from accounts of the period: "A&P Stores Come . . . ," *HDC*, 1 May 1930, 15; "Atlantic & Pacific Lives Up . . . ," *HDC/HES*, 29 May 1930, 10; *HDC*, 18 July 1930, 13; "Three New Stores . . . ," *HDC/HES*, 30 Oct. 1930, II-13; *HDC*, 26 Feb. 1931, 15; "A. and P. Store . . . ," *BHC*, 14 Sep. 1933, 19; *HDC*, 13 Oct. 1933, 17; *HDC/HES*, 12 Apr. 1934, 1; "Two More A&P Stores . . . ," *HDC*, 4 June 1931, 15; *HDC/HES*, 19 Sep. 1935, 1; *LAT*, 20 Sep. 1935, I-7; *Tide* 9 (Oct. 1935), 27; "Building to House . . . ," *LAT*, 26 Jan. 1936, V-4; *SWW*, 25 Sep. 1936, S2; Allen G. Siple, "Supermarket for Atlantic & Pacific," *Architectural Concrete* 3 [1937], 6–8; "A&P Super Stores . . . ," *CSA/GE* 14 (Feb. 1938), 24–25; and "A and P Super Market . . . ," *SWW*, 21 Apr. 1939, 16.

49

Zimmerman, "Super-Markets," (9 July 1936), 10.

50

For some early examples, see "New Surv-All Food Market . . . ," *HDC*, 21 May 1931, 13; *LAT*, 9 July 1931, V-3; "Contract Let . . . ," *SWW*, 31 July 1931, 11; "Building Considered . . . ," *SWW*, 2 Oct. 1931, 1,2; "Green Spray Market . . . ," *HDC*, 17 Dec. 1931, 19; "Penny Market to Open . . . ," *BHC*, 9 June 1932, 12; "ABC Market . . . ," *HDC*, 30 June 1932, 16; "Family Market Opens . . . ," *BHC*, 5 June 1933, 4; "Berk Brothers Stage . . . ," *SWW*, 31 Mar. 1933, 13; *LAT*, 14 May 1933, I-19; "Program to Mark . . . ," *GNP*, 25 May 1933, 5; "Saving Center Market . . . ," *SWW,* 6 Oct. 1933, 1–8; *LAT,* 3 Dec. 1933, I-19; and "New Linden Food Store . . . ," *BHC,* 7 Dec. 1933, 6.

51

The large Sunfax Market in Hollywood (1934), for example, cost about $40,000; see *LAT,* 1 July 1934, I-15. See also Walter H. Leimert, "The Super Markets of Los Angeles," *Freehold* 4 (15 Mar. 1939), 200.

52

For an early example, see *LAT,* 14 May 1933, I-19; and Donna Collister, "Inside Story of a Supermarket," *PG* 13 (Aug. 1934), 40–41, 92, 94, 98.

53

For background on Davidson, see Esther McCoy, *The Second Generation* (Layton, Utah: Peregrine Smith Books), 1984, 2–35.

54

Leimert, "Super Markets," 60; "Today's Supermarkets," 23–25; and Zimmerman, "Cross Country," 37, 40–41, 53.

55

Luis Gibson, "What Type of Super-Market Will Survive?" *SMM* 3 (Sep. 1938), 26; Holden, "Super-Markets," 58; Leimert, "Super Markets," 200–201; O'Connor, "Super Markets," 73; Holden, "Price-Wrecking," 94.

56

Correlating market advertisements through the 1930s in the *East Side Journal, Belvedere Citizen,* and *Montebello Messenger* (collectively covering a major blue-collar part of the metropolitan area) with information on Sanborn fire insurance atlases indicates that few stores occupied more than 5,000 square feet and many were smaller. See also J. Gordon Wright, "Belvedere Gardens Offers Best in Low Income Section," *SMM* 3 (Sep. 1938), 14, 53, 55.

57

Collister, "Inside Story," 58; Schwartz interview. Schwartz recalled that produce departments often were leased by Japanese Americans, whose internment during World War II constituted the unfortunate circumstances that facilitated grocers' consolidating departmental ownership.

Useful accounts of the Los Angeles super's business structure include M. J. Rowoldt, "How Supers Operate in California," *PG* 16 (Oct. 1937), 29–30, 86, 90; idem, "How Supers Operate Meat Departments," *PG* 16 (Dec. 1937), 39–40, 56; idem, "Delicatessen Big Factor in Super-Market Success," *PG* 17 (Mar. 1938), 59–60, 90, 93.

58

Davidson, "What about Supermarkets?" 82–83; James Turnbull, "The Supermarket," *Appraiser Journal* 7 (Oct. 1939), 348.

59

Turnbull, "Supermarket," 352–353. Focusing on Los Angeles, this concise account is one of the most neutral and informative of its kind from the period. For a more optimistic portrayal, see M. J. Rowoldt, "Inside Figures of a Los Angeles Super," *PG* 16 (Jan. 1937), 43, 108, 111.

60

Concerning Allen & Huck, see "It's Ready! . . . ," *SWW,* 16 June 1933, 16; "Allen and Huck Acquire . . . ," *SWW,* 25 Jan. 1935, 1; "Observes Eighth Anniversary," *SWW,* 19 June 1936, S2; J. J. S., "Special Promotions Increase Sales . . . ," *SMM,* 2 (July 1937), 4–5; and "Allen and Huck Markets' . . . ," *SWW,* 14 June 1940, 21.

Fred L. Roberts, president of the Roberts Markets chain of moderate-sized stores, took over the Beverly Farms Market on Crenshaw Boulevard in 1934 ("Smashing News . . . ," *SWW,* 18 May 1934, 15). That same year, Don Caler, head of Caler's Food Centers, purchased a large drive-in market on N. Vine Street to augment his supermarket operation on N. La Brea Avenue (*HDC/HES,* 9 Aug. 1934, 1). In 1939, Jess Willard's Food Department Store, also in Hollywood, was reincarnated as the Radio Center Market (*HDC,* 13 Sep. 1939, 15).

61

Prior to this venture, Young's had significantly reduced the number of its existing outlets. Telephone directories list seventeen such establishments in the city of Los Angeles in 1926, and eight in 1932.

62

Concerning Seelig, see "Brea-Wilshire Mart . . . ," *HDC,* 10 Mar. 1932, 17; "Sam Seeling, Pioneer . . . ," *LAT,* 12 Mar. 1937, I-6, 7; "New 'Foodland' Market . . . ," *LAT,* 11 June 1937, I-6, 7; and J. Gordon Wright, "Attention to Details Spell Success for Seelig," *SMM* 3 (Jan. 1938), 30, 58. Concerning Von's, see *LAT,* 17 Aug. 1939, IV (whole sect.); and J. Gordon Wright, "75,000 Help Celebrate . . . ," *SMM* 4 (Nov. 1939), 12, 38–39, 59.

63

"New Surv-al Market . . . ," *HDC,* 16 May 1931, 11; "New Surv-All Food Market . . . ," *HDC,* 21 May 1931, 13; Charles Gormack, "Enter New Locality and Develop It . . . ," *SMM* 3 (May 1938), 6–7.

64

The new stores included ones at 240 E. San Fernando Road, Burbank (1935); Philadelphia and Comstock streets, Whittier; Third Street and Wilshire Boulevard, Santa Monica (1936); 9331 Wilshire Boulevard, Beverly Hills; 4841 Lankershim Boulevard (1937); 3003 W. Manchester Avenue (1939); 3635 Crenshaw Boulevard; 1416 E. Colorado Boulevard, Glendale (1940); 8575 W. Third Street; and 14049 Ventura Boulevard (1941). Accounts include "Ralphs Stages Food Show," *HDC,* 23 Oct. 1936, Souvenir Sect.; "New Ralphs Grocery . . . ," *BHC,* 11 June 1937, Souvenir Sect.; "Ralphs Purchase Market Site . . . ," *SWW,* 20 Sep. 1938, 2; *LAT,* 28 Apr. 1939, IV; "Massive Ralphs Store . . . ," *SWW,* 28 Apr. 1939, Ralphs Sect.; "New Store Thronged," *LAT,* 3 May 1939, II-2; J. Gordon Wright, "Ralphs Twentyseventh Unit Makes Debut," *SMM* 4 (June 1939), 10, 19; "Ralphs Acquires . . . ," *LAT,* 13 Aug. 1939, II-8; "Ralphs Finest Store . . . ," *SWW,* 26 Jan. 1940, 17; "Ralphs Opens . . . ," *LAT,* 18 Jan. 1940, I-14; "Ralphs Opens 28th Super Unit," *SMM* 5 (Mar. 1940), 14–15, 19; "Arrangement of New Store . . . ," *HDC,* 18 Apr. 1941, 12; "Market Building at Glendale . . . ," *SWBC* 97 (21 Mar. 1941), 25–26; *HDC,* 18 Apr. 1941, Special Sect.; "Newest, Largest Ralphs . . . ," *BHC,* 18 Apr. 1941, III-1; *HDC,* 24 Oct. 1941, Ralphs Special Sect. See also nn. 63 and 65.

One unit was added between the two building campaigns, in 1933, when Ralphs took over space in part of the Chapman Park Market, which is discussed in chapter IV. This appears to have been the only instance when the company leased space rather than purchased the property.

65

General accounts include Wright, "Food and Functionalism," 28, 36; O'Connor, "Super Markets"; and O'Connor, "Planning the Super-Market," 14–19.

66

"False Front . . . Taboo," *BHC,* 11 June 1937, Souvenir Sect., 2; Wright, "Sharing Economies," 8.

67

In addition to sources cited in nn. 64 and 65 above, see "Insulex Glass Block Panels . . . ," *SMM* 5 (May 1940), 28; "Sunlight Pours . . . ," *CSA/GE* 17 (Jan. 1941), 48; and "Let's Light the Middle of the Market," *SMM* 7 (Mar. 1942), 19.

68

Wright, "Sharing Economies," 8; "Study Features . . . ," *BHC,* 11 June 1937, Souvenir Sect., 2; "Area Experiencing Rapid Expansion," *LAT,* 28 Apr. 1939, IV-18; "Ralphs Twenty-eighth Unit," 19; Zimmerman, "Cross-Country," 41.

69

Schwartz interview. According to Schwartz, some house builders were so eager to have a Ralphs store near their projects that they offered the site for a small sum or no money at all. Concerning the adjacent development at Crenshaw and Exposition boulevards, see Longstreth, *City Center to Regional Mall,* 194–195. Ralphs did not build units as part of shopping centers until after World War II.

70

For background, see "The Cheapy Thrives," *Business Week* 6 Feb. 1933, 11–12; Frank E. Landau, "Is the Price-Wrecking Market Here to Stay?" *CSA/GME* 8 (Mar. 1933), 78, 80, 99–101; Zimmerman, "Super-Markets," 9 July 1936, 10, 90–92; 23 July 1936, 53; "Slashing of Prices in Supermarkets," *Literary Digest* 22 (19 Sep. 1936), 45–46; "King Kullen, the Trail Blazer," *SMM* 2 (June 1937), 3–5, 25; Zimmerman and Grant, "Warning," 21; Furnas, "Super Market," 25–38; Zimmerman, *Super Market,* 31–39; Charvat, *Supermarketing,* 18–19; Randolph McAusland, *Supermarkets: 50 Years of Progress* (Washington: Food Marketing Institute, 1980), 14–15; Liebs, *Main Street,* 124–125; and Mayo, *Grocery Store,* 140–144.

71

"King Kullen," 25.

72

By 1937, the number had risen to seventeen, with ten more planned. Cullen, who died the previous year, had envisioned a national chain, but the company never expanded beyond the metropolitan area. See "Kullen's Kingdom," *Tide* 7 (May 1933), 32, 34.

73

For background, see "The Cheapy Thrives"; "Big Bear . . . Wrecking Competitors' Prices," *Retailing,* 6 Mar. 1933, 12; "Bears & Bulls," *Tide* 7 (Mar. 1933), 14–16; Alexander Kaylin, "'Supermarkets' Scare," *Retailing,* 18 Feb. 1933, 2; Frank Brigham, "Supermarket Grocery Chain Mechanically Merchandised," *Retailing,* 27 May 1935, 4; Zimmerman, "Super-Markets," 16 July 1936, 53, 56, 58–59, 62; "Slashing of Prices," 44–45; Zimmerman and Grant, "Warning," 21–22, 96–97; Furnas, "Super Market," 25, 38; Zimmerman, *Super Market,* 39–43; Charvat, *Supermarketing,* 18–19; McAusland, *Supermarkets,* 18–19; Liebs, *Main Street,* 125–126;

and Mayo, *Grocery Store,* 141, 144.

74

Big Bear's sales are discussed in Zimmerman, "Super-Markets," 16 July 1936, 56. *PG* noted that supermarkets in Los Angeles making approximately $500,000 worth of sales annually were not unusual in 1934 ("Inside Figures Concerning a $500,000 Super Market," 14 [Apr. 1935], 40−42). A writer for *CSA* found average sales of Los Angeles supers to be only slightly less (Holden, "Super-Markets," 58). A large supermarket could bring in considerably more: E. F. Smith's facility on W. Sixth Street earned $1,800,000 its first year (Collister, "Inside Story," 92).

75

"'Super' Market Makes Good in Kansas City," *Retailing,* 23 Oct. 1933, 12; Ralph F. Linder, "Is the Supermarket Coming or Going?" *PG* 13 (Feb. 1934), 32, 68, 72; "Dawson's Trading Post, A Pioneer's Vision Fulfilled," *SMM* 1 (Dec. 1936), 6−7, 16.

76

Linder, "Coming or Going?" 76; "Is the Super-Market Dressing Up?" *CSA/GE* 11 (Apr. 1935), 41; Zimmerman, "Super-Markets," 23 July 1936, 60; "Supers' Status," *Tide* 11 (1 Apr. 1937), 27−28; "Super-Store Trend Takes Shape under Chain Leadership," *CSA/GE* 13 (Sep. 1937), 20−21.

77

Basic differences in the operational structure are noted in Zimmerman, "Super Markets," 23 July 1936, 62. For examples, see Malcolm Kinney, "Barnum and Bailey Stuff," *CSA/GE* 7 (Apr. 1931), 5−6, 26; F. I. Harley, "Amend's Has a Way of Making Motorists Stop," *PG* 10 (Oct. 1931), 24−27; Carl W. Dipman, *The Modern Grocery Store* (New York: Progressive Grocer, 1931), 189; "The Romance of the Super Market, #1, George A. Steindl," *SMM* 1 (Nov. 1936), 9, 24; "Dawson's Trading Post"; "The Romance of the Super Market, #3, John E. Livingstone," *SMM* 2 (Jan. 1937), 7−8; "Cifrinos Made $3,000 Grow to $3,000,000," *SMM* 2 (May 1937), 6−7, 24; "Ablers Super Race Ahead on Sales Volume," *SMM* 3 (Jan. 1938), 10, 42, 44; Gerald Leavitt, "Palmer Woods Super Largest in Middle West," *SMM* 3 (Sep. 1938), 20, 40; "Humpty Dumpty, One of Southwest's Finest," *SMM* 6 (Mar. 1941), 23.

78

Among the notable exceptions was Big Chain Stores in Shreveport, Louisiana. See chapter IV.

79

See, for example, Dwight G. Baird, "From Tiny Store to Deluxe Market in 10 Years," *PG* 14 (Jan. 1935), 1−15, 80, 82, 84. Early on, Big Bear sought to upgrade the image of its new stores; see B. Sumner Gruzen, "Automobile Shopping Centers," *AR* 76 (July 1934), 43−48; idem, "Shopping Centers," *AR* 81 (Jan. 1937), 18BT−22BT; and idem, "Specifications for the Modern Super," *SMM* 4 (May 1939), 8, 10, 33−34, 37.

80

"Is the Super-Market Dressing Up?" 41−42; "Chains Go Supermarket," *Business Week* 1 May 1937, 44−47; "Supermarkets Now Feel Competition of Grocery

Chains," *Retailing,* 16 Aug. 1937, 4, 14; "Super-Store Trend Takes Shape under Chain Leadership," *CSA/GE* 13 (Sep. 1937), 20, 50, 52; Zimmerman, *Super Market Grows Up,* 11–17. For illustrations of buildings, see *CSA/GE* 14 (Feb. 1938), 71; *CSA/GE* 14 (Apr. 1938), 31; E. C. Barrett, "Beaumont Has Latest Piggly Wiggly Super," *SMM* 3 (Sep. 1938), 35; *CSA/GE* 15 (Jan. 1939), 59; Robert Margolius, "The Supermarket Grows Up," *Retailing,* 20 Feb. 1939, 3, 13, and 27 Feb. 1939, 14–15; "A&P Sales Reported as Highest in History," *PG* 20 (Aug. 1941), 55; "Big Market Building Boom Result of War Conditions," *PG* 20 (Nov. 1941), 56–57; and Sidney R. Rabb, "Super Markets—Past, Present and Future," *Twenty-third Annual Boston Conference on Distribution,* 1951, 66.

81

The best historical account of this phenomenon is in Liebs, *Main Street,* 55–58. Contemporary literature on the subject is vast. See, for example, Kenneth Kingsley Stowell, *Modernizing Buildings for Profit* (New York: Prentice-Hall, 1935); and *52 Designs to Modernize Main Street with Glass* (Toledo: Libby Owens Ford Glass Co., ca. 1935).

82

The image appears to have been taken directly from the Andrew Williams Food Market, which opened in Oakland, California, earlier that year—a scheme that owed its principal debt to Morgan, Walls & Clements's latest work for Ralphs. Concerning the market itself, see "65,000 Throng Williams' Food Market in Gala Oakland Opening," *SMM* 2 (May 1937), 2, 23.

83

See, for example, "Constans Opens New Duluth Market," *SMM* 3 (Aug. 1938), 8, 30; "Carl's Market Opens with 324 Carloads of Food," *SMM* 4 (Feb. 1939), 6, 43; "New Goldman Market Shows Efficiency Features," *SMM* 5 (Feb. 1940), 10, 41; "Movements in the Super Market World," *SMM* 6 (Dec. 1941), 52; "New Super Called '1950 Store,'" *PG* 20 (Feb. 1941), 42–46; "Efficient Shopping Is Keynote of New Super-Market," *CSA/GE* 17 (Feb. 1941), 58–62; Harry Padgett, "Denver's Newest Super," *SMM* 6 (Feb. 1941), 94–95; Fred G. Galer, "Super Appearance as Sales Promotion," *SMM* 6 (Mar. 1941), 56–57, 71; "Standard Opens Its Twenty-fifth Super," *SMM* 7 (July 1942), 47; and "Humpty Dumpty's New Units Answer Defeatists," *SMM* 7 (Sep. 1942), 36–37.

84

Concerning the Standard stores, see *Indianapolis Star,* 17 Apr. 1942, 7; and "Standard Opens Its Twenty-fifth Super," *SMM* 7 (July 1942), 47. Compare with examples of the company's first supermarkets as illustrated in *SMM* 3 (Jan. 1938), 32. Concerning Weingarten's, see "New Weingarten's Store . . . ," *HP,* 14 Feb. 1937, II-7; B. J., "Weingarten's 'Parade of Progress,'" *SMM* 4 (Mar. 1939), 6, 8, 70–71; "Glass Block Provides Natural Lighting . . . ," *CSA/GE* 15 (June 1939), 24–25, 63; "'Supers' Seek New Fields," *Retail Executive* 27 Sep. 1939, 6. Henke & Pillot followed a similar course several years later; see *HP,* 21 Apr. 1940, I-18; *HP,* 1 Nov. 1940, Henke & Pillot Sect.; "Spaciousness Marks New Super-Market," *CSA/GE* 17 (Mar. 1941), 54; and "Modern Features Keynote Henke & Pillot's Newest Unit," *SMM* 6 (Jan. 1941), 12, 14, 16.

IV *Is Main Street Doomed?*

NOTES

2 1 2

1

Crag Dale, "Is Main Street Doomed?" *PM* 55 (May 1931), 765. Roadside stands proliferated during the interwar decades; many of them did not start as filling stations, however, and the extent to which they became competitors with merchants in town is questionable. For an account of the period, see "Roadside Markets the Modern Solution of the Marketing Problem," *CHM* 6 (Aug. 1922), 180–181. See also Chester H. Liebs, *Main Street to Miracle Mile: American Roadside Architecture* (Boston: New York Graphic Society, 1985), 21–22.

Wright's ideas on the subject may have been derived empirically, for he was probably among the few architects of the period to motor long distances on a regular basis. His twice-a-year trip between Wisconsin and Arizona, as well as other motoring ventures, gave him ample opportunity to inspect the dramatic changes that were occurring along U.S. highways between the world wars.

2

Frank Lloyd Wright, *The Disappearing City* (New York: Wilson Farquhar Payson, 1932), 16–17, 76; "Broadacre City: An Architect's Vision," *New York Times Magazine,* 20 Mar. 1932, 8–9; and "The City of Tomorrow," *Pictorial Review* 34 (Mar. 1933), 4–5. Recent accounts of the complex history of the Broadacres plan include Donald Leslie Johnson, *Frank Lloyd Wright versus America: The 1930s* (Cambridge: MIT Press, 1990), 108–141; and Anthony Alofsin, "Broadacre City: The Reception of a Modernist Vision, 1932–1988," *Center* 5 (1989), 8–43.

3

Frank Lloyd Wright, "America Tomorrow," *American Architect* 141(May 1932), 17.

4

Wright, *Disappearing City,* 69.

5

See Frank Lloyd Wright, "Broadacre City: A New Community Plan," *AR* 77 (Apr. 1935), 243–254. Wright designed another, quite dissimilar configuration for a roadside market in 1932; see Johnson, *Wright,* 131–133, 138.

6

For definitions of community and regional shopping centers, see Richard Longstreth, *City Center to Regional Mall: Architecture, the Automobile, and Retailing in Los Angeles, 1920–1950* (Cambridge: MIT Press, 1997), 222.

7

A detailed account of the Broadacres market is given in an expanded version of *The Disappearing City* entitled *When Democracy Builds* (Chicago: University of Chicago Press, 1945), 93–95. To my knowledge this latter publication was the first occasion when the market complex itself was shown, although photographs taken a decade earlier document that it was part of the original 1934–1935 model and presentation site plan. Appearing right at the start of the post–World War II era, this image may have directly influenced the new generation of architects who designed many shopping centers, reinforcing the pragmatic concerns of retailing that governed their work.

8

For a case study of a major example of the postwar era, see Richard Longstreth, "The Mixed Blessings of Success: The Hecht Company and Department Store Branch Development after World War II," in Elizabeth Collins Cromley and Carter Hudgins, eds., *Shaping Communities: Perspectives in Vernacular Architecture, VI* (Knoxville: University of Tennessee Press, 1997), 244–262; and idem, "Silver Spring: Georgia Avenue, Colesville Road and the Creation of an Alternative 'Downtown' for Metropolitan Washington," in Zeynep Celik et al., eds., *Streets: Critical Perspectives on Public Space* (Berkeley: University of California Press, 1994), 247–258, 294.

9

For discussion, see Longstreth, *City Center to Regional Mall,* chaps. 6, 9; and idem, "The Diffusion of the Community Shopping Center Concept during the Interwar Decades," *JSAH* 56 (Sep. 1997), 268–293.

10

For background, see Richard Longstreth, "The Neighborhood Shopping Center in Washington, D.C., 1930–1941," *JSAH* 51 (Mar. 1992), esp. 6–7.

11

In Los Angeles and other urban areas, the scale of taxpayer blocks tended to increase during the interwar decades. A facility containing a number of stores and some additional feature, such as a neighborhood movie house, was not uncommon. Such complexes were seldom, if ever, operated as integrated businesses and thus were not shopping centers in the modern sense of the term. For examples, see "New Business Building . . . ," *LAT,* 17 July 1921, V-2; *LAT,* 28 Aug. 1921, V-4; *LAT,* 16 Dec. 1923, V-2; "Alhambra Has New Theater," *LAT,* 16 Nov. 1924, V-3; and J. Harold Hawkins, "The Community Store Group," *American Builder* 42 (Nov. 1926), 144–145.

12

The best source of information on these complexes is the *Country Club District Bulletin,* which was published between 1919 and 1931. See also William S. Worley, *J. C. Nichols and the Shaping of Kansas City* (Columbia: University of Missouri Press, 1990), chap. 8. I am grateful to Lee Fowler of the J. C. Nichols Company for supplying me with additional material on the subject.

13

Without detailed study of outlying retail development in other cities, it is impossible to ascertain precisely the degree to which these experiments were unique to southern California. A city such as Houston, which shared many urban characteristics on a smaller scale, may well have been host to similar endeavors. Investigations elsewhere, including Houston, conducted during the course of this study failed to reveal analogous examples; however, the southern California buildings themselves received meager coverage when built and are completely forgotten today. More probing is needed in other localities before a solid comparative base can be established.

14

"New Market Is Pleasing Idea," *GNP,* 8 Jan. 1927, 2. Genevieve Lund, perhaps the only female designer of a drive-in market, apparently intended to expand upon the scheme using a block-and-a-half stretch of her own property just to the south. See also *GNP,* 1 Jan. 1927, Rotogravure Sect., 12; and *GNP,* 26 Aug. 1928, II-9.

15

"Market-Place of Unique Character . . . ," *PSN,* 6 Feb. 1926, 37; "Large Market Unit . . . ," *LAT,* 7 Feb. 1926, V-11.

16

"Artistic Covent Garden Market . . . ," *PSN,* 25 Sep. 1926; "Mother Goose Market . . . ," and "Mother Goose Pantry . . . ," *PSN,* 31 Aug. 1927, 22–23; "Development of Market . . . ," *PSN,* 26 May 1928, 31.

17

"Ten English Shops . . . ," *HDC,* 28 Aug. 1924, 2; "Grand Opening . . . ," *HDC,* 12 Dec. 1924, 2. As built, the scheme was more regularized in its massing and composition. Tenants included four food stores and shops for a barber, beautician, artworks, flowers, electrical and plumbing needs, and sewing goods as well as the offices of Mauzy's realty firm and the project's architect.

A decade later, the complex became part of an unplanned retail development called Sunset Center. Popularly known as "The Strip," this loosely knit grouping of stores, restaurants, and nightclubs was among the most fashionable in the metropolitan area before and immediately after World War II. See "Small Shops with Architectural Distinction," *California Arts & Architecture* 48 (Dec. 1935), 21–22, 35; "Making History . . . ," *HDC,* 13 Dec. 1935, 13–18; *BHC,* 20 Nov. 1936, 21–27; and "The Strip," *Freehold* 7 (15 July 1940), 54–57.

18

For discussion, see Longstreth, *City Center to Regional Mall,* 276–278.

19

"Largest Drive-In Market Rising," *LAT,* 21 Oct. 1928, V-6; "Drive-In Market . . . ," *LAT,* 16 June 1929, II-2; Olive Gray, "New Market . . . ," *LAT,* 20 June 1929, II-2; Frank H. Williams, "495 Autos Can Park in This New Drive-In Market," *PG* 8 (Oct. 1929), 30–31, 130; Willard D. Morgan, "The Super Drive-In Emerges from the Competitive Whirl," *CSR* 3 (Oct. 1930), 10–12.

20

For discussion, see chapter III.

21

Morgan, "Super Drive-In," 10–11. In 1933, the largest of these market spaces was leased by Ralphs, whose presence appears to have precluded the others from remaining on the premises.

22

The earliest street directory I have been able to locate (Jan. 1935) lists the store tenants as a bakery, brassiere shop, laundry, florist, beauty shop, and a shop purveying painted fabrics.

23

The estimate of 495 cars given by Williams and the large numbers cited in other contemporary accounts appear to have been based on daily averages rather than the capacity at any given time. Still, the size was considerable. Ralphs's largest lots then held around forty cars, as noted in chapter III.

24

"City Market Buys . . . ," *LAT,* 14 Mar. 1909, V-1; "Huntington Backs . . . ," *LAT,* 2 May 1909, V-1, 24. Some working drawings for the project can be found among the Morgan, Walls & Clements materials at the Huntington Library.

25

Plans for the complex were begun as early as 1909; see "Largest Market . . . ," *LAT,* 1 Jan. 1910, 4. However, the scheme was not finalized nor was construction begun for another seven years. See "Excavating for Foundations . . . ," *LAT,* 11 Feb. 1917, II-8; "Building of Huge Shipping Terminal . . . ," *LAT,* 13 May 1917, II-13; "Rushing Work on Terminal," *LAT,* 18 Nov. 1917, V-1; L. A. Waterbury, "Market and Warehouses Form Large Building Group," *Engineering News-Record* 80 (24 Jan. 1920), 167–168; "Great Terminal Market Opened . . . ," *LAT,* 12 May 1918, V-1; "How Los Angeles Handles Its Wholesale Produce Market," *MA* 37 (26 Feb. 1920), 33; "Addition Will Cost Million," *LAT,* 18 June 1920, II-1; Gerald Fitzgerald, "Concrete Carries Heavy Traffic at Wholesale Terminal," *CHM* 5 (Sep.–Oct. 1921), 103–105; *LATMN,* 1 Jan. 1924, I-23; and *LATMN,* 1 Jan. 1925, II-15.

26

Concerning Chapman, see William A. Spalding, *History of Los Angeles City and County,* 3 vols. (Los Angeles: J. R. Finnell & Sons, 1931), 3: 587–591; Edward Palmer, *History of Hollywood,* 2 vols. (Los Angeles: Arthur H. Cawston, 1937), 2: 49–52; and Ralph Hancock, *Fabulous Boulevard* (New York: Funk & Wagnalls, 1949), 292–293. In the year of the market's construction, Goodwin was preparing what became the definitive trade book on the subject: *Markets: Public and Private* (Seattle: Montgomery Printing Co., 1929); see p. 72 therein.

27

"Mammoth Market . . . ," *LAT,* 28 Dec. 1928, V-2. A similarly ambitious complex was planned over a year later on the edge of downtown Long Beach. In this case, however, a large market did not provide the anchor unit. See "New Shopping Center . . . ," *Long Beach Press-Telegram,* 22 June 1930, A-1, A-10. The courtyard arrangement was also used for proposed shopping complexes in San Antonio (1928) and Milwaukee (1931); see Longstreth, "Diffusion," 285–286.

28

Neither Lexington newspapers nor material in the Neutra archive at UCLA have yielded any information on this project other than what can be gleaned from the drawings, which suggest that it never progressed beyond a preliminary stage. The stock market crash occurred shortly after the drawings were prepared in August 1929 and may have precipitated the abandoning of the endeavor. The site lay just east of the city center, indicating it was to function as an extension to that core rather than as a discrete peripheral node. The design was published in "Drafting and Design Problems: Neighborhood Shopping Centers," *AR* 71 (May 1932), 331–332. See also Thomas S. Hines, "Designing for the Motor Age: Richard Neutra and the Automobile," *Oppositions* 21 (Summer 1980), 45–46.

Neutra also prepared preliminary plans for a smaller drive-in market for the same client, to have been located at Main, Ransom, and Shreve streets in Lexington. The site plan is preserved in the architect's papers at UCLA.

29

Richard J. Neutra, *Amerika: Die Stilbildung des Neuen Bauens in den Vereinigten Staaten* (Vienna: Anton Schroll, 1930), 84–85. For background on the complex, see

"Three-Million-Dollar Terminal," *LAT,* 29 May 1927, V-7; "Terminal Open To-day," *LAT,* 27 Nov. 1927, V-8; and G. W. Hegel, "The Los Angeles Produce Termi-nal," *CHM* 12 (Apr. 1928), 82–83. The importance Neutra placed on vehicular as well as pedestrian movement in shaping such a design is evident in his "Termi-nals?—Transfer!" *AR* 68 (Aug. 1930), 90–104.

30

The subject is discussed at length in Longstreth, *City Center Regional Mall,* chap. VII. Aside from automobile service facilities, the other type of drive-in establish-ment then common in southern California was the restaurant. These buildings, however, failed to gain currency as a general model. Drive-in facilities could also be for a few additional functions, but examples were rare before World War II. See Richard Longstreth, "Don't Get Out: The Automobile's Impact on Five Building Types in Los Angeles, 1921–1941," *Arris,* Journal of the Southeast Chapter of the Society of Architectural Historians, 6 (1997), 32–56.

31

Longstreth, "Neighborhood Shopping Center," 11–17.

32

"Big Chain Grocery . . . ," *Shreveport Times,* 30 Dec. 1928, 8; *Shreveport Times,* 28 June 1929, Big Chain Ed.; George Malcolm, "'Big Chain' Typifies Trend to the Complete Market," *CSR* 3 (Feb. 1930), 49–51; *CSA/GME* 6 (Apr. 1930), 47.

33

K. Lonburg-Holm, "Planning the Retail Store," *AR* 69 (June 1931), 499; "Draft-ing and Design Problems," 325–327. The latter article also contained illustrations of the Munsey Park Business Center at Manhasset, Long Island (1930–1931) and the Radburn Plaza Building at Radburn, New Jersey (1928–1929), both of which provided for some off-street parking in front but lacked the forecourt arrangement; and a complex in New Canaan, Connecticut, that had parking in the rear.

In confirming his responsibility for the drawings and coauthorship of the ar-ticle, Frey noted the paucity of examples from which they could draw at that time (letter to author, 12 Oct. 1989). He and Kocher were aware of the drive-in markets through illustrations published in *AR* over a year earlier. Subsequently, Frey saw a number of examples firsthand during his July-August 1932 trip to southern Califor-nia, as discussed in chapter II, and used three of the drawings prepared for his *AR* ar-ticle in an essay describing those markets published the following year (Albert Frey, "Amerikanische Notizen," *Werk* 20 [Oct. 1933], 314). I am aware of no other such drawings to appear in any type of publication prior to the mid-1940s save for those in Clarence S. Stein and Catherine Bauer, "Store Buildings and Neighborhood Shopping Centers," *AR* 75 (Feb. 1934), 179, 181, 184–185. At that time it was still a standard practice for architects to maintain reference files on building types that were primarily comprised of articles and illustrations clipped from professional jour-nals. Thus it is probable that many practitioners would have kept Frey and Kocher's material and would have consulted it when designing a small retail complex.

34

Stein and Bauer, "Store Buildings," 185. The photograph of the Palm Market had been taken by Frey during his 1932 trip to California and is reproduced herein as figure 65.

35

William L. Pollard, "Determining the Amount, Character, and Location of Business Property a Subdivision Needs," *Annals of Real Estate Practice* (Chicago: National Association of Real Estate Brokers, 1928), 621–632.

36

Harland Bartholomew, "Business Zoning," *Annals of the American Academy of Political and Social Science* 155 (May 1931), 101–102. See also idem, *Urban Land Uses . . .* (Cambridge: Harvard University Press, 1932), 71–72; and Paul J. Fitzpatrick, "What Factors Make a Successful Store Location," *Journal of Retailing* 9 (Oct. 1933), 90–91.

37

See, for example, Robert Kingery, "Determining the Size of Retail Districts in Zoning Cities and Villages," *AC* 36 (Feb. 1927), 246–248; Coleman Woodbury, "The Size of Retail Business Districts in the Chicago Metropolitan Region," *Journal of Land and Public Utility Economics* 4 (Feb. 1928), 85–91; and "How Much Business Frontage Shall the Developer Set Aside?" *CHM* 12 (Feb. 1928), 36–37 (Chicago); "County Zoning under Way in Wisconsin," *AC* 38 (Feb. 1928), 143–144; and Charles B. Bennett, "Local Business Centers for Milwaukee," *City Planning* 5 (Jan. 1929), 47–50 (Milwaukee); and Charles F. Fisher, "Planning Local Business Districts," *City Planning* 5 (Apr. 1929), 106–109 (Akron).

38

Gordon Whitnall, "Place of Subdivision in Community Expansion," *Community Builder* 1 (Dec. 1927), 15–20; *AC* 38 (Feb. 1928), 144; Huber Earl Smutz, "Zoning Business Frontage," *City Planning* 5 (Oct. 1929), 269–271; "Business Area Analysis Made," *LAT,* 13 Oct. 1929, V-1, 2. The scheme may have been partially based on an earlier one for Chicago, which called for commercial building setbacks, but no additional parking space; see Jacob L. Crane, Jr., "Recent Theories in Street and Block Planning," *AC* 33 (Aug. 1925), 144. Somewhat similar proposals continued to be made for other cities into the 1930s. See, for example, H. W. Alexander, "Designing a Suburban Commercial Center," *AC* 47 (July 1932), 67, reprinted as "A Suburban Commercial Center," *AR,* 72 (Aug. 1932), 75–76.

39

A Comprehensive Report on the Regional Plan of Highways, Section 2-E, San Gabriel Valley (Los Angeles: Los Angeles County Regional Planning Commission, 1929), 60; Charles H. Diggs, "Zoning by Design," *Annals of the American Academy of Political and Social Science* 155 (May 1931), 83–84.

40

Perry's writings on the subject include "The Relation of Neighborhood Forces to the Larger Community," *Proceedings of the National Conference on Social Work, 1924* (Chicago: University of Chicago Press, 1924), 415–421; "The Neighborhood Unit," in *Neighborhood and Community Planning* (New York: Regional Plan of New York and Its Environs, 1929), 25–83; and *Housing for the Machine Age* (New York: Russell Sage Foundation, 1939). Recent scholarly analysis includes Howard Gillette, Jr., "The Evolution of Neighborhood Planning from the Progressive Era to the 1949 Housing Act," *Journal of Urban History* 9 (Aug. 1983), 421–444; and Christopher Silver, "Neighborhood Planning in Historical Perspective," *Journal of the American Planning Association* 51 (Spring 1985), 161–174. An indication of the longevity of Perry's work in southern California is apparent in Mel Scott, *Metropolitan Los Angeles: One Community* (Los Angeles: Haynes Foundation, 1949), chaps. VII–VIII.

41

In fairness to Perry, once he became aware of the Park and Shop, he promoted it as a model solution for commercial development. See *Housing for the Machine Age,* 70.

42

Catherine Bauer, "When Is a House Not a House?" *The Nation* 136 (25 Jan. 1933), 99. Wright, of course, was unmoved by such comments and continued to present the idea in his writings for some years to come. See, for example, *The Future of Architecture* (New York: Horizon, 1953), 176.

43

For background on the FHA's propagation of the concept, see Longstreth, "Neighborhood Shopping Center," 18–20. See also "Suggests Control of Shopping Areas," *New York Times,* 13 Aug. 1939, XI-4.

Other important federal initiatives in this sphere were the Resettlement Administration's Greenbelt towns program and the commercial center at the Tennessee Valley Authority's town of Norris, illustrated in E. S. Draper, "Town Stores and Office Building, Norris, Tennessee," *AR* 80 (Aug. 1936), 139–142; and Giorgio Ciucci, et al., *The American City: From the Civil War to the New Deal* (Cambridge: MIT Press, 1979), 354. I am grateful to the late Frederick Gutheim for his discussions with me concerning the importance of the Park and Shop on the thinking of planning reformers of the period, and on the direct connection between it and subsequent federal undertakings.

The greatest number of FHA-related projects came after the war. The role of the federal government in fostering shopping center development has generally been ignored and warrants further study.

44

See, for example, "Suburban Shopping Centers," *National Real Estate Journal* 39 (Dec. 1938), 29–33; "Forum: Shopping for the Upper Classes," *Freehold* 4 (15 Jan. 1939), 54–57; "Taking the Business out of Traffic," *CSA/AE* 15 (Dec. 1939), 8, 23; Carl Feiss, "Shopping Centers," *House and Garden* 76 (Dec. 1939), 48–49, 66; "Community Shopping Centers," *AR* 87 (June 1940), 99–120; and Harry E. Martin, "Trends in Decentralization of Shopping Centers," *CSA/AE* 17 (Apr. 1941), 12, 34, 36, 38, 40–41.

45

For discussion, see Longstreth, "Neighborhood Shopping Center," 17–33.

46

A list of Washington-area centers is contained in Longstreth, "Neighborhood Shopping Center," 33–34. Those built in conjunction with FHA-insured housing projects include Colonial Village Parking Stores (1935–1936), Beverly Plaza (1937–1938), Buckingham Shopping Center (1938–1939), Brentwood Shopping Center (1939–1940), Woodmoor Shopping Center (1938, only a few units realized), Arlington Village Shopping Center (1939), Westmont Shopping Center (1939–1941), Westover Hills Shopping Center (1940), River Terrace Shopping Center (1940), Greenway Shopping Center (1940–1941), Fairfax Village Shopping Center (1941), and Arlington Forest Shopping Center (1941).

47

Material gathered over the past dozen years has yielded a wealth of information on the subject but is far from complete, and thus the conclusions offered here must remain tentative. In addition to consulting pertinent journals, reports, and books, I conducted searches through the real estate sections of newspapers in Washington, Cleveland, Detroit, Dallas, and Houston—cities known to have had early activity in this field. Additional information was gathered from miscellaneous sources for work in Baltimore, Richmond, Philadelphia, Atlanta, Columbus, Louisville, and St. Louis.

Direct ties to Washington are not easy to document. The Buffalo real estate firm of Guelich & Boebbel developed several complexes in upstate New York that they called "park-and-shop centers," suggesting the paradigmatic value of counterparts so termed in Washington; see Richard H. Guelich, Jr., "Little Lessons in Planning Park-and-Shop Centers," *Freehold* 6 (1 June 1940), 378–381; and "New Shopping Centers Offer Good Locations," *PG* 20 (Feb. 1941), 52–53, 56, 60. The center at Olentangy Village, an FHA-insured garden apartment complex at Columbus, Ohio, was designed by Raymond Snow, who was then practicing in Washington and had designed a somewhat similar group there; see "Taking Business," 8; *AR* 84 (Sep. 1938), 122–123; and "FHA Rental Project Spotlights Columbus," *Architectural Forum* 70 (May 1939), 372–373. Another such development, Northwood, in Baltimore, was also by Snow; see "Neighborhood Shops . . . ," *Freehold* 7 (15 Oct. 1940), 278–281.

For other examples, see Leon Brown, "Super Architects Put Beauty to Work," *SMM* 6 (July 1941), 22 (Philadelphia); "A New Model Shopping Center Developed by Realtor Firm," *National Real Estate Journal* 39 (Jan. 1938), 46–48; "A Shopping Center . . . ," *AR* 83 (Feb. 1938), 134; "5 Traffic Arteries Merge at Shopping Center," *CSA/AE* 18 (Feb. 1942), 12 (Birmingham); "$50,000 Community Center . . . ," *HP* 4 Feb. 1940, II-8; and "The Store-Theater Idea," *Freehold* 8 (Apr. 1941), 32–38 (Houston).

48

In addition to articles cited in nn. 31 and 33 above, coverage of Washington-area neighborhood centers includes "Washington Gets New 'Park and Shop' Market," *CSA/GE* 7 (July 1931), 4–5, 32; "Terminal Facilities—Motor Transport's Greatest Need," *AC* 49 (Feb. 1934), 70; "'But Where Will We Park?'" *Printer's Ink* 36 (Oct. 1937), 13; "Park and Shop," *AC* 52 (Oct. 1937), 71–72; F. Wallace Stoever, "Park-and-Shop Projects for Neighborhood Improvement," *Real Estate Record* 141 (5 Feb. 1938), 30–31; "Suburban Shopping Centers," 32–33; Perry, *Housing for the Machine Age,* 70; "The Roadside Picture . . . ," *Landscape Architecture* 30 (Oct. 1939), 34; Feiss, "Shopping Centers," 49, 66; and "Community Shopping Centers," 119–120.

49

Feiss, "Shopping Centers," 49, 66. See also "Taking Business," 8. Even after World War II, a drive-in market was illustrated as a "shopping center" in Nelson A. Miller et al., *Grocery Store,* Industrial (Small Business) Series No. 21, U.S. Department of Commerce (Washington: U.S. Government Printing Office, 1946), 34.

50

For background on the development, see Don Riddle, "'Homes to Last for All Time': The Story of Houston's River Oaks," *National Real Estate Journal* 30 (4 Mar. 1929), 28; and Charles Orson Cook and Barry J. Kaplan, "Civic Elites and Urban Planning: Houston's River Oaks," *East Texas Historical Journal* 25:2 (1977), 29–37.

51

Concerning Potter's views on the economic situation, see "City Planning Needed, Potter Tells Rotarians," *Houston* 7 (Oct. 1936), 14–15. For discussion in greater detail, see Richard Longstreth, "River Oaks Shopping Center," *Cite,* Journal of the Rice Design Alliance, 36 (Winter 1996), 8–13.

52

Letter from Hugh Potter to Oliver Winston, 4 Oct. 1936. This and other correspondence between the two parties over the next three months helps indicate the complicated sequence of River Oaks's design. I am grateful to Mrs. Oliver Winston of Peterborough, New Hampshire, for sharing this material with me. Much additional information was supplied by Milton and Burke McGinty (interview, Houston, 8 May 1989).

53

One scheme was published in *AR,* June 1929, as well as in *CSR,* Sep. 1928. Neutra is quoted at length on his ideas for a drive-in market in Willard D. Morgan, "At Last—A Place to Park!," *American Builder* 47 (July 1929), 59–60. Winston surely would have seen the Neutra design published in the June 1929 issue of *AR,* but whether he knew more of Neutra's work in this vein, directly or otherwise, is unknown. Milton McGinty's brother and associate, Burke, recalled that this scheme was well known among the students at Rice University's School of Architecture (where Winston taught prior to his move east) during the 1930s (interview with Milton and Burke McGinty).

54

"River Oaks Shopping Center Sets the Pace for Better Stores," *American Builder* 65 (July 1943), 40–41; Robert W. Dowling, "Neighborhood Shopping Centers," *Architectural Forum* 79 (Oct. 1943), 77; *Urban Land* 3 (Oct.-Nov. 1944), 1; J. Ross McKeever, "Shopping Centers: An Analysis," *Urban Land Institute Technical Bulletin* 11 (July 1949), 36–37; *The Community Builders Handbook* (Washington: Urban Land Institute, 1950), 104. The River Oaks center was expanded in a less physically integrated fashion after the war; see J. Ross McKeever, "Shopping Centers: Principles and Policies," *Urban Land Institute Technical Bulletin* 20 (July 1953), 36–37.

55

For discussion, see Longstreth, *City Center to Regional Mall,* 185–196, 265–266.

56

Concerning the rise of the shopping center after World War II, see Longstreth, *City Center to Regional Mall,* chaps. IX and XI. Those chapters, however, focus on regional centers, not the smaller community and neighborhood ones discussed here. To date, no systematic historical study has been done of the latter two during the postwar era.

    River Oaks and other drive-in centers were not the only precedent for postwar work. In both their size and scope of tenants, larger complexes of earlier years also provided a key foundation. For background, see Richard Longstreth, "The Diffusion of the Community Shopping Center Concept during the Interwar Decades," *JSAH* 56 (Sep. 1997), 268–293.

57

S. O. Kaylin, "Major Factors Chains Should Check in Evaluating the Planned Shopping Center," *CSA/AE* 30 (May 1954), 13. See also idem, "The Chain Store in the

Planned Shopping Center," *CSA/AE* 29 (May 1953), 23–58; and "Appraising the Shopping Center," *SMM* 18 (Mar. 1953), 35–42, 44–45. Kaylin's figures may be exaggerated. Five years later, the *Directory of Shopping Centers in the United States and Canada* (Chicago: National Research Bureau, 1959) estimated that 2,400 centers existed in the two countries combined, but the listing omits many smaller examples. Even rough estimates are difficult to tally, given the differing views of precisely what constituted a shopping center. Nevertheless, accounts of the 1950s are in accord that the growth rate was remarkable.

In 1954, the introduction of accelerated depreciation to the Internal Revenue Service Code significantly enhanced the already thriving trend. See Thomas W. Hanchett, "U.S. Tax Policy and the Shopping-Center Boom of the 1950s and 1960s," *American Historical Review* 101 (Oct. 1996), 1082–1110.

58

Los Angeles markets continued to be seen as industry leaders. See, for example, "New Von's Combines Size plus Service," *SMM* 13 (Apr. 1948), 50–51, 53–54; "Largest and Lightest for Ralphs," *CSA/GE* 24 (Aug. 1948), 68–69, 113; Lucius S. Flint, "More Large Stores for California," *CSA/GE* 25 (May 1949), 82–83, 138, 140, 142, 144; idem, "The Los Angeles Super," *CSA/GE* 26 (June 1950), J34–J35; "Von's New Super, Model of 'Ultra-Refrigeration'," *SMM* 16 (Mar. 1951), 136–137; "Largest for Ralphs," *CSA/GE* 16 (June 1951), W2–W3; "Ralphs Marks 75 Years of Dynamic Building," *SMM* 17 (Mar. 1952), 56–57; Nathaniel Schwartz and Richard G. Zimmerman, "Los Angeles Sets Super Pace," *SMM* 18 (Feb. 1953), 109, 111, 113, 116, 118, 121, 124, 127, 129, 131; "Super Markets Take on 'New Look'," *SMM* 19 (Aug. 1954), 50–51, 53.

59

"What Progress in Self-Service Meats?" *SMM* 7 (Jan. 1942), 19–22, 66; S. N. Goldman, "Self-Service Produce Can Speed Sales," *SMM* 7 (Apr. 1942), 24–26, 28–29; "Self-Service Boosts Dairy Sales," *SMM* 7 (May 1942), 14–16; La Verne R. Eastman, "Self-Service Meats Makes Los Angeles Debut," *SMM* 7 (July 1942), 22, 24–25; Lucius S. Flint, "Self-Service Produce Spreads in Los Angeles," *SMM* 7 (Aug. 1942), 18–22; S. N. Goldman, "Operating Self-Service Produce and Meat Departments," *SMM* 7 (Oct. 1942), 71, 73–74; Lucius S. Flint, "Labor Short-Cuts in Western Markets," *SMM* 8 (Aug. 1943), 18–23; Hubert E. Bice, "400 Customers Look at Self-Service," *SMM* 9 (Feb. 1944), 16, 18, 20–21; "Some Thoughts on Post-War Planning," *SMM* 9 (May 1944), 64–66; M. M. Zimmerman, "Re-Appraising the Industry's Thinking," *SMM* 9 (Aug. 1944), 11–12, 14, 16; idem, "All-Self-Service Meat Departments a Post-War Certainty," *SMM* 9 (Oct. 1944), 13–14, 16, 18–23; idem, "Food Industry Asks Fair Climate for Post-War Expansion," *SMM* 9 (Nov. 1944), 13–14, 16–17; "Meat Self-Service Seen Growing," *CSA/GE* 20 (Nov. 1944), 101; Stephen F. Elms, "Merchandising Self-Service Baked Goods for Volume," *SMM* 10 (Jan. 1945), 19–22; "Self-Service Gains in Consumers' Preference," *SMM* 10 (Feb. 1945), 46–47; John W. Ernest, "A Basic Course in Grocery Merchandising," *SMM* 11 (Mar. 1946), 121–122, 124, 126, 128, 130; "Self-Service Meats to Date," *SMM* 13 (Oct. 1948), 77, 80; "Growth of Self-Service Meat," *CSA/GE* 25 (Apr. 1949), 76–78, 111. Not every company saw the advantages of combining self-service with a single checkout area. A 1946 unit of All American Markets in Los Angeles County was completely self-service, but had the space divided into four distinct zones. See "All American Unit 100% Self-Service," *SMM* 11 (Aug. 1946), 40–43; and Blayne Hutchison, "100% Self Service Pays Off," *CSA/GE* 23 (Aug. 1947), 40–41, 104–105.

60

For purposes of continuity, however, many of the examples selected for discussion are from southern California.

61

For a sampling of Los Angeles examples, see *LAT,* 5 Sep. 1920, I-7; *LAT,* 3 Feb. 1923, I-3; "Departmental Drug Store . . . ," *HDC,* 5 July 1923, 12; "California's Finest Owl . . . ," *HDC,* 3 Feb. 1928, Owl Drug Sect.; "Owl Drug Stores . . . ," *HDC,* 31 July 1930, 9; and James G. Danley, "When Is a Drug Store?" *Pacific Coast Record* 21 (Feb. 1921), 11–13. See also "Drug Store Merchandising," *Commercial America* 24 (Nov. 1927), 17, 19–20, 32.

62

See chapters II and III.

63

Kansas City Star, 2 Aug. 1934, 3; "Where Buildings Less . . . ," *Kansas City Star,* 5 Aug. 1934, 6D; "Katz's Super," *Tide* 8 (Sep. 1934), 56–57; *Kansas City Star,* 6 Dec. 1934, Katz Sect.; "Katz Opens . . . ," *Women's Wear Daily,* 17 Dec. 1934, 18.

64

Kivett's most overt borrowing, however, was the vertical pylon, a miniature of that on the Hall of Science at the Chicago Century of Progress Exposition. The architect was responsible for many of the later Katz stores as well. After World War II, he founded what became the largest firm in the region. George Ehrlich graciously supplied me with material on his career.

65

Kansas City Star, 25 June 1941, 12–13; *Kansas City Star,* 5 June 1941, 6–7; "New Waldo Building . . . ," *Kansas City Star,* 9 Nov. 1941, 7D; "New Self-Service Stores Planned and Manned for Big Volume," *CSA/DE* 17 (Dec. 1941), 14–15, 50.

66

Longstreth, *City Center to Regional Mall,* 136–137.

67

"Drug Firm Announces . . . ," *HDC,* 20 Dec. 1935, 15; "Beach City Store . . . ," *LAT,* 28 June 1936, V-5; "Thrifty's Modern . . . ," *SMEO,* 16 Dec. 1936, 16; "Drug Store Organization's . . . ," *LAT,* 26 Dec. 1937, V-2; "New Sontag Store . . . ," *SWW,* 9 Dec. 1938, 23; "Owl Opens . . . ," *SMEO,* 17 Aug. 1939, Von's Market Sect., 9; "Three New Stores for Thrifty," *Architectural Concrete* 6:1 [1940], 34–35; "Thrifty Opens . . . ," *LAT,* 9 June 1940, V-2; "Thrifty Opens . . . ," *LAT,* 11 Aug. 1940, V-2; Willis H. Parker, "From Pine Board to Streamlined Stores," *CSA/DE* 16 (Sep. 1940), 26–27; "Store Added . . . ," *LAT,* 22 Sep. 1940, V-3; "Modern Lines Characterize New Unit," *CSA/DE* 16 (Dec. 1940), 25; "Drug Chain Opens . . . ," *LAT,* 22 June 1941, V-3; "Drugstore Chain Launches . . . ," *LAT,* 29 June 1941, II-2; *SWW,* 11 July 1941, 13. The figures cited in the text pertain to the city of Los Angeles alone.

68

For a sampling of accounts, see "Thrifty Opens . . . ," *LAT,* 26 Nov. 1948, I-8; "Owl Rexall . . . ," *LAT,* 3 Feb. 1949, II-2; "Thrifty Drug . . . ," *LAT,* 27 June 1950, II-2; "New Thrifty Drugstore . . . ," *LAT,* 8 July 1951, V-6; "Building Will Be . . . ," *LAT,* 2 Sep. 1951, V-10; "Owl Drug Co.'s . . ." *LAT,* 7 May 1952, III-12; "Thrifty Opens . . . ," *Los Angeles Examiner,* 7 Aug. 1952, I-16; "Sav-On to Open . . . ," *LAT,* 4 Nov. 1953, II-2; and "Two New Stores . . . ," *Los Angeles Examiner,* 11 Aug. 1954, III-2.

69

"Owl Drug Co.'s . . . ," *LAT,* 7 May 1952, III-12; "'Stupendous' Describes Opening . . . ," *Norwalk Advertiser,* 8 May 1952, 1, 12. The Greater Norwalk Shopping Center, of which the store was to be a part, was never developed further, eclipsed by the nearby Norwalk Square, also begun in 1951. Here, too, the initial units were a supermarket and drug store. See "Market Basket Opening . . . ," *Norwalk Advertiser,* 10 Jan. 1951, 1, 13; "Sav-On Opening . . . ," *Norwalk Advertiser,* 29 Nov. 1951, 1.

70

"Owl Drug Co. . . . ," *LAT,* 14 Dec. 1949, II-2; *PSN,* 14 Dec. 1949, Alpha Beta Sect. Soon thereafter, Owl embarked on a second venture, this time with Mayfair Markets in Santa Ana. See "Owl-Mayfair Opening . . . ," *LAT,* 14 Dec. 1950, II-17; "Spectacular Stores from California," *CSA/GE* 27 (Mar. 1951), 84−85; and Edwin J. Fox, "Owl-Mayfair Join in 'Tomorrow's Market'," *SMM* 16 (Apr. 1951), 41−45, 47, 49. The coupling occurred in other parts of the country as well, but proved short-lived; see John G. Poulos, "10 Trends in Self-Service Merchandising," *CSA/DE* 29 (Apr. 1953), 55.

71

I. H. Bander, "Mass Merchandising: Five Reasons for Greater Profits," *Drug Store Retailing* 6 (Aug. 1935), 22−25; "Scientific Store Planning," *NARD* 58 (6 Aug. 1936), 1074−1078; "Makes Most of Strategic Location," *CSA/DE* 15 (Dec. 1939), 13; Milton Figen, "Modernization Plus," *American Druggist* 102 (Jan. 1941), 64−66; "Open Display Keynotes New Super Store," *CSA/DE* 18 (May 1942), 32−33; "New Michigan Drug Store: A Dream Come True," *NARD* 67 (3 Dec. 1945), 2116−2117; ". . . Drug Store of Tomorrow," *NARD* 68 (7 Jan. 1946), 30−31; "Tomorrow's Drug Store Will Gleam with Light," *NARD* 68 (20 May 1946), 923−936; A. F. Loewe, "Light for Competitive Selling," *NARD* 68 (2 Sep. 1946), 1616−1617, 1640; "New Store Layout Makes Shopping Easy," *CSA/DE* 23 (May 1947), 76; "Let There Be Light!" *NARD* 67 (21 July 1947), 1304, 1336; "Master Drug Store," *CSA/DE* 23 (Oct. 1947), 82; "Modern in Color and Design," *CSA/DE* 24 (Jan. 1948), 90; "Streamlined for Service," *CSA/DE* 24 (Mar. 1948), 67; "'World's Most Easily Shopped Drug Store,'" *NARD* 70 (3 May 1948), 700−701, 718, 720; ". . . Modernizing," *NARD* 70 (17 May 1948), 782−783; "Full Vision in Full Swing," *CSA/DE* 24 (Aug. 1948), 40−43; Charles E. Roseman, Jr., "Make Mine Modern!" *CSA/DE* 25 (July 1949), 167; "Emphasis on Open Display," *CSA/DE* 25 (Aug. 1949), 45−46; "Modern Pharmacy in Shopping Center," *NARD* 72 (21 Aug. 1950), 1254−1255; "Merchandising to Be Spotlighted," *NARD* 72 (18 Sep. 1950), 1422; Raymond Schuessler, "Women Prefer to Buy . . . ," *NARD* 73 (19 Feb. 1951), 268, 294; "Designed for the Suburbs," *CSA/DE* 27 (Aug. 1951), 122; Milton C. Elsberg, "'That's My Business'," *CSA/DE* 29 (Aug. 1953), 49−50, 115−116.

72

LAT, 18 Aug. 1948, I-13; "Owl-Rexall Store . . . ," *LAT,* 20 Aug. 1948, II-2. See also references cited in n. 68 above. Concerning the Broadway-Crenshaw Center, see Longstreth, *City Center to Regional Mall,* 227−238.

73

"Drug Firm Enters Self-Service Field," *SMM* 6 (Aug. 1941), 24; Hix Smith, "Dallas Approves New Drug Supers . . . ," *SMM* 7 (July 1942), 42−45; John G. Poulos,

"How Far Self Service?" *CSA/DE* 28 (Mar. 1952), 62. See also "Omaha Drug Super Opens," *SMM* 10 (Feb. 1945), 35–37. Skillern's was among those to retreat after a few years; see Rae E. Skillern, "For More Profit Departmentalize!" *CSA/DE* 24 (Nov. 1948), 43–45. Katz, on the other hand, continued its practices; see M. R. Shlensky, "Semi-Self-Service Is Our Answer for Modern Drug Store Merchandising," *CSA/DE* 28 (Apr. 1952), 66–67, 86d.

74

"Self-Service Store . . . ," *LAT,* 12 Aug. 1942, I-12; "Service and Self-Service on Sundries," *CSA/DE* 24 (Feb. 1948), 67, 132; Lucius S. Flint, "Review of Self-Service on West Coast, *CSA/DE* 25 (May 1949), 59–60, 109–110.

75

For discussion, see Poulos, "How Far," 62–108; idem, "10 Trends," 50–62; Lynn H. Stiles, "What About Self-Service?" *CSA/DE* 30 (Mar. 1954), 64, 132, 135–136, 138; John G. Poulos, "Self-Service Gathers Momentum," *CSA/DE* 30 (Jul 1954), 42–58; "What Do They Ask about Self-Service?" *CSA/DE* 30 (Nov. 1954), 51; John G. Poulos, ". . . What Kind of Self-Service?" *CSA/DE* 31 (July 1955), 30–41; and "Trends in Self-Service," *CSA/DE* 31 (Nov. 1955), 47, 88, 91.

76

Hess Kline, "Glassware Merits Permanent Spot in Super . . . ," *SMM* 8 (Sep. 1943), 75–77; "Glimpsing the Post-War Super," *SMM* 9 (Sep. 1944), 40; "$120,000,000 Post-War Plum in Super Drugs," *SMM* 9 (Oct. 1944), 44–47; M. M. Zimmerman, "Drug-Cosmetic Sales Climb Steadily in Super Markets," *SMM* 10 (Mar. 1945), 13–14, 16, 18–20; "Drug Sales Key to Super's Sensational Rise," *SMM* 10 (Nov. 1945), 19–22; Maurice Warshaw, "Building Profit with Self-Service Drugs," *SMM* 11 (July 1946), 46–48; H. A. Swainsgood, "Self-Service Drug Operation," *SMM* 11 (Sep. 1946), 43–45; Forrest J. T. May, "Expanding into Drugs and Toiletries," *SMM* 16 (Feb. 1951), 99, 101–102, 104, 106–107, 110–112, 114, 124; Glenn Horsley, "Super Expansion into Housewares," *SMM* 16 (Sep. 1951), 163–164, 168, 171, 175; (Oct. 1951), 99–100, 103, 105–106, 108, 110, 114, 117.

77

For background, see Godfrey M. Lebhar, "The Story of Variety Chains," *CSA/VS* 26 (June 1950), J1–J5, J70–J71; Ben Gordon, "From Five and Dime to Family Shopping Centers," *CSA/VS* 26 (June 1950), J6–J9, J72; and Lawrence R. Robinson and Eleanor G. May, *Self-Service in Variety Stores,* Bureau of Business Research, Bulletin #147 (Boston: Harvard University Graduate School of Business Administration, 1956), 4–6.

78

See, for example, "McCrory Opens No. 300, Syracuse," *CSA/VS* 24 (Oct. 1948), 56–57, 115; "Woolworth's Largest, #28, Opens in Newark, N.J.," *CSA/VS* 24 (Dec. 1948), 47, 112; "Variety's Biggest," *CSA/VS* 29 (Aug. 1953), 80; "Woolworth Opens Its Biggest Southeastern Store . . . ," *CSA/VS* 30 (Oct. 1954), 12–13; "Grant Opens Huge New Store . . . ," *CSA/VS* 30 (Dec. 1954), 58–59. The most extensive pictorial coverage on new stores is in the monthly issues of *VSM.*

79

These figures were gleaned from city and telephone directories.

80

Akron Beacon Journal, 7 Nov. 1940, Scott Store Sect.; *Women's Wear Daily,* 26 Nov. 1940, 25; *VSM* 19 (Jan. 1941), 34–35.

81

Scott was exceptional in this regard. A similar configuration existed at a unit that opened in Kansas City, Missouri, several months later (*VSM* 20 [July 1941], 74–75). For other examples, see *VSM* 15 (Nov. 1938), 22–23; "Grant's 'Store of Tomorrow'," *VSM* 17 (Dec. 1939), 62–63; "Newberry Opens New Store at Tampa," *VSM* 21 (Oct. 1941), 38–39; "Woolworth Opens Harrisburg 'Super'," *VSM* 21 (Nov. 1941), 26–27.

82

"Newberry's Biggest Self-Service Store," *CSA/VS* 30 (Jan. 1954), 20–21. For other examples, see "Fisher-Beer Reopens Hempstead," *VSM* 35 (Nov. 1948), 94–96; "Kresge Reopens . . . ," *VSM* 36 (Jan. 1949), 106–109; "Head's Denver, Colo., Goes Modern," *VSM* 36 (June 1949), 23; "Kresge's New Baltimore Units," *VSM* 39 (Sep. 1950), 25; and "McCrory Opens Its 'Model Store'," *CSA/VS* 28 (Dec. 1952), 142.

83

"Sprouse-Reitz Tests Self-Service '5&10'," *VSM* 18 (May 1940), 24–25, 114, 116; Otis R. Tyson, "'Self-Service' in Operation at 40 Sprouse-Reitz Stores," *VSM* 20 (July 1941), 80–81, 132, 134. See also Robinson and May, *Self-Service,* 6; and "Sprouse-Reitz Pioneered Variety Self-Service . . . ," *CSA/VS* 29 (Nov. 1953), 78, although their dates do not correspond to those in period sources. Another chain pioneer was Winn Stores of San Antonio, Texas; see Murray Winn, Sr., "Women Like Self-Service in Variety Stores," *CSA/VS* 18 (June 1942), 26, 64, 66; and "Tomorrow's 'Dream' Stores Today at Winn Chain," *CSA/VS* 21 (May 1945), 68–70, 133–134. Concerning postwar attitudes, see "Is Self-Service Profitable for Variety Chains?" *CSA/VS* 21 (Dec. 1945), 44–46; "Self-Service vs. High Selling Costs," *CSA/VS* 25 (Oct. 1949), 51; and "Self-Service . . . Survey of a Trend," *CSA/VS* 25 (Nov. 1949), 36–39, 107–108, 110, 113, 115, 120, 123–124.

84

Robinson and May, *Self-Service,* 8.

85

J. P. Rome, "'Self-Service'—Story of Trend," *VSM* 40 (Mar. 1951), 102–105, 172; "Ben Franklin Variety Stores Get Set for Self-Service," *VSM* 43 (Sep. 1952), 139–144; "Report on Self-Service," *CSA/VS* 29 (Nov. 1953), 56–78; "Self-Service Promises More Net Profits . . . ," *CSA/VS* 30 (Apr. 1954), 60–63, 72; "Self-Service . . . Where Do We Go from Here?" *CSA/VS* 32 (Jan. 1956), 36–39; Godfrey M. Lebhar, "Progress Report on Self-Service," *CSA/VS* 32 (Aug. 1956), 51–82; Robinson and May, *Self Service.*

86

For background, see Bernice L. Thomas, *America's 5&10 Cent Stores: The Kress Legacy* (New York: John Wiley & Sons, and Washington: National Building Museum, 1997).

87

Preston J. Bell, "History and Growth of the Variety Chains . . . ," in *Variety Store Merchandiser Directory,* 1954, 31. The comparison with department stores was expressed most overtly in literature that was widely read by department store executives. See, for example, Henry Wolfson, "Chains Palatial Business Homes . . . ," *Women's Wear Daily,* 6 Oct. 1937, II-10; "Woolworth's Unit . . . ," *Retailing,* 7 Mar. 1938, 11; "Grant Unit Makes News in Display," *Bulletin of the National Retail Dry Goods Association* 22 (Jan. 1940), 24–25. See also *Woolworth's First 75 Years: The Story of Everybody's Store* (New York: F. W. Woolworth Co., 1954).

88
For discussion of a similar remodeling, see "Newberry's Ten-Day Self-Service Conversion Yields 50% Gain in Space," *CSA/VS* 30 (Mar. 1954), 20–21.

89
"Shopping Centers: A Way to More Sales If You Know How to Use Them," *Tide* 28 (24 Apr. 1954), 21.

90
According to a 1953 survey of community- and regional-sized centers, supermarkets occupied the second largest amount of square footage, exceeded only by department store branches. Variety stores were a close third. See S. O. Kaylin, "The Chain Store in the Planned Shopping Center," *CSA/AE* 29 (May 1953), 50–51. For background, see ibid., 23–49; "The Variety Chain in Shopping Centers," *CSA/VS* 29 (May 1953), 52–59; and S. O. Kaylin, "The Planned Shopping Center," *CSA/AE* 30 (May 1954), 13–19.

91
For examples, see "Kresge's New Baltimore Units," *VSM* 39 (Sep. 1950), 25; "Newberry Returns to Seattle . . . ," *VSM* 39 (Nov. 1950), 30–31; "McCrory's Opens Its 'Model Store'," *CSA/VS* 28 (Dec. 1952), 142; "Neisner, Woolworth, Grant Open in Buffalo's Thruway Plaza," *CSA/VS* 28 (Nov. 1952), 44–45; "FWW Opens Unit in Expanding San Angelo, Texas," *VSM* 44 (May 1953), 10–11; "FWW Opens Unit in Akron Shopping Center," *VSM* 44 (June 1953), 10–11; "McCrory's First Self-Service Unit . . . ," *VSM* 45 (Aug. 1953), 18; "Buffalo Suburbs Get Self-Service Woolworths," *VSM* 45 (Aug. 1953), 10–11; and "'Coexistence' for Downtown and Out-of-Town Stores," *CSA/VS* 31 (Feb. 1955), 116, 160.

BIBLIOGRAPHICAL NOTE

As in City Center to Regional Mall, *I have had to rely primarily on a large number of period accounts, many of them short in length and limited in scope. Thus, a subject guide to the sources cited in the notes is presented instead of a conventional bibliography. Roman numerals refer to chapters; the following arabic numbers refer to individual notes.*

ARCHITECTURE/ARCHITECTS, MISCELLANEOUS

II *38, 39, 43–45, 47–50*

III *21, 26, 53*

IV *2*

COMMERCIAL ARCHITECTURE/RETAILING, MISCELLANEOUS, SOUTHERN CALIFORNIA

Intro *3*

I *1, 4, 42*

II *4, 33, 54, 59, 61*

IV *11, 17, 26, 29, 61, 67–70, 72, 74, 82*

COMMERCIAL ARCHITECTURE/RETAILING, MISCELLANEOUS, U.S.

Intro *1, 4*

I *6, 7*

INDEX

In this index, cities, districts of cities, and towns are listed by name, as are a relatively small number of individuals, agencies, businesses, publications, and other named entities. Other proper names are grouped under the following broader categories: architects; car washes; commercial districts, outlying; designers/builders; drug stores; gasoline stations; grocers; markets; parking; planned residential communities/tracts; planners; real estate agents/developers; shopping centers; and variety stores. The index also includes general topics such as automobiles; depression, effects on retailing; gender, relation to building/retail practices; and traffic congestion. All buildings are located in Los Angeles unless otherwise noted. Page numbers in italics indicate material in illustrations.

selling space in, 165, 169–170

Skillern's Drug Stores, 169

Sontag Drug Co., 166

Thrifty Drug Co., 166, 170

    4901 Whittier Boulevard, East Los Angeles, *167*

    332 Wilshire Boulevard, Santa Monica, *166*

Hollywood (Los Angeles), 12, 14, 17, 18, 20, 25, 27, 35, 39, 57, 59, 68, 86, 90, 98, 111, 115, 120, 129, 144, 205 (n. 43), 207 (n. 51), 208 (n. 60)

I
———

K
———

L
———

DATE DUE

WITHDRAWN

Printed
in USA